A. Toomer Porter

History of the Holy Communion Church Institute

Of Charleston, South Carolina

A. Toomer Porter

History of the Holy Communion Church Institute
Of Charleston, South Carolina

ISBN/EAN: 9783337062842

Printed in Europe, USA, Canada, Australia, Japan

Cover: Foto ©Lupo / pixelio.de

More available books at **www.hansebooks.com**

LIFE OF

JANE WELSH CARLYLE

BY

MRS ALEXANDER IRELAND

'All at once they leave you; and you know them'
BROWNING'S *Paracelsus*

WITH A PORTRAIT AND FACSIMILE LETTER

NEW YORK
CHARLES L. WEBSTER & COMPANY
1891

PREFACE

I HAVE wished for some years to write about Jane Welsh Carlyle, were it only to echo from my heart the opinions of those who were privileged to know her—those whose eyes were open to her deep, isolated nature, her shining gifts, her unique charm, and her life of pain.

My first step was to apply to Mr. Carlyle's literary executor, Mr. FROUDE, for permission to avail myself of his exhaustive volumes, without which my task could not possibly have been attempted. This permission was most kindly granted me, and it must be observed that all quotations, passages from letters, &c., in this memoir—unless specially indicated as drawn from other sources—may be referred to Mr. Froude's pages.

I am indebted to Mr. D. G. RITCHIE, Fellow and Tutor of Jesus College, Oxford, for valuable aid. Through his courtesy I secured the consent of his publishers, Messrs. SWAN SONNENSCHEIN, to use certain passages from the 'Early Letters of Jane Welsh Carlyle.' He has kindly made the Index to the present volume.

Mr. Ritchie also gave me information which resulted in my obtaining access to the hitherto unpublished letters from Mrs. Carlyle to Mrs. Dinning, the 'Grace Rennie' of the old Haddington days. For the permission to publish these letters, as well as for the sight of the originals, I am directly indebted to Mrs. ANTHONY F. NICHOL, of Bradford House, Belford, Northumberland. This lady is a grand-daughter of Mrs. Dinning.

I have received much aid, in more directions than one, from Mr. HENRY LARKIN, the devoted friend of both Mr. and Mrs. Carlyle. He it is whose article, 'A Ten Years' Reminiscence'—published some years ago in the 'British Quarterly Review'—shows such understanding and sympathy. To Mr. Larkin I also owe the letter of Mrs. Carlyle to himself, which is here given in facsimile.

Mr. JOHN STORES SMITH, of The Laurels, Chesterfield, literary executor to the late Miss Jewsbury, kindly placed in my hands the letter from Mrs. Carlyle to this beloved friend of hers. The letter, though undated, and without post-mark, bears indisputable testimony as to the time at which it was written, namely within a very few months of Mrs. Carlyle's death.

I am also grateful to Mr. DAVID DOUGLAS, publisher, Edinburgh, for permission to use certain extracts of singular interest from Lieutenant-Colonel Davidson's 'Memorials of a Long Life.'

The Collotype photograph has been executed by Messrs. Elliott & Fry, from a portrait of Mrs. Carlyle, taken about the year 1850. It is pronounced by one who knew her well, to be one of the most characteristic presentments possible.

ANNIE E. IRELAND.

May 1891.

CONTENTS

PART I

GIRLHOOD

CHAPTER I

A. D. 1801-1819

PAGE

Early days in Haddington—The Welsh family—Dr. John Welsh—His marriage—John Welsh of Liverpool—The home at Haddington—The only child—Her beauty and talent—The rival grandfathers—Schooldays at Haddington—Jeannie's love of danger and adventure—Edward Irving as private tutor—Early signs of originality in the 'only child'............... 1

CHAPTER II

A. D. 1819-1821

Strong attachment between the father and daughter—The last talk—Sudden illness and death of Dr. John Welsh—Jeannie's 'Paganism'—Serious thoughts—'Early letters' to Eliza Stodart—Boarding-school in Edinburgh—Active tendencies—Teaching—Characteristics more plainly shown—The loss of the father's influence—Haddington felt to be dull—Early lovers—Power of language............................ 16

CHAPTER III

A. D. 1821

First meeting with Thomas Carlyle—Introduction by Edward Irving—The May evening—Irving's attachment to Miss Welsh—Carlyle and Margaret Gordon—Isabella Martin—George Rennie—Miss Welsh's early impressions of Carlyle—Literary ambitions and projects—Irving's engagement to Miss Isabella Martin—Miss Welsh's hesitation in accepting Carlyle as a lover—Miss Welsh's readings of Rousseau—George Rennie's departure—Visit of Carlyle to Haddington—Possibilities.... 25

CHAPTER IV

A. D. 1821-1825

Miss Welsh's German studies—Projected literary work—Irving's anxieties as to Miss Welsh's reading—Remonstrances — Irving goes to London—He introduces Carlyle to the Bullers—The tutorship—More intimate correspondence between Carlyle and Miss Welsh—Friendship the footing prescribed by Miss Welsh—Irving's marriage to Miss Martin—Continuation of the Buller engagement—Carlyle's wooing, and its results—Stoical acceptance of repulse—Dr. Fyffe—Miss Welsh's admiration for genius—The letter from Goethe to Carlyle—Sympathy on Byron's death—' Benjamin B——' —Miss Welsh does not pay a visit to the Irvings in London.................... 34

CHAPTER V

A. D. 1825

Carlyle in London—Thoughts of marriage—Difficulties—Mrs. Montagu—'Barry Cornwall'—Allan Cunningham—The breaking off of the Buller engagement—Irving's hospitality—Serious reflections—Consultations with Miss Welsh—The idea of 'living on a farm'—Miss Welsh's very different project—Carlyle's independent spirit—Exceptional position of affairs—Miss Welsh's delicate health—The proposal to farm Craigenputtock—Final decision left to Miss Welsh—Suspense—Discussion—Modest wants of Carlyle—Miss Welsh demurs at the essential conditions, but still proffers friendship—Carlyle's renewed professions of attachment........................ 43

CHAPTER VI

A. D. 1825

Carlyle at Hoddam Hill—Miss Welsh's transference of Craigenputtock to her mother—Carlyle's personal appearance at this time—Miss Welsh's beauty—Letter from Mrs. Montagu to Miss Welsh—Reference to Edward Irving—An independent spirit—Second letter of Mrs. Montagu—Results—Miss Welsh informs Carlyle of her old attachment to Irving—A woman's appeal—Carlyle's reply—Imperfect understanding—Exciting correspondence—Engagement of Miss Welsh and Thomas Carlyle—Visits to Hoddam Hill and Mainhill—Difficulties as to future residence—Incompatibility between Carlyle and Mrs. Welsh—Misgivings—Correspondence with the Carlyle family—Their removal to Scotsbrig............................. 60

CHAPTER VII

A. D. 1825-1826

PAGE

Loyalty of Miss Welsh—Her sense of being bound to the engagement with Carlyle—Proposal to live at Scotsbrig—The actual *versus* the ideal—Miss Welsh's mind made up—Carlyle's determination not to live in the house with Mrs. Welsh—A daughter's devotion and appeal—Renunciation of the cherished wish—The point yielded.................................... 71

CHAPTER VIII

A. D. 1826

Mrs. Welsh decides to further the marriage—Her decision to live with her father at Templand—The Carlyle parents see the impossibility of their son's bride living at Scotsbrig—A new home to be chosen—Impossible conditions—Blindness of Carlyle to the actual situation—Trying uncertainty—The idea of the home at Haddington as a residence for the newly-married pair—Painful objections—The idea abandoned—Recurring failure of plans—And a dissimilarity in ideas—The proposed cottage in Annandale.................................... 77

CHAPTER IX

A. D. 1826

The home at Haddington broken up—Comely Bank furnished by Mrs. Welsh—Immediate difficulty over—Miss Welsh happier—Her pride in Carlyle's genius—Her estimate of him—The marriage at Templand—Natural cravings for the affection of Carlyle on the part of his bride-elect—Her unconventionality—State of mind as to the approaching ceremony—Miss Welsh prepares to put off her mourning for the occasion—The 'three cigars'—Good resolutions—White gowns—A post-chaise to Comely Bank.................................... 83

PART II

EARLY MARRIED LIFE

CHAPTER X

A. D. 1826

Comely Bank—Good resolutions—Social opportunities—A wifely letter—Narrow income—Visit of Dr. John Carlyle—The daily life—The little 'Wednesday evenings'—Friendship with

Jeffrey—Brighter prospects—Household activities on Mrs. Carlyle's part—Renewed ideas of living at Craigenputtock—Its unsuitability to Mrs. Carlyle's needs—Carlyle visits it with his brother Alick—The tenant about to leave—Letter from Mrs. Carlyle—Loving response....................... 95

CHAPTER XI

A. D. 1827

Alexander Carlyle and his sister Mary go to live at Craigenputtock—The visit of the Carlyles to Templand, Scotsbrig, &c.—Prospect of some professorship for Carlyle—Disappointment—Decision for Craigenputtock—A sacrifice—Bleak and barren situation of the new home—Jeffrey's disapproval of the plan—Mrs. Carlyle's courage—House-moving—Carlyle's despair—Correspondence of Mrs. Carlyle with her old friend, Miss Eliza Stodart—Ideals of married life relinquished—Carlyle's frequent depression and absorption in his work—The wife's isolation.. 103

CHAPTER XII

A. D. 1827–1829

'Cares of bread'—The first loaf—Visit of the Jeffreys to Craigenputtock—Mrs. Carlyle's preparatory ride to Dumfries—Friendly advice of Jeffrey to Carlyle—Invitation to Moray Place—The two mountain ponies—Mrs. Carlyle's loneliness—'Brother Alick'—A visit to Templand—Letter from the wife to the husband—Visit of the Carlyles to Edinburgh—22 George Square—Return to 'The Desert'—Serious illness of Mrs. Carlyle — Visit of Mrs. Welsh — Permanently weakened health.. 110

CHAPTER XIII

A. D. 1830–1831

Alexander Carlyle leaves Craigenputtock—Second visit of the Jeffreys to the Carlyles in their solitude—Mrs. Carlyle confesses her unhappiness to Jeffrey—The eventless life again sets in—The Jeffreys go to London—Carlyle's generosity to his brothers—He accepts help from Jeffrey, and goes to London to push his literary enterprises—A hard and sad time for Mrs. Carlyle—Ill-health and anxiety—Her verdict on 'Sartor'—Letters from Carlyle to his wife—Irving in the region of the supernatural—Caution of publishers—Good appointment for Dr. John Carlyle—Thoughts of living in London—Tender letters from Carlyle—Solitude doing its work on the delicate constitution of Mrs. Carlyle—Kindness of Carlyle's mother—Mrs. Carlyle's determination to join her husband in London—Encouragement...................... 118

CHAPTER XIV

A. D. 1831

Mrs. Carlyle's arrival in London—Ampton Street—The Irvings—Ill-health of Mrs. Carlyle—Position with Mrs. Montagu—Meetings with congenial spirits—Carlyle still restless—Death of his father—Impending return to Craigenputtock—Misgivings—A sad return—Solitary habits—Realisation of the actual by Mrs. Carlyle—Jeffrey's anxiety about Mrs. Carlyle. 125

CHAPTER XV

A. D. 1832-1834

Carlyle's letter to his mother—Mrs. Carlyle's overstrained nerves and failing strength—Her letter to Eliza Stodart—Mrs. Welsh's delicate health—Death of Walter Welsh of Templand—The Carlyles plan a long visit to Edinburgh—The home at 18 Carlton Street, Stockbridge—The 'disgraceful home march'—An 'angel's visit' at Craigenputtock—Meeting of Emerson and the Carlyles—The relapse into solitude—Living in London seriously contemplated—Preparations.................. 133

PART III

LIFE IN LONDON

CHAPTER XVI

A. D. 1834-1836

The new, yet old life—Unalterable conditions—The removal to London—Leigh Hunt—John Stuart Mill—Allan Cunningham—The circle of friends—Edward Irving's visit—George Rennie and his sister—Eliza Miles—Burning of the MS. of Vol. I. of 'French Revolution'—Wifely sympathy—'The Sterlings'—Sprinklings of foreigners—Domestic difficulties—Visit of Mrs. Welsh—Maternal counsels from Scotsbrig—Godefroi de Cavaignac....................................... 145

CHAPTER XVII

A. D. 1836–1840

Retrospect on the Scotch journey—Return to Chelsea—Mrs. Carlyle's letter to Sterling — Carlyle's supposed 'lady-admirers' — The lectures—Success and congratulations—Second visit of Mrs. Welsh—Flight of Carlyle into Annandale —'The bird and the watch'—Regrets and ill-health of Mrs. Carlyle—Cheque from Emerson, being proceeds of 'French Revolution'—John Sterling's health—Reflections thereon—Carlyle again in Scotland—Letter to John Forster: 'Why do women marry?'—The 'Lion's wife!'.......................... 154

CHAPTER XVIII

A. D. 1841–1846

Trouble at Templand—Sudden alarm—Summons too late—Mrs. Carlyle receives the news of her mother's death when on her way to nurse her—Carlyle goes to Templand to wind up the estate—Mrs. Welsh buried at Crawford—Heartstricken letter to Mrs. Russell of Thornhill—Troston Rectory and the Bullers —Lady Harriet Baring—Mrs. Carlyle's return to Cheyne Row —First meeting with Miss Jewsbury and the Paulets—'The three-cornered alliance'— Household 'earthquaking' in Cheyne Row—Mrs. Carlyle's first expressed judgment of Lady Harriet Baring—Stay at Ryde—Father Mathew—Loss of strength—Need of a quiet place for Carlyle to write in—Failure of the attempt—Letter to John Welsh of Liverpool—Carlyle's hopefulness of his wife's health—Her visit to Liverpool and Seaforth (the Paulets)—Visit to the Grange—Painful thoughts—'Cromwell' concluded.......................... 168

CHAPTER XIX

A. D. 1846–1847

The dark cloud—Carlyle's anxiety—Mrs. Carlyle seeks counsel —Mazzini's honourable and noble advice—The flight to Seaforth—Birthday gift and gentle words—Renewed counsels—Renewed bitterness—Lord Houghton's estimate of Lady Harriet Baring—Contrasts—Sad thoughts—Clough's Poem—Visit to W. E. Forster—Again at Addiscombe—Hopeless misunderstanding—The healing of the wound rendered impossible.... 186

CHAPTER XX

A. D. 1847-1849

Return to Cheyne Row—Renewed illness—Bitter reflections—Disappointment—Confidences to Uncle John Welsh—A winter's visit of Carlyle to the Barings—Mrs. Carlyle remaining at Cheyne Row—Remonstrances of Miss Jewsbury—Long illness of Mrs. Carlyle—Consultations with John Forster—Visit to Addiscombe—Death of Lord Ashburton—Carlyle's tour in Ireland—The forgotten plaid—Mrs. Carlyle visits Lady Harriet Baring (now Lady Ashburton) at Alverstoke—Brilliant society but no sleep—Death of John Sterling—Declining health of Jeffrey—Haddington—Betty Braid, the 'old nurse'—Scenes of childhood revisited—'Mathew Baillie'—Mrs. Carlyle visits her father's grave—Sunny Bank—Sad and loving meetings—'Old Jamie'—Manchester and Miss Jewsbury—Illness of Helen Welsh of Liverpool.................. 197

CHAPTER XXI

A. D. 1849-1851

Introduction to James Anthony Froude—Arthur Clough—Spedding—Froude's impressions—Mutual loneliness of the Carlyles—Mrs. Carlyle's letter to Mrs. Aitken—Note to John Forster—Visit to the Grange by Carlyle—'Nero' and 'Shandy'—Nero's letter—Failing ideas—Society felt to be hard work by Mrs. Carlyle—Latter-day pamphlets concluded—Carlyle in Wales—Renewed household 'earthquakings' at 5 Cheyne Row—Failing strength of Mrs. Carlyle—Sad thoughts—Fruitless regrets and good resolutions.................. 207

CHAPTER XXII

A. D. 1851-1853

Carlyle's visit to the Marshalls—Tennyson and his bride—Disgust at the Exhibition of 1851—Visit to Malvern—Verdict thereon—Miss Gully's letter—Mrs. Carlyle again at the Grange—Repairs at Cheyne Row—Visit to Macready—Carlyle's 'Life of Frederick'—He sails for Rotterdam—A serious undertaking—Mrs. Carlyle visits Lady Ashburton—Carlyle's second German tour—Discomforts—Return to 5 Cheyne Row of Mrs. Carlyle—Further 'earthquakings'—A second visit of Mrs. Carlyle to the Lady Ashburton—Sleeplessness—Depression—The old letter—Carlyle's return—Commencement of 'Frederick'—Mrs. Carlyle with the John Carlyles at Moffat—Return to softer conditions at Chelsea............. 219

CHAPTER XXIII

A. D. 1853-1856

Declining health of old Mrs. Carlyle at Scotsbrig—Mrs. Carlyle hastens to her—Womanly tenderness—The danger staved off—Return to Chelsea—Death of John Welsh of Liverpool—Visit of the Carlyles to the Grange—The 'soundless' room at Chelsea—Return of Mrs. Carlyle—Noises—Death of Helen Welsh—Death of Carlyle's mother—Wifely sympathy—Miss Jewsbury comes to live in London—Miss Fox—Mazzini's farewell—Mrs. Carlyle's Journal—Deep misery—Sympathy—Budget of a ' Femme Incomprise '........................ 229

CHAPTER XXIV

A. D. 1856-1858

Position between Mrs. Carlyle and Lady Ashburton—The Scotch journey—Carlyle at 'The Gill'—Mrs. Carlyle at Auchtertool—'Seeking and finding'—Sunny Bank—Tender Remembrances—The return to London—Death of Lady Ashburton—Tribute to her—Bitter reflections—Scotland again—First readings of a portion of 'Frederick'—Wifely pride—Mrs. Carlyle's return to Cheyne Row—Discouragement—The kindness of Mr. Henry Larkin—Another visit to Germany—Mrs. Carlyle at Lann Hall—Holm Hill—Letters to Mr. Larkin—Cheyne Row once more—Second marriage of Lord Ashburton—Mrs. Carlyle's thoughts of her mother—The visit to 'Humbie' and Auchtertool—Carlyle again in Annandale with his own people.................................... 243

CHAPTER XXV

A. D. 1859-1860

Life in Cheyne Row—Mrs. Carlyle's return—George Rennie's death—Letters of Mrs. Carlyle on the subject to Mrs. Dinning of Belford, Northumberland—Carlyle at Thurso Castle—Mrs. Carlyle, with Lady Stanley of Alderley, *en route* for Scotland—Holm Hill—Misunderstanding as to date of Carlyle's return—Mrs. Carlyle returns to Cheyne Row unnecessarily—Carlyle's remorse—Two servants kept....................... 249

CHAPTER XXVI

A. D. 1861-1863

Mrs. Carlyle's craving for her ' one little maid-servant '—Death of Arthur Hugh Clough—Mrs. Carlyle's visit to Ramsgate with Miss Jewsbury—Sleeplessness—Longings to visit Mrs.

Russell—Estimate of men—Miss Barnes' marriage—Deaths of dear friends—Folkestone—Mrs. Carlyle accomplishes her visit to Holm Hill and Craigenvilla—'Old Betty'—Visit to Auchtertool—Home again—Illness of Lord Ashburton in Paris—Mrs. Carlyle's wish to go and be useful—Sad letter to 'Old Betty'—The Carlyles at the Grange—Neuralgia or rheumatism causing Mrs. Carlyle increasing pain—The accident soon after the return to Cheyne Row—Carlyle's account —Mr. Froude's account—Mr. Larkin's account.............. 267

CHAPTER XXVII

A. D. 1863-1864

Consequences—The first re-appearance of the invalid—Mr. and Mrs. Froude spend a bright evening with the Carlyles—Mr. Simmonds—Ominous signs—Death of Grace Welsh—Decreasing strength of Mrs. Carlyle—Passage from the 'Reminiscences'—Unaidable pain—Maggie Welsh—The strange nurse— Invitation to St. Leonards................................. 278

CHAPTER XXVIII

A. D. 1864

Mrs. Carlyle's resolution—Mr. Larkin—The terrible journey— Maggie Welsh—Carlyle at Chelsea—Regrets—Despair—The furnished house—Maggie Welsh recalled to Liverpool—Mary Craik—Sad bulletins—Carlyle's visits—Calls of friends—The sufferer too weak to see them—Mrs. Carlyle writes to her aunts—Insomnia—Heavy days—Futile plans of change—Mrs. Carlyle's horror of returning to Chelsea—Miss Bromley's kindness—Mrs. Carlyle starts for Scotland with Dr. John Carlyle—Spending a night in London on her way—Mrs. Austin—Removal of Mrs. Carlyle to Holm Hill—Her dread of travelling home—The return—The worst over.............. 285

CHAPTER XXIX

A. D. 1864-1865

The brougham—Mrs. Carlyle's joy at her husband's gift—Illness again—Visit of the Carlyles to Lady Ashburton at Seaton, Devon—Soothing impressions—Discomfort again at Cheyne Row—The 'hereditary housemaid'—At Holm Hill once more —Suffering health—Erskine of Linlathen—Home duties at Cheyne Row—Depression—Letter to Miss Jewsbury........ 294

CHAPTER XXX

A. D. 1865-1866

PAGE

Carlyle offered the Lord Rectorship of Edinburgh University—His wife's wish that he should accept it—His election—His journey northwards with Professor Tyndall—The last parting—Professor Huxley—Mr. Erskine of Linlathen and Carlyle's brothers gathered in Edinburgh—The great day—Immense success—The telegram—The dinner at Forster's—Interview with Professor Tyndall—Excitement—The projected tea-party—The afternoon drive—Sudden death of Mrs. Carlyle—Carlyle receives the news at Dumfries—The unopened letter—Funeral at the Abbey Kirk of Haddington—Epitaph—Reflections.. 301

APPENDIX

I. THE WELSH ANCESTRY................................... 309

II. DR. JOHN WELSH.. 310

III. THE DEATH OF DR. JOHN WELSH..................... 311

IV. MRS. CARLYLE AND DE QUINCEY..................... 313

V. CARLYLE'S ACCOUNT OF THE BAKING OF THE FIRST LOAF.. 314

VI. VERSES BY MRS. CARLYLE............................ 315

VII. CARLYLE LOCALITIES IN EDINBURGH................ 316

VIII. A REMEMBRANCE OF SUNNY BANK.................. 319

IX. LETTER TO MRS. CARLYLE FROM HER HUSBAND....... 320

X. EXTRACT FROM A LETTER TO MR. CARLYLE ON HIS WIFE'S DEATH.. 321

XI. CARLYLE AT THE GRAVE OF HIS WIFE................ 323

INDEX.. 325

LIFE OF
JANE WELSH CARLYLE

PART I

GIRLHOOD

CHAPTER I

A. D. 1801—1819

Early days in Haddington—The Welsh family—Dr. John Welsh—His marriage—John Welsh of Liverpool—The home at Haddington—The only child—Her beauty and talent—The rival grandfathers—School-days at Haddington—Jeannie's love of danger and adventure—Edward Irving as private tutor—Early signs of originality in the ' only child.'

HUMAN BEINGS whose gifts and qualities barely reach the average level of mediocrity are, now and then, apt to acquire, during their lifetime, a factitious halo of importance or of interest, attaching to them less through any special merit of their own, than through some circumstance of a passing or local nature extraneous to their veritable character. Possibly, however, it is of more frequent occurrence that those who are really remarkable, who are undoubtedly 'giants among the pigmies' by virtue of surpassing intellectual and moral attributes, fail of a true appreciation among their fellows, or receive but partial recognition, even at the hands of those privileged to intimacy with them. It would seem that these brilliant natures, specially open to unfavourable influences as they too often are, seldom realise their own highest possibilities—do not come to blossoming, but, obeying an ironical decree of fate, veil their bright presence in some mysterious cloud of suffering or inevitable misinterpretation, and so move amongst us, hidden from our true sight, till the end comes, when they suddenly stand revealed to our unobservant eyes. Such has been the case, to a large extent, with the subject of this memoir.

Nearly a quarter of a century has passed away since the death of Jane Welsh Carlyle, and, except among those who knew her intimately—a sadly-diminished number, alas!—there has been comparatively scant recognition of her brilliant powers and altogether unique and charming personality. The publication by Mr. Froude, in 1883, of the 'Letters and Memorials,' gave us a revelation. These letters, so truly remarkable for style and power, for humour, pathos and originality, were read with the deepest interest. In their conciseness and keen intellectuality, in their vivid word-painting, in their fearless frankness, they present a Rembrandt-like portrait of a woman, touched with strongest lights and deepest tragic shades—a faithful and an unerring portrait, self-depicted.

Jane Baillie Welsh was born at Haddington on July 14, 1801. Her ancestors on the father's side could be traced back to a certain famous John Welsh, minister of Ayr, who married the youngest daughter of John Knox. Then came a long line of John Welshes who, through many generations, had been lairds of Craigenputtock, that 'Hill of the Hawk' so impressed on our minds, the high moorland farm standing bleak on the Dunscore Moors, sixteen miles from Dumfries, with its dark sheltering pines and its few acres of grass-land—a green island set in a wilderness of heathery hills, sheep-walk, and undrained peat-bog.

In the rebellion of 1745, the then John Welsh, laird of Craigenputtock, was among the sympathizers, and narrowly escaped committing himself. The son of this same laird died young, leaving his widow at Craigenputtock with one child, another John Welsh, whom she, by-and-by, sent to a tutor in Nithsdale, and afterwards to Tynron school, which was in good repute in those days. But the young laird's education ended somewhat abruptly with his marriage, at seventeen years of age, to a Miss Hunter, a year younger than himself, daughter of the farmer with whom he boarded whilst attending Tynron school. This girl-bride was the grandmother, in later days, of Jane Baillie Welsh, and her bridegroom was afterwards John of Penfillan—that grandfather so beloved by his bright little granddaughter.

In the early days, Craigenputtock was the home of this very youthful couple. In that solid, gaunt farmhouse, with a small income and many struggles, the adventurous pair contrived to bring up their large family of fourteen children. We are not surprised that pecuniary straits compelled the young man to sell part of the estate, namely Nether Craigenputtock, in order to pay his sister's portion, and, long years afterwards, Craigenputtock proper, to his own eldest son, John Welsh, then Dr. John Welsh of Haddington, and father of Jane Baillie Welsh.*

This eldest son was born at Craigenputtock in 1776, and early went to Edinburgh University, where his intelligence and distinguished merits were not overlooked. He was apprenticed to one of the celebrated brothers, John or Charles Bell; Mr. Froude thinks most probably to Dr. John Bell, as Sir Charles Bell was only two years the senior of John Welsh. When but twenty years of age, the young surgeon was recommended for a commission in the Perthshire Fencibles, a post which he held for two years. In 1798 he came to Haddington, and shortly thereafter joined Mr. George Somner, a surgeon in that town, in partnership. The practice was carried on very successfully, under the title of Somner Welsh. Mr. Somner, however, died in June 1815, Dr. Welsh having previously assumed as a partner Mr. Thomas Howden, a former apprentice of the firm. An annuity of 200*l.* a year was paid by Dr. Welsh to his retired partner for some years,

* See Appendix I.

and on the death of Dr. Welsh, Mr. Howden assumed as a partner Benjamin Welsh, M. D., the younger brother. This partnership continued till 1826, when Dr. Benjamin Welsh died.

Dr. John Welsh was a surgeon of great skill, always ready to relieve suffering humanity; he was greatly loved and esteemed by all who came in contact with him. He was a man of fine disposition, stately presence and gentle manners, unselfish and noble-minded. He rapidly made a fortune, and, as we have seen, in order to help his numerous brothers and sisters, actually purchased the family estate of Craigenputtock before it should come to him by inheritance, paying off all incumbrances, with the intention of retiring to it himself, on relinquishing his medical practice. He, no doubt, looked forward to carrying on the family tradition by settling in his birthplace, and in due time leaving another John Welsh there to succeed him. But this was never realised.

In the year 1800 Dr. John Welsh married. He chose a wife who was also a Welsh, though the families were entirely unrelated. Miss Grace Welsh boasted as famous an ancestry as himself, if tradition could be trusted. Dr. John Welsh could trace his descent to John Knox, and the lady he married traced her pedigree, through her mother, once the beautiful Miss Baillie, back to William Wallace. Grace Welsh's father, Walter Welsh, was a prosperous stock-farmer, then living at Capelgill, on Moffat Water. When his daughter Grace, or, as the Scotch sometimes call this pretty name, 'Grizzie,' married her young doctor, and went to live at Haddington, old Walter moved into Nithsdale, and took the farm then known as Templand, near Penfillan. Thus the two grandfathers of the yet unborn Jane Baillie Welsh, connected only through the marriage of their children, became close neighbours and friends.

The beautiful Miss Baillie, Walter Welsh's wife, died early. She it was who came of Wallace. It was a son of hers and

Walter's, another John Welsh, who went into business in Liverpool, where, after a time of prosperity, he fell into trouble through the dishonesty of a partner, who, alas! was also his brother-in-law-elect. Left to bankruptcy, with a debt of 12,000*l*., John Welsh gallantly remade his fortune, and after eight hard years' struggle invited his creditors to dinner, and each man found under his cover a cheque for the full amount of his claim. There must have been good fighting material, and honour withal, in the Welsh blood that came of Wallace.

But let me turn to the home in Haddington, where Dr. John Welsh brought his beautiful bride; for, by all accounts, Mrs. Welsh must have been a lovely woman, 'tall, aquiline, and commanding.' In character she seems to have been emotional and sensitive, easily saddened, and variable, perhaps, in her moods. More is known of Dr. John Welsh, who must in every way have realised his wife's preconceived ideals, of which, doubtless, she had many and lofty ones. From the description of him handed down by those who knew him, he was of noble, distinguished presence, tall, highly graceful, self-possessed, dignified, strikingly handsome, with black hair, bright hazel eyes, and lively and expressive features. More noteworthy, however, were his moral character and his medical sagacity, which combined in the consistent and honourable man, faithful at all points, and universally esteemed. The home in Haddington was not only comfortable and well appointed—elegance and refinement were added to ease of circumstances.

Dr. Welsh led a busy life in his profession, his fatigues being much increased by the many miles of riding incidental to a country practice, which caused him to have never less than three strong saddle-horses at his command. He was punctual to a minute in the keeping of appointments, inflexible where right was concerned, and possessed of the strong pride of independence. He was a loving and wise husband to his beautiful Grace, and a devoted father to the one child born to them—the little Jeannie, whose birth, on July 14, 1801, has been already chronicled.

This only child must have shown to the eyes of those who loved her, very early indications of her uncommon nature and qualities—points no less noticeable than, and far outweighing in importance, the unusual beauty apparent from the beginning. She was the child of remarkable people, and traced her ancestry through generations of original and strikingly superior characters; it was not wonderful that she should present a remarkable, almost unique type in her own person. Her curling black hair, large black eyes, now shining with soft mockery, now softly sad; clear pale skin, broad forehead, and nose the least bit *retroussé*, give us a picture of this arch, gay, mobile little creature, with her slight, airy, and graceful figure in harmony with the spiritual face. Those who knew her, speak of her as beautiful to the very end of her life. Such beauty as could call forth this universal tribute must have been undeniably pronounced. Such beauty as could survive in triumph the long martyrdom of suffering to which this bright creature was predestined, must have traced its truest source to the spirit within, whence it could still shine forth amid ruins. Even in early childhood it was felt by those around her that the most remarkable gifts of this fairy-like Jeannie were those of the mind. Her extreme intellectual vivacity startled them all. And no wonder! It does not seem, however, that the lively child was spoiled by over-indulgence, had the mother inclined to that fault.

Dr. John Welsh watched with ceaseless care over this precious only child, and strict obedience was the rule in the Haddington household. Still, there was scope enough for natural playfulness. The nearness of two grandfathers must have offered many opportunities for the little lady, and she was a special favourite of Walter of Templand, whom she occasionally visited. Her 'little name' of 'Pen' meant 'Penfillan Jeannie,' by which old Walter always called her.

* See Appendix III.

No doubt there was a certain rivalry between the two grandfathers in attracting the notice of this precocious and gifted little child; a born coquette we may suppose her, even from her babyhood, with that wonderful caprice of baby-girls so intensely amusing to grown-up people, so half-pathetic and altogether human when considered from some points of view. Who has not seen the dimpled despot of a year old, safely enthroned in the arm of mother or father, give, or passionately refuses the kiss, contract the whole face with sudden frown, or dispense bewitching smiles, and offer or sharply withdraw the dimpled rose-leaf hand?

Some such picture might be drawn of this baby Jeannie, this only one, this sole tyrant in the house at Haddington. Old Walter had certain peculiarities of speech, had a 'burr' in pronouncing his 'r,' and spoke in the old style generally, which was duly noted by the quick little child. When about six years old, her grandfather had taken her with him for a ride on a quiet little pony. When they had gone as far as was desirable, Walter, in his own characteristic dialect, said: 'Now we will go back, by so-and-so, to *vah-chry the shane!*' 'And where did you ride to, Pen?' asked the company at dinner. 'We rode to *so*, and then to *so*,' she answered punctually, 'and then returned by *so* to *vah-chry the shane!*' At which, no doubt, old Walter joined the general gaiety, with that laugh of his characterised later on by Carlyle as one of the prettiest laughs in the world, with 'something audible in it, as of flutes and harps, as if the vanquished themselves were invited or compelled to partake in the triumph.'

Something of old Walter's nature was, undoubtedly, inherited by Jeannie Welsh. He is described by Carlyle as of 'hot, impatient temper, breaking out into flashes of lightning if you touched him the wrong way; but they were flashes only, never bolts.' A lovable man he must have been, with his 'laughing eyes, beautiful, light humour, and features, massive yet soft, so quickly lighted up by a bright, dimpling chuckle.'

Less is known of Jeannie's other grandfather, John of Penfillan, who is described as a singular and interesting man, devout, upright, honourably respected and esteemed, and certainly beloved by Jeannie as she grew older. His marriage into the Hunter family had possibly failed to develop what was most attractive in him, as we are told that Jeannie never liked the Hunters, and used in later days to divide her uncles into ' *Welshes* ' (these were uncles on her mother's side of the house) and 'Welshes with a cross of Hunter' (these were the members of the Penfillan family).

Time passed on, and Jeannie began to attend Haddington school, which stood only a furlong from her father's house. Here boys and girls were taught, but in separate schoolrooms for the most part; only arithmetic and algebra, in which the little girl became specially proficient, they learned together.

Jeannie had many devoted slaves among the boys. But she was of a fiery temper, and could not always keep the peace. Differences arose now and then. A lad one day was impertinent. She doubled her little fist, hit him hard on the nose, and made it bleed. The penalty for fighting in school was flogging. At the noise of the scuffle the master came in, saw the marks of the fray, and asked who was the delinquent. All were silent. The boys could not tell tales of a girl. The master threatened to thrash the whole school, when the small Jeannie looked up, and said: ' Please, sir, it was I!' The master's gravity gave way, and, laughing, he told her she was 'a little deevil,' and sent her back to the girls' room.

There is a lifelike description of Jeannie about this time from Carlyle's pen. She may have been seven or eight years old, and was attending the Haddington school.

Thither daily, at an early hour, might be seen my little Jeannie, tripping nimbly and daintily along, satchel in hand, dressed by her mother, who had a great talent that way, in tasteful simplicity—neat bit of pelisse, light blue sometimes, fastened with black belt; dainty little cap, perhaps beaver-skin, with flap turned up, and, I think, one at least with modest little plume in it.

The child was ambitious as well as keenly intelligent. She rapidly mastered the ordinary branches of learning, and demanded to 'learn Latin like a boy!' But there was a difference of opinion on the subject at home. Mrs. Welsh opposed her; but her father, who thought well of her talents, was willing she should have her way. Jeannie took the matter into her own hands. She found out a lad in Haddington school who taught her to repeat a Latin noun of the first declension. Armed with this weapon, she hid herself, one night when she was supposed to be in bed, under the drawing-room table. When opportunity offered, her small voice, from under the tablecover, broke silence with—'*Penna*, a pen; *Pennæ*, of a pen,' &c. And, amid the general amusement, she crept out, ran to her father, and repeated her simple petition, 'I want to learn Latin; please let me be a boy!' and was no doubt caught up in his arms amid kisses, which settled the Latin question.

But this desire for manly learning, and this ability to dispense salutary chastisement with her little doubled fist, did not preclude Jeannie's very feminine qualities from early declaring themselves. It was a woman's soul, a woman's nature, essentially, in this Ariel of a child with the deep dark eyes and fiery temper. A very characteristic anecdote of her childhood finds place here.

There was a dancing-school in Haddington, when Jeannie, then not more than six, had been selected to perform some 'Pas seul,' beautiful and difficult; she was anxious in her little heart to do it well. Dressed to perfection, she was carried across the muddy street in a clothes basket. All went well till her turn came. The little child stood waiting the music. Music began. Alas! the wrong music; impossible to dance that 'Pas seul!' to it. She made signs of distress—music ceased—took counsel, and began again; again wrong, helplessly, flatly impossible.

Beautiful little Jane, alone against the world, forsaken by the music, but not by her presence of mind, plucked up her little skirt, flung it over her head, and curtseying in that veiled manner, withdrew from the adventure, amid general applause.

There is great significance in this incident: the brave, dignified reception of defeat, the controlling of the child-heart in its bursting pain of disappointment, the ready device to hide the tears of mortification—all these were unusual signs in a child of tender years, when most youngsters would have openly blubbered. And perhaps mothers would rather see their own little ones comfort themselves thus.

Jeannie Welsh could not so disburden her child-heart! Later on in her life, when its deep music went hopelessly wrong, when it became manifestly impossible to fit in its difficult evolutions to any harmony of existing accompaniment, when preconceived schemes were defeated, and the eager heart could plan no more, it was granted to her, vanquished, to withdraw swiftly, silently into impenetrable shelter. Now the child-spirit was endlessly brave, and feared nothing. Very amusing is the account of her attack on a horrid and alarming turkey-cock she was apt to encounter at a gate through which she passed on her way to school. Her alarm at this hideous bird grew almost overpowering, and she hated the thought of living in fear of him. On one occasion, as she passed this gate, several labourers and boys were near, who seemed to enjoy the thought of seeing the ill-conducted bird run at her. Jeannie's spirit was roused. She gathered herself together, and made up her mind. The turkey ran at her, gobbling and swelling; she suddenly darted at him, seized him by the throat, and swung him round—no small feat for a slender little lady of her age.

But from the first she loved a sense of danger. Near the school was the Nungate Bridge, whose arch overhangs the water at a considerable height. There was a narrow ledge on the parapet, the crossing of which was an uncommonly dangerous feat, to which the boys now and then dared one another. One fine morning Jeannie got up early, went to the Nungate Bridge, lay down on her face on this ledge, and crawled from one end to the other, at the imminent risk of breaking her neck by a fall into the river beneath. This exploit, with others like it, must be taken as plain proof of a dauntless courage which gave way only under trial of unusual severity, and presented to the end some of the old daring, which was never extinguished altogether.

With such energy of character, it is not surprising that at nine years old Jeannie was reading 'Virgil.' Her first teacher was Edward Irving, the Annandale youth, whose brilliant promise was not yet darkened by the shadow of disaster. Irving had been sent in 1810, by two learned professors, to teach school in Haddington. Fresh from collegiate honors, attractive and gifted, Irving was soon intimate in Dr. Welsh's family, which took the lead in Haddington, socially as well as intellectually. Dr. Welsh recognized Irving's fine qualities, and treated him as an elder son. He was trusted with the private education of Jeannie, as well as with the management of the school. He carefully watched over the little girl's studies, and would take her out on fine nights to show her the stars, and teach her wonderful things about them. More interesting master and pupil surely were seldom known than these two, both so ignorant of the wild and dark future looming ahead of them. These peaceful, unawakened days in sleepy little Haddington must often have come back in memory to them both in the days when the 'tangled skein of life' proved utterly confused.

Edward Irving, when appointed master of what was called the mathematical school in Haddington, was, as Mrs. Oliphant tells us, between seventeen and eighteen years of age, a handsome, ruddy youth, boyish still, in spite of his inches; ardent and full of hope. His personality was at all times a striking one, his manner, in these early days, frank and winning; he was, indeed, singularly attractive. Born in August 1792, he had been sent when yet almost a child to the University of Edinburgh, and had done well; but it early became necessary that he should be placed in some position of usefulness, and, recommended by Sir John Leslie and Professor Christison, he obtained the mastership in the new school in Haddington, his first appointment. He was well able to give what was then considered the decidedly masculine education desired by Dr. John Welsh for his only daughter. Such an education would not provoke comment in these days, when girls aspire to, and attain, university honors.

It was otherwise in Jeannie Welsh's childhood, and Mrs. Welsh considered Latin and mathematics sadly out of place in the little girl's education. Herself an accomplished and somewhat intellectual woman, she had kept to the old traditions, and desired nothing further for Jeannie. But the father divined his child's unusual capacity, and determined that it should have scope. The opportunity of private teaching from the young divinity student was all that could be desired. Irving was expected to leave a daily report of his pupil's work and progress. It is recorded that on one occasion, when the work had been eminently unsatisfactory, he paused remorsefully, and at last, with a pitiful look at the eager face beside him, cried, 'Jane! my heart is broken, but it must be *pessima*'—a terrible blow to the small offender, no doubt, but more painful to the tutor.

Edward Irving was then a young man, his pupil only a child, but doubtless those subtle links of sympathy which bound these two natures so closely together in later life were formed in those early days, when the impetuous, bright child sought her knowledge from the tall, handsome youth, and ripened her powers under the deep interest which entered into his teachings. Jeannie worked with eagerness and concentration. She would rise at five in the morning to study, and in the fear of sleeping too long, would tie a weight to one of her ancles that she might awake. She was at this time a most healthy little girl, but did much to injure her health, in her zeal and her ignorance. She took greatly to mathematics, and would, if undetected, sit up half the night over a problem. A story is told of her being greatly perplexed by a proposition in Euclid, and going to bed at last in despair over it. In a dream, it is said, Jeannie got up and did it, and went to bed again. And in the morning, when the consciousness of the dream had vanished, there stood the solution of the problem as testimony of what she had done. No need to point out that Jeannie's brain, eager little soul, was too active—and such it was to the end!

Under Irving's tutorship she advanced rapidly in Latin, and the effect of 'Virgil' and other studies was, she says in one of her old note-books, to change her religion, and make her into a sort of Pagan.

It is strictly true (she says), and it was not alone my religion that these studies influenced, but my whole being was imbued with them. Would I prevent myself from doing a foolish or cowardly thing, I didn't say to myself, 'you mustn't, or if you do you will go to hell hereafter,' nor yet, 'if you do you will be whipt here'; but I said to myself, simply and grandly, 'a Roman would not have done it,' and that sufficed under ordinary temptations. . . . But the classical world in which I lived and moved was best indicated in the tragedy of my doll. It had been intimated to me by one whose wishes were law [probably Edward Irving], that a young lady in 'Virgil' should, for consistency's sake, drop her doll. So the doll, being judged, must be made an end of; and I, 'doing what I would with my own,' like the Duke of Newcastle, quickly decided how. She should end as Dido ended, that doll—as the doll of a young lady in 'Virgil' should end. With her dresses, which were many and sumptuous, her four-posted bed, a faggot or two of cedar allumettes, a few sticks of cinnamon and a nutmeg, I, *non ignara futuri*, constructed her funeral pile—*sub auras*, of course; and this new Dido, being placed in the bed with my help, spoke through my lips the sad last words of Dido the First, which I had then all by heart. . . . The doll having thus spoken, *pallida morte futura*, kindled the pile, and stabbed herself with a penknife, by way of Tyrian sword. Then, however, in the moment of seeing my poor doll blaze up—for, being stuffed with bran, she took fire, and was all over in no time—in that supreme moment my affection for her blazed up also, and I shrieked, and would have saved her, and could not, and went on shrieking till everybody within hearing flew to me and bore me off in a plunge of tears—an epitome of most of one's 'heroic sacrifices,' it strikes me, magnanimously resolved on, ostentatiously gone about, repented of at the last moment, and bewailed with an outcry. Thus was my inner world at that period three-fourths old Roman and one fourth old Fairy.

It is hardly fair to relate this remarkable and touching story, with the addition of bitter comment added by afterwisdom and experience. Mothers, as a rule, would prefer their little girls to adopt a less heroic, simpler, and more merely mischievous method of destroying their dolls. I cannot but suppose Irving to have been the person whose wishes were law in the matter of the doll. So harsh an edict sounds less like the father than the schoolmaster. The note-book which contains this tale of the funeral pyre contains also a long story of her first child-love, told with infinite grace.

When Jeannie was fourteen she wrote a tragedy, with certain youthful faults, it is true, but still showing ability that was remarkable for her age. This was her only dramatic effort; but she often wrote verses, inheriting this pleasant gift from her mother. Mrs. Welsh's verses seem to have been simply soft, sweet, and musical, after the manner, perhaps, of poor 'L. E. L.'; while there was depth and power, and altogether wider intellectual range, in those of Jeannie herself. The verses written in later life, and sent to Lord Jeffrey, are perfect in literary form, and possess the higher charm of strong pathos. But there was never anything commonplace in Jane Welsh.

In considering the home influences under which she spent her early years, I cannot imagine that the relation between mother and daughter was perfectly harmonious. Mrs. Welsh was capricious and arbitrary, beautiful, impulsive, and not overwise perhaps. Her father-in-law, John of Penfillan, is reported to have observed her 'in fifteen different humours in one evening'; though this was, probably, to some extent, mere satirical exaggeration. Still, there was, presumably, some basis for the remark, and fewer humours than fifteen will result in collision in family life, where the elements are strong, fiery, and few. Mrs. Welsh probably shared the faults of many beautiful women—was somewhat hard to please, variable, not easy to live calmly and evenly with. And as she grew older she may have been exacting, unreasonable in some respects, though always of good and exemplary conduct.

When Jeannie was a girl, the two strong wills must certainly have clashed now and then, and the result would hardly show itself in meek filial submission. But there was a deep, almost a passionate, attachment between the mother and daughter, a fact not in any way inconsistent with the want of perfect harmony, but rather explanatory of it: as it is only between those who love each other that such critical sensitiveness is ever developed. Indifference is an easier atmosphere in which to live at peace; and no indifference was possible between these two natures of quick affections and quick tempers. The experience is a common one, and readily understood.

CHAPTER II

A. D. 1819—1821

Strong attachment between the father and daughter—The last talk—Sudden illness and death of Dr. John Welsh—Jeannie's 'Paganism'—Serious thoughts—'Early letters' to Eliza Stodart—Boarding-school in Edinburgh—Active tendencies—Teaching—Characteristics more plainly shown—The loss of the father's influence—Haddington felt to be dull—Early Lovers—Power of language.

BUT Jeannie's strongest attachment was to her father. Dr. John Welsh must have inspired, not only deep, admiring reverence in his child, but a love that was truly the strongest feeling in her heart, the master-passion in her young nature for many years—one of those unique sympathies, never to be replaced, even by tender ties of another kind. This loyal nature of Jane Welsh preserved through life the freshness of these natural affections; could never bear to see even the chimney-tops of Templand, after her mother had died there, and returned to mourn at her father's grave in Haddington, thirty years after his death, with all the pain and faithful love that a recent loss could have called forth.

She lost her father just at the time when his influence would have been most valuable and active in forming her character. It was when Jane Welsh was little over eighteen years of age that, one September afternoon, she had an ever-memorable drive with her father, who had a distant patient to visit. It was not unusual for him to take his daughter with him on these country drives. But this was destined to be a special day; for it was, in fact, the end of that close and loving intercourse of father and daughter, and not, as the eager girl supposed, only the beginning of a deeper and yet dearer link between them; for on this day the usually silent man spoke much, and long, and eloquently, to his Jeannie, and with a depth of feeling which struck her, at the time, as something new and impressive.

He told her she was a good girl, capable of being useful and precious to him and the circle she would live in; that she must summon her utmost judgment and seriousness to choose her path, and be what he expected of her; that he did not think she had yet seen the life-partner that would be worthy of her—in short, that he expected her to be wise, as well as good-looking and good; all this in a tone and manner that filled her poor little heart with surprise, and a kind of sacred joy, coming from the man she, of all men, revered.*

These fatherly counsels, so heartfelt, so entirely suited to Jeannie's needs, were all she ever had from that time—for ever. He had spoken his last to her; on the morrow, possibly on the same evening, Dr. Welsh developed symptoms of malignant typhoid fever, caught from a patient. The illness being of so deadly a kind, he at once, with a physician's instinct, gave orders that Jeannie should not enter his room. Unselfish to the last, he denied himself the solace of her bright presence. The girl, in her violent grief and anguish, did, however, on one occasion, force herself into the sick-room, but he ordered her to leave it, and she obeyed. But all that night she lay on the stairs, outside his door, in agony. On the fourth day he passed away. The treatment of this terrible disease was but imperfectly understood at that time, even by the best medical authorities. A brother of Dr. John Welsh, himself a medical man, was called in, and, in his anxiety to save life, had bled the sufferer profusely, which may or may not have hastened the fatal event. Thus, at forty-three years of age, Dr. John Welsh was cut off, in September 1819, and the home at Haddington broken and changed.†

* ' Reminiscences,' II. 94.
† Appendix 3, on ' Dr. John Welsh's Illness and Death.'

Before sorrow had been tasted, the lively girl had spoken laughingly of her 'Paganism'; but other thoughts now quickened within her. As is often the case with bright and mobile natures, there lay in Jane Welsh a real seriousness, too deep for words, and only evident when she was stirred by passionate emotion. Writing to Mrs. Welsh of Penfillan a fortnight after Dr. Welsh's death, she says:—

This has indeed been an unexpected and overwhelming blow. My father's death was a calamity I almost never thought of. If on any occasion the idea did present itself to me, it was immediately repelled as being too dreadful to be realized for many, many years, and too painful to occupy any present place in my thoughts. Until this misfortune fell upon me I never knew what it was to be really unhappy. . . .

You, my dear grandmother, have had many trials; but, if I mistake not, you will still remember the bitterness of the *first*, above all others; you will still be able to recall the feeling of disappointment and despair which you experienced when calamity awoke you from your dream of security, and dispelled the infatuation which led you to expect that you alone were to be exempted from this world's misery. But you are good, and I am judging of your feelings by my own. When young as I am, perhaps you were not, as I am, thoughtless, and unprepared for the chastisement of the Divine Power.

Here we find the little formality of expression induced by the fact of writing to an elderly relative, though the pain of the young heart, even here, speaks clearly through the careful phrases. A much more natural expression of grief is found in the first of that most valuable collection of 'Early Letters of Jane Welsh Carlyle,' edited by David G. Ritchie, fellow and tutor of Jesus College, Oxford. These letters, the bulk of which are addressed to Mr. Ritchie's great-aunt, form a most important addition to our knowledge of Jane Welsh. In fact, they represent absolutely all the actual material for any account of her during the years when most of them were written. And they are highly significant, as well as characteristic.

Miss Eliza Stodart, great-aunt of the editor, was a niece of Mr. Bradfute, a partner in the firm of Bell and Bradfute, of Edinburgh. The young lady lived with her uncle at 22 George Square, and there was a very close friendship between her and Jane Welsh. The friendship included Mr. Bradfute, who is often named 'Bradie' in these letters, and has sundry kisses sent him in Jane's letters to Eliza, or her 'Dear Bess,' or 'Dear Angel Bessy,' as she often calls her friend.

It is only since the publication of the 'Early Letters' that Mr. D. G. Ritchie has received information which clears up a point that was doubtful in Jane Welsh's earlier history. A correspondent—Mr. A. K. Mackenzie, of Ravelrig, Balerno, Midlothian—places it beyond all doubt that Jane Welsh was at a boarding-school in Edinburgh. Mr. Mackenzie's wife's aunt, Mrs. Walrond, of Calder Park, (maiden name, Jane Hastings), was at Miss Hall's boarding-school in Edinburgh *with Jane Welsh.* 'Miss Hall's,' writes Mr. Mackenzie, 'was a well-known school, latterly in Great King Street; but as that street could scarcely have been built before 1820, it must have been elsewhere before that.' Here is one little point in Jane Welsh's history fortunately cleared up. Evidently Mrs. Welsh had been anxious that her brilliant daughter should have what was then termed a '*finishing*'—an opportunity, namely, of acquiring certain feminine accomplishments and elegances not easily attainable in the Haddington school, yet needful to blend with the rather masculine education she had already received.

We find a confirmation of this episode of ' boarding-school' in an allusion in a letter written by Mrs. Carlyle, and dated Craigenputtock, November, 1829. She writes to Miss Stodart: 'I liked Edinburgh last time as well as I did at sixteen! (you know how well that was), and cried as much at leaving it.' We see the reference now, and how natural it was that Jeannie Welsh, while at Miss Hall's school, may have occasionally gone ' to 22 George Square on Saturdays, and taken her gloves and stockings to be mended,' for this was always the tradition in the Stodart family, and appears well supported by fact. This fixes the date of 'boarding-school' as probably 1817-18. No doubt those were happy days. Eliza Stodart, the recipient of Jane Welsh's early letters, was evidently much trusted and loved by her friend.

The grief of the young is sharp and bitter. We do not wonder to find Jane Welsh cast down by her father's death, and passionately sad. She describes the first drive to Haddington Church after the funeral; the hatefulness of the changed, yet familiar aspect of the scene. Colour and warmth had left the well-known surroundings looked on by those haggard young eyes. 'I looked out only once,' she says, 'and I thought the stones were covered with snow, everything looked so white and bleak!' And this was in early golden-autumn days. In her next letter she says, 'God bless you, and preserve you from such a loss as mine.'

But hers was not a nature to sink into apathy and mere selfish repining. It was not long ere her instincts of activity reasserted themselves in the efforts she made to teach her Aunt Elizabeth—French, drawing, and geography. Two other pupils, young girls, joined in receiving the lessons. Nor was the fair instructress herself idle in self-improvement, but energetically studied Italian and French, always with the sense that it was something done in memory of her 'adored father,' and 'first blessing!'

Jane Welsh was keenly sensible of the advantages she owed to the sound education with which her father had provided her. The habits of study in which she had been trained, were now priceless, and helped her to begin life without that father, whose life had such a hold upon her own. The mother and daughter continued for some time at Haddington, able to live in comfort, even with elegance. After settling a small annuity on his widow, Dr. Welsh left everything belonging to him to his daughter. Thus she was, in a moderate sense, an heiress, and the object of numberless matrimonial designs and speculations.

The withdrawal of the father's influence while she was yet so young, at such a critical time of life for the development of character, was a great drawback to her. Mrs. Welsh, sunk in her own grief, possessed but little influence on her daughter, whose *esprit fort* rapidly asserted itself, and resulted in one of the most marked individualities ever clothed in delicate and fascinating exterior.

The early letters to Eliza Stodart show a power of sarcasm, a caustic wit; waywardness too, and impatience. The lovely girl is sharp with her pen, presumably no less so with her tongue. She displays a strong Scotch plainness and hardness of speech, a cutting, common-sense judgment, and was not apt to attribute lofty or beautiful motives to any one, be their conduct what it might. The shrewdness and incisive wit would have been altogether detestable, taken apart from the brilliant intellectual gifts and the truly feminine charm of the lovely girl who had such an armoury of powerful weapons at command. It was a strange combination, one that boded ill for the future.

Her uncompromising habit of denunciation was manifest even in these early days. It was at first merely that wonderful, untempered severity of youth, which disposes of the claims of others with such triumphant despatch. It might, under other auspices, have mellowed into a gentle and wise toleration; but that was not to be.

Jane Welsh was effusive at times, but not tender. Her health, never robust, was always delicately balanced, her temperament too finely strung for undisturbed normal physical well-being. She was fiery, quick, and keen. Her untried heart was ignorant as yet of the sacred 'strength of that love or divine charity which 'beareth all things, hopeth all things, suffereth long, and is kind.' Hers was quite another idea of life and its potentialities. The world—her little world-sphere—was to be subjugated, made to bend low to that imperious will of hers, and her little foot was to be firmly planted on its neck. And the thought of love and marriage was much in her mind. It is satisfactory to find, however, that the 'Robert' who is described as 'looking divine' was an uncle, not a lover. 'Benjamin B——' she calls 'one of the most frank, unaffected young men I have seen.' And a year or two later she speaks of meeting him 'on the opposite bank of the river.'

Let any human being (she says) conceive a more tantalising situation!—I saw him, and durst not make any effort to attract his attention, though, had my will been consulted in the matter, to have met him *eyes* to *eyes* and *soul* to *soul* I would have swam—ay, swam across, at the risk of being dosed with water-gruel for a month to come! . . .

Providence has surely some curious design respecting this youth and me! It was on my birthday we parted—it was on my birthday we met, or (but for that confounded river) should have met again.

This letter is addressed to Eliza Stodart from Templand, the home of Walter Welsh, with whom his widowed daughter was staying. Jane adds, in her plain, uncompromising frankness of language: 'I wonder what the devil keeps my mother here!' Years afterwards, in 1825, Jane Welsh writes to Eliza Stodart, betraying at once her feminine unstability, and her knowledge of Latin: '"Times are changed, and we are changed in them." Mr. Benjamin B—— is become the most disagreeable person on this planet.' This little episode is taken as one of many.

But we return to the year 1820, when, after a journey to Liverpool, where some time was spent with her mother's brother, Mr. John Welsh, and other visits involving an absence of some months, Mrs. Welsh and her daughter returned to their lonely home in Haddington. The restless spirit of Jane Welsh was sorely tried by this return to familiar things.

Well, my beloved cousin (she writes to Miss Stodart), here

I am once more at the bottom of the pit of dulness, hemmed in all round, straining my eyeballs and stretching my neck to no purpose.

Was ever starling in a more desperate plight? But I *will get out* —by the wife of Job, I will!

An eloquent abuse of her native town is followed by:—

After all, there is much in it that I love. I love the bleaching-green, where I used to caper and tumble and roll . . . in the days of my *wee existence;* and the school-house, where I carried away prizes . . .; and, above all, I feel an affection for a field by the side of the river, where corn is growing now, and where a hay-rick once stood. You remember it. . . . I was very happy then. All my little world lay glittering in tinsel at my feet! But years have passed over it since, and storm after storm has stripped it of much of its finery.

We quote this to illustrate the character which, at twenty years old, could describe the scenes of her childhood as 'glittering in tinsel.' Why not have called them pure gold? What a scepticism of happiness is betrayed in this expression! what absence of the heart-free, sound, wholesome joy of life! The passage is most significant.

In this very letter the young girl's mood promptly changes, as she goes on to discuss 'my quondam lover, the "goosish" man,' whose attempt at serious wooing was met with scorn and derision. He had arrived in hot haste, 'twelve hours after he received my answer to his letter . . . and in the morning sent a few nonsensical lines to announce his nonsensical arrival.' Poor young man! His chance was indeed small. Little wonder that, in his nervous trepidation before this beautiful young angel with the two-edged sword, his power of expression should fail him, and he should gravely announce having been at a party some days before 'with his arm under his hat,' and, desperately correcting himself, 'with his *head* under his *arm*'; the lively girl's comment being, ' it was of very little consequence *where* his head was!' This ill-starred suitor found that even two waistcoats, one of figured velvet, and one of sky-blue satin, failed to plead his cause. Gossamer silk hose and morocco slippers were all in vain; he departed, presumably 'a sadder and wiser man.' Jane Welsh adds: 'A visit from a man with any brains in his head would really be an act of mercy to us here.' With what emphasis that wish was presently to be granted!

We may note that the 'cousinship' with Eliza Stodart seems to have been merely a term of good-will and liking, as Jane Welsh always mentions Mr. Bradfute as 'your uncle.'

It would seem that Jane Welsh was not inclined to domestic interests in these days. She manifests much impatience at being made the medium of some homely and housewifely messages from Mrs. Welsh to her 'Angel Bessie.' Advice as to the quantity of sugar needful to make marmalade, and directions with regard to the management of sick hens, cause quite an outburst of wrath in the young amanuensis. After the words, 'Moreover—Oh! she has plenty of cursed, ugly, wee black "pigs" [jars for the said marmalade] at your service,' she adds, 'Not one word more will I write for her, by——!'

Even in those days this must have been unusual language for a young lady to use. And the existence of it, in many of these early letters, must guard us from supposing that Jane Welsh learned her use of expletives and her tremendous force of language from Carlyle, whom she had as yet never seen. This peculiarity of strong language, far stronger than occasion demanded, was one of those extraordinary resemblances between these two persons, who, while presenting some noticeable points of difference, were yet strangely, altogether unaccountably alike in many ways. With them both it was the *fortiter in re*, not the *suaviter in modo*, which ruled their outward manifestations. In them both lay deep tenderness—the deepest—ill-developed, and huddled into a corner, its diviner outcomes smothered and choked; but it was there, and at moments of strong emotion it came forth, full-grown, unmistakable in its strength and beauty.

CHAPTER III

A. D. 1821

First meeting with Thomas Carlyle—Introduction by Edward Irving—The May evening—Irving's attachment to Miss Welsh—Carlyle and Margaret Gordon—Isabella Martin—George Rennie—Miss Welsh's early impressions of Carlyle—Literary ambitions and projects—Irving's engagement to Miss Isabella Martin—Miss Welsh's hesitation in accepting Carlyle as a lover—Miss Welsh's readings of Rousseau—George Rennie's departure—Visit of Carlyle to Haddington—Possibilities.

BUT to return to Jane Welsh. It was late in the month of May, 1821, that Thomas Carlyle appeared on the scene. Mrs. Welsh had given Edward Irving leave to bring his gifted friend over to Haddington and introduce him. This, accordingly, was carried out by Irving on one of his occasional holiday sallies from Glasgow, now the scene of his labours. It was at Haddington he sometimes recruited his strength, and he was always a welcome guest in Mrs. Welsh's house, for the sake of old times. It all came about in the most natural manner possible. Irving was now engaged to be married: his betrothed, Miss Martin, being the daughter of the minister in Kirkcaldy, where Irving had taken an appointment as schoolmaster on leaving Haddington. It was natural that Irving should wish to introduce Thomas Carlyle to these dear, valued friends of his. He knew how keenly the intellectual Miss Welsh would enjoy the original genius of his friend. And Irving was proud of Carlyle, and no doubt longed to show him off where he was sure of appreciation.

But let us consider the real position of these three people

—their inner standpoint, not apparent in their outward seeming. Thomas Carlyle, the rugged, fiery peasant, had passed through his one tender passage, his love for Margaret Gordon, to whom, but for the interposition of friends, he would probably have been affianced. She must have loved him, to read his powers so clearly in an exterior that ill-expressed him. 'Genius will render you great' she had written to him. 'May virtue render you beloved! Remove the awful distance between you and ordinary men by kind and gentle manners!' An angel could not have counselled Carlyle better. Small wonder that, many years later, in 1840, when he met her, then Lady Bannerman, riding in Hyde Park, her eyes mutely recognized him. He seems to have had no other attachment till he met his fate in the bright eyes of Jane Welsh. He had not yet transacted what he called his 'conversion,' or 'new birth'—had not yet 'authentically taken the devil by the nose.' 'Doubt had darkened into unbelief.' That was his own account of his state. He was indeed forlorn and needing comfort.

There is no mystery whatever as to the fact that Edward Irving loved Jane Welsh, whatever his actual position with the Martins may have been. The fact of his finding an attached and amiable wife in Miss Martin, and proving a good and loving husband to her, can in no way alter what is known to have been his devoted love for his old pupil.

Folded among Irving's letters to Miss Welsh is a passionate sonnet addressed to her, and on the other side of it (she had preserved his verses and so much of the accompanying letter as was written on the opposite page of the paper) a fragment, evidently written at this period (about 1820), in which he told her that he was about to inform Miss Martin, and possibly her father, of his feelings.

We have seen how that ended. Miss Welsh nobly refused to listen to the addresses of a man who was not free; and Irving, though he afterwards confessed that the struggle had almost made his 'faith and principles to totter'—to use his own words—submitted to the inevitable. In a letter he wrote to Miss Welsh after the matter was decided he says:—

My well-beloved Friend and Pupil,—When I think of you, my mind is overspread with the most affectionate and tender regard, which I neither know how to name nor to describe. One thing I know—it would long ago have taken the form of the most devoted attachment but for an intervening circumstance, and shown and pleaded itself before your heart by a thousand actions, from which I must now restrain myself. Heaven grant me its grace to restrain myself; and, forgetting my own enjoyments, may I be enabled to combine into your single self all that duty and plighted faith leave at my disposal. When I am in your company my whole soul would rush to serve you, and my tongue trembles to speak my heart's fulness. But I am enabled to forbear, and have to find other avenues than the natural ones for the overflowing of an affection which would hardly have been able to confine itself within the avenues of nature, if they had all been opened.

But I feel within me the power to prevail, and at once to satisfy duty to another and affection to you. I stand truly upon ground that seems to shake and give way beneath me, but my help is in Heaven.

Edward Irving had, as we have seen, left Kirkcaldy an engaged man, pledged to Miss Isabella Martin, who afterwards became his wife. Yet was there an unsatisfied longing in his heart also, for the image of the bright, eager face of Jeannie Welsh, his former pupil, haunted his mind and thoughts, and refused to be banished. Parting from her while she was still almost a child, he had yet had opportunities of seeing her while she ripened into her lovely womanhood, and he had learned to know his own heart, whose deep strong love was, alas! given to her, and not by any means to be taken away and bestowed on Miss Martin, or any other woman. Irving knew it, blinded himself to it, perhaps, in a measure, and at one time desperately hoped against hope. But the days of hope were over before 1821, and he knew he was only looking at the roses in another man's garden. Still, he saw Jane Welsh, and time drifted on.

What, then, of her, at this momentous time? She shared the knowledge and the sorrow. The ardent girl had learned that Irving loved her; she returned his love, and no doubt blindly hoped, as he had hoped, that the Martins would set him free from his engagement. That suspense was all over now, and stern reality had looked her in the face. Proud and honourable, she had received his tale of love with the understanding that, unless he were absolutely free, there must be no such footing between them as that of lovers. And he was not free, never *would* be free to offer his love —and there was an end of it.

There is no doubt, therefore, that a mutual attachment existed between these two young people. Yet we cannot predict that Jane Welsh would have found *happiness* had her fate united her to this religious and enthusiastic nature. There would probably, as she herself said in later life, have been '*no tongues.*' But we cannot see that there was a strong likelihood of happiness between them, as her mocking wit and fine sense of the ludicrous, would have harmonised imperfectly with his simple, devout earnestness. And she might have come to despise him for his blind faith; whilst she never could despise Thomas Carlyle. That bitterness, at least, was spared her, in the ill-prospering of her first love. So there was in her an emptiness of heart and a seeking out for some deeper interest in life, when first she met Carlyle.

No wonder the proud, brilliant girl looked with immense contempt on her many would-be admirers, and thought within herself that it was all mockery and sham. It was to literature that she now looked for an opening for her ambition, and an interest that should not fail her; and it was as a literary man of genius that Carlyle was presented to her, in her then empty and dissatisfied state of mind and heart.

Truly they were three remarkable personalities who met

in that drawing-room which looked out into the flower-garden, with its trim box-edgings and slender birch-trees, on that sweet May evening, so memorable a date in the lives of two, at least, of the three who formed the little company. Mrs. Welsh was now in the third year of her widowhood; 'an air of deep sadness lay on her,' says Carlyle, 'and she soon withdrew.'

So the three craving, unsatisfied natures, the three rare intellects, the three who knew each other so little, and themselves so infinitely less, spent their first hours together. 'The summer twilight,' says Carlyle, 'was pouring in rich and soft; I felt as one walking transiently in upper spheres.' Probably none of the three ever forgot that hour. The memory of it was in Carlyle's mind when, not long after, he wrote that exquisite passage in 'Sartor Resartus' beginning, 'The conversation took a higher turn: one fine thought called forth another.' . . .

This visit lasted three or four days. Writing of it in later times Carlyle says: 'There were others besides the one fair figure most of all important to me. We met often, in her mother's house—sat talking with the two, several hours, almost every evening. The beautiful, bright, earnest young lady was intent on literature, as the highest aim in life.' Was this so? Was it natural that it should be so? Was Carlyle so far deceived as to believe this astounding fiction, from the lips of the young creature, just newly blossomed into life, and ignorant of so much that goes to form happiness?

Later on, he was undeceived on one point at least—he knew from her own pen that she had loved Irving 'passionately,' had hidden that love, had jested at Irving's expense to mislead Carlyle and to shield her own heart—like that bird which starts up in solitary moorland places with shrill cries, hovering over the place where its nest is NOT, to protect the precious nook where it IS!

This womanly instinct must not be harshly dealt with. It

bears a sacred tenderness in it, and has no real kinship with voluntary untruth or misleading. Jane Welsh, sternly honourable, as she was to the last fibre in her nature, laid down this love for Irving, and gave it up, and in time it ceased to exist—as an attachment. She would not love another woman's husband. But a love such as hers had been, is not put off as we put off a garment; the nature and character receive certain undeniable impressions, and it could never be with Jane Welsh, as though she had not met Edward Irving.

Many persons are disposed to say that, in this bright, quick nature of hers, whatever impression there was, must have been a transient one: that many young girls were in love with the winning young man; that, as one of them said in later life, 'Oh! we were *all* in love with him!' It may have been so; but from the documentary evidence in existence we are forced to believe that in the case of Jane Welsh, it was a far deeper feeling at one time, and, had Carlyle been more like other men, the letter in which Miss Welsh confessed to her former feeling for Edward Irving, might certainly have made him pause in his wooing. But he was *not* like other men, and regarded the matter with totally different judgment. It was by no means unnatural that Miss Welsh should, finally, think a marriage with Carlyle possible. She may have cherished a dream of close companionship with a brilliant mind, the realisation of a satisfied ambition fed with aliment that should not fail. She sought, perhaps, some reliable, tangible basis of happiness.

Some such thoughts may have animated Carlyle at this time of first impressions; though, in truth, he hardly knew what a companionship was, and often needed, as an old friend said, 'a solar system to himself'—so that invisible agencies would noiselessly minister to his personal needs.

On this visit, Carlyle, charged by Irving with the direction of Jane Welsh's studies, introduced some of his favourite German authors to her notice, and obtained permission to send her books now and then, which gave occasion to 'bits of writing to and from'; and when she visited the Bradfute household, in George's Square, Edinburgh, Carlyle was allowed to call. And thus the memorable acquaintance progressed.

I was not her declared lover (says Carlyle), nor could she admit me as such in my waste and uncertain posture of affairs and prospects; but we were becoming thoroughly acquainted with one another, and her tacit, hidden, but to me visible, friendship, for me was the happy island in my otherwise dreary, vacant, and forlorn existence in those years.

The German studies were more wholesome literary food for Miss Welsh than some of the books she was reading about this time. The reading of 'La Nouvelle Héloïse' hardly suggested valuable ideas; perhaps the least hurtful effect of such reading was to foster a contempt in Jane Welsh for the raw Scotch youths who admired her.

No lover (she writes to Eliza Stodart early in 1822) will Jane Welsh ever find like St. Preux, no husband like Wolmar (I don't want to insinuate that I should like them *both*), and to no man will she give her heart and pretty hand, who bears to these no resemblance. George Rennie! James Aitken! Robert Macturk! James Baird! Robby Angus! O Lord! O Lord! Where is the St. Preux? Where is the Wolmar?

We admire the *naïveté* with which Jane Welsh tells her 'Angel Bessy,' commenting on Rousseau's heroine, Julie Étange, that she, Jane Welsh, 'does not wish to countenance such irregularities among her female acquaintances,' but qualifies this gentle condemnation by the admission that 'were *any* individual of them to meet with *such* a *man*, to struggle as she struggled, to *yield* as she yielded, and to repent as she repented,' she 'would love that woman better than the chastest, coldest prude between John o' Groat's House and Land's End.' To such sentiments had she 'screwed up her violin strings' after reading the 'fatal Book.' It is amusing, too, to hear her apostrophise the race of old maids as 'virtuous, venerable females,' and express pity for her aunt, who, 'poor thing! does not understand love.'

In this same letter she describes Carlyle, from whom she had just had a letter announcing a visit to Haddington. She says:—

He is something liker to St. Preux than George Craig is to Wolmar. He has *his* talents, *his* vast and cultivated mind, *his* vivid imagination, *his* independence of soul, and *his* high-souled principles of honour. But then—ah! these *buts*—— . . . Want of elegance! Want of elegance, Rousseau says, is a defect no woman can overlook.

It must be remembered that, at this time, there was a rather serious love-affair between Jane Welsh and George Rennie; it had been the most serious of the many 'affairs,' and was drawing to a somewhat unexpected close. Strange to say, in this case, from some unexplained reason, it was the gentleman who withdrew from the adventure. Carlyle speaks of him in the 'Reminiscences' as 'a clever, decisive, very ambitious, but quite unmelodious young fellow, whom we knew afterwards here [in Chelsea] as sculptor and M. P.' Tender passages would seem to have taken place between this 'decisive' young man and Jane Welsh, perhaps without much depth of feeling. But she says: 'O wretch! I wish I could hate him, but I cannot. . . . And when Friday comes, I always think how neatly I used to be dressed, and sometimes I give my hair an additional brush and put on a clean frill, just from habit. Oh! the devil take him!'

There was certainly, at the time, some feeling on Jane Welsh's part for this 'unmelodious young fellow,' for when he was going abroad she writes to Miss Stodart: 'I had not heard his voice for many a day, but then I had heard those who had conversed with him. I had seen objects he had looked on, I had breathed the air that he had breathed.' And when the young man called to take leave of her, Jane Welsh says, 'I scarcely heard a word he said, my own heart beat so loud.' The young lady promptly discards this unwonted mood of tenderness, and goes on, in the same letter, to describe a visit from Carlyle:—

Mr. Carlyle was with us two days (she writes), during the greater part of which I read German with him. It is a noble language; I am getting on famously. He scratched the fender dreadfully; I must have a pair of carpet-shoes and handcuffs prepared for him the next time. His tongue only should be left at liberty; his other members are most fantastically awkward.

In concluding the same letter she says : ' I will be happier contemplating my beau-ideal than a real, substantial, eating, drinking, sleeping, honest husband !'

To us, these expressions about George Rennie seem rather intended to mislead than enlighten Miss Stodart, for the name that was never written—the name of Edward Irving—was linked with a deeper, unspoken feeling; and the friendship for George Rennie, which outlasted time and change, was of another kind, since, many years later, when he lay dying in London, with wife and family about him, Mrs. Carlyle went, at Mrs. Rennie's wish, and watched her old companion and playfellow in his last hours on earth. This, we would affirm, she *could* not have done in the case of Edward Irving; and this paradox is no paradox to those who know women's hearts. But Jane Welsh was loyal, and deeply kind-hearted, and there was nothing to render that last tender and sacred office of friendship impossible.

CHAPTER IV

A. D. 1821-1825

Miss Welsh's German studies—Projected literary work—Irving's anxieties as to Miss Welsh's reading—Remonstrances—Irving goes to London—He introduces Carlyle to the Bullers—The tutorship—More intimate correspondence between Carlyle and Miss Welsh—Friendship the footing prescribed by Miss Welsh—Irving's marriage to Miss Martin—Continuation of the Buller engagement—Carlyle's wooing, and its results—Stoical acceptance of repulse—Dr. Fyffe—Miss Welsh's admiration for genius—The letter from Goethe to Carlyle—Sympathy on Byron's death—'Benjamin B——'—Miss Welsh does not pay a visit to the Irvings in London.

THE thought of Edward Irving as a lover was put away, and in time took its place with the sad, beautiful things that were not to be—'Es wär zu schön gewesen!' Meantime George Rennie was on the high seas, and Miss Welsh busy with her German studies, laughingly considering some literary work that should tend to the 'immortalising of old maids.' She declined an offer made her by one of the editors of a proposed local magazine, and was ready to swear that the first number would be the last. The offer in question, made by Mr. George Cunningham, was that she should assist the projected literary work with her pen; and certainly she would have been a brilliant contributor, but her powers were destined to be otherwise employed. Her interest in German was very genuine. In an enforced absence from her studies she says, writing to Miss Stodart, 'Oh my beloved German! my precious, precious time!'

These German readings with Carlyle were a source of fresh anxiety to Edward Irving.

I would like (he writes to Thomas Carlyle) to see her surrounded with a more noble set of companions than Rousseau (your friend), and Byron, and such-like—— . . . And I don't think it will much mend the matter when you get her introduced to Von Schiller and Von Goethe, and your other nobles of German literature. I fear Jane has already dipped too deep into that spring, so that, unless some more solid food be afforded, I fear she will escape altogether out of the region of my sympathies, and the sympathies of honest, home-bred men.

Irving also feared the influence of some of the German writers as likely to undermine Miss Welsh's religious convictions, which he had himself laboured to establish in what he felt more and more convinced was the only true form. It was natural, no doubt, that he should view Carlyle as a dangerous teacher; but it is no less true that Carlyle's own principles, as applied to life and morals, were as pure in their results as can be inspired by the most orthodox creed in existence.

In 1822 an important change took place in Carlyle's circumstances. Since his retirement from his post of schoolmaster in Kirkcaldy, in 1818, he had led a struggling life in Edinburgh, writing, reading, translating, at very moderate remuneration, borne down by poverty and dyspepsia. But at this time his constant friend, Edward Irving, was invited as minister to the Caledonian chapel in Hatton Garden, and his subsequent brilliant success as preacher there brought him in contact with many distinguished persons. Among these was Mrs. Charles Buller, a wealthy lady with sons. Recommended by Irving, Thomas Carlyle became tutor to two of these lads, and was at once in easy circumstances, and nobly helped his family.

The correspondence with Haddington continued, and grew even more intimate. Mr. Froude says: 'The relations between tutor and pupil developed, or promised to develop, into a literary partnership.' As such it might have been a success. There was no sign of tender feeling on Jane Welsh's part, and a decided check imposed on the earliest indication of gallantry. *Friendship*, the beautiful girl maintained, was the only footing possible between them. And Carlyle acquiesced, without a suspicion. It was, perhaps, not difficult for him to observe this wish of hers.

Edward Irving was in London, out of the way, but took his trouble with him, and did, it seems, contemplate even now informing Miss Martin and her father of his feelings. But the Martins had justice and custom on their side, and, though actually appealed to, stood firm to their contract. A letter from Irving to Jane Welsh after the final decision was made is painful in its forced tone of resignation, its mixture of passionate love and religious formula—simple, true, and manly as is the attitude adhered to.

Upon Irving the effect of this disappointment was undoubted and abiding. A few months later he married Miss Martin, and entered on a new life. His old self was left behind. As Mr. Froude says, 'the old, simple, unconscious Irving ceased to exist.' But there were other potent causes in Irving's career from this point which rendered simplicity and unconsciousness difficult to maintain, though his married life was calm and loving; more peaceful than it could have been with the quick, fiery-hearted, brilliant Jane Welsh. And she surely would not have found her beau-ideal in Edward Irving; nor was she formed for that simple and uncomplicated happiness which suffices to so many women and wives. 'Where the light is brightest the shadows are deepest,' so say the Germans; and both were very vivid in this remarkable girl. It would be hard to say what Jane Welsh would have really considered as happiness.

In any case, she now turned to her strange relation with Carlyle, which offered interest of no common kind. He wrote her his discontented and yet brilliant letters during the Buller engagement—admitted that he had 'quiet, and free air, and returning health '—and besought her not to be in pain for him.

In October 1822 he paid a hasty visit to his faithful and

beloved old mother, always dearer, practically, to him, than any one on earth. Here, in Mainhill, a most rudimentary little farmhouse, he tried to comfort his mother as to his spiritual state; no doubt, over their midnight pipes, they exchanged much earnest talk, and these must have been among the most precious hours ever spent by Thomas Carlyle. Meanwhile, the 'paragon of gifted young girls' abode with her dignified, sad, and beautiful mother, in the comfortable house at Haddington, among what Carlyle called the 'elegant whim-whams' of a refined home, fastidious as to the binding of her 'wee, wee Cicero,' playing the piano, singing Moore's melodies, and sending kisses to 'Brady.' There had been a visit of 'Uncle Robert,' once spoken of as 'perfectly divine,' now evidently fallen from that giddy elevation. 'There' (she says) 'was my precious uncle, sneezing, snarling, and sometimes snoring; the Lady [her aunt] dressing, yawning, and practicing postures; our mother wearying her heart to entertain them, all in vain, and our sorrowful self casting many a wistful glance towards the little table where Schiller and Alfieri lay neglected.'

Thus opened the year 1823. In May, Carlyle spent a week in Annandale, and wrote to Miss Welsh: 'Here I purpose to spend my leisure, and to think sweetly of friends that are far away.' Such thoughts must have been mostly of the charming girl he was addressing. The position could not possibly remain at a fixed point of friendship and literary sympathy. Such terms become flimsy pretences between a man and a woman unless each has some deep, abiding haven of the heart, whence, safely anchored, they can ' sport upon the shore;' and neither Thomas Carlyle nor Jane Welsh had such abiding-place. She truly sought none such, but was amused, flattered, perhaps at times touched, to see this man of genius at her feet. And his social status seemed, no doubt, to her a very real barrier against the idea of a marriage between them. It was a temptation hard for the lively girl to resist—that of playing with the feelings of this uncouth and remarkable man, and it is not to be wondered at that she should yield to it. So he was 'caressed or chidden by the dainty hand,' and was well contented.

He was ever ready to listen to her lively sallies; and in the summer of 1823, when staying in some house she particularly disliked, Miss Welsh, dating her letter, in her forcible language, as from '*Hell*,' must have somewhat overstated her gratitude for Carlyle's affection for her. She must have expressed herself with less reticence than usual, carelessly perhaps; but by Carlyle, little practised in the ways of woman, what she said was eagerly taken as a willingness on her part to become his wife. Nothing could have been further from the young lady's thoughts, and she lost no time in explaining herself, so as to do away with the effect of what she had done.

My friend! (she said) I love you—I repeat it, though I find the expression a rash one. All the best feelings of my nature are concerned in loving you. But were you my brother, I should love you the same. No! Your friend I will be, your truest, most devoted friend, while I breathe the breath of life. But your wife, never! Never! not though you were as rich as Croesus, as honoured and renowned as you yet shall be!

This sounds decisive, and Carlyle took it as a conclusive settling of the point, and bore it as a brave man should, replying in terms which, *had Miss Welsh loved him*, would indeed have broken off the intimacy once for all. 'My heart,' he said, 'is too old by almost half a score of years' (he was only twenty-eight), 'and is made of sterner stuff than to break in junctures of this kind.' One might naturally ask, In what kind of juncture, then, would his heart have broken? But he continues: 'I have no idea of dying in the Arcadian shepherd's style for the disappointment of hopes which I never seriously entertained, or had no right to entertain seriously.'

As we have said, between *lovers* such words as these would either have been impossible to be spoken, or impossible to be forgiven; but between this strange pair they produced little effect. Jane Welsh was *désœuvrée*; her life did not give her that whereby her eager, restless nature could live. She could not 'live by bread alone.' She could not lay down the romantic idea of aiding the upward striving of this man of extraordinary genius; there were interest, excitement, occupation of thought, literary sympathy—elements which made life worth living—and the correspondence between herself and Carlyle continued. In a letter to Miss Stodart on March 31, 1823, Jane Welsh writes: 'Often at the end of the week my spirits and my industry begin to flag; but then comes one of Mr. Carlyle's brilliant letters, that inspires me with new resolution, and brightens all my hopes and prospects with the golden hues of his own imagination.'

At this time she busied herself with certain humble *protégés*: A beggar-boy of fifteen—taken on trust as a genius, but with an aversion to all kinds of mortal labour, which could not do away with faults of a less exalted character, such as lying and refusing to wash his face—was one of these. A second pensioner, described as being 'eight years old and a few inches high,' proved more respectable and satisfactory.

These benevolent occupations were supplemented by her 'translating German.' 'As busy at this,' she says, 'as if my fortune in this world and my salvation in the world to come depended on my proficiency in that enchanting tongue.' This devotion to German showed that she wished to please Carlyle, who was also deep in the language.

Jane Welsh was sharp as ever in her sarcasm. She speaks of the 'little gunpowder-man of medicine' (Dr. Fyffe) in singularly cutting terms:—

Now, when he perceives (she writes) that he may bleed or boil himself to the day of Pentecost without interesting this *hard and stony heart* of mine the least in his favour, he is adopting another mode of attack. Instead of *shaving his whiskers*, and using all possible expedients to give him the aspect of a woe-begone man, he is now trying to dazzle my wits with a white hat, silver-headed jockey whip, and bits of leggings of so bright a yellow that it does me ill to look at them.

In this letter she asks her ' dear, dear Angel Bessie ' to do her two tremendous favours, one being to send a book to Dr. Carlyle's lodgings. Dr. John Carlyle was now studying medicine at Edinburgh University, and Miss Welsh had forgotten the name of the people with whom he was lodging. The other favour requested, savours of the mysterious: 'You are to be so very kind as to order for me at Gibson and Craig's one of the best gentlemen's hats, of the most fashionable cut, *not* broad-rimmed. The *outside* measure is enclosed. It is to be a present to my intended husband, so do see that they send a Jemmy one.'

Mr. Ritchie gives the date of this letter as doubtful, and we are inclined to think that it must have been written in 1826 when Carlyle really was Miss Welsh's 'intended husband,' and she may have had some feminine view of smartening him up. Things had not gone so far as this in 1824, when Miss Welsh tells her 'dearest Eliza' how for two weeks she never wearied of her cousin—played chess with him, strolled through the woods with him, or sat on a green bank talking sentiment with him, and, whilst admitting his nature to be most affectionate, his spirit magnificent, his intellect clear and quick, his fancy lively, and himself beautiful, brilliant, graceful, and courtly, yet deplored his not possessing *genius*, that fatal gift, necessary, as she adds, to the destiny of her life. And this was evidently the fact, for, when the momentous choice was at length made, Jane Welsh elected to choose genius, without some of these gracious and attractive accompaniments. Her longing after genius was a real and an unquenchable one; genius in her life-partner was her *sine qua non*, and, for the time, at least, this longing outweighed and dominated all other desires. And the gods heard, and she had her wish.

It would seem that in 1824 Jane Welsh's decision still hung in the balance, however. ' I begin to think,' she says, 'that men and women may be very charming without having *any genius*. Who knows but I shall grow reasonable at last, and descend from my ideal heaven to the real earth—marry —and, O Plato ! make a pudding.' But Jane Welsh acted out her ideal, and proved its real nature and consequences. Her various love-affairs ruffled, but did not stir her. She overwhelmed her unlucky suitors with satirical invective. But she could not treat Thomas Carlyle so. His hold on her lay out of the reach of her mocking spirit. In December 1824 he sent her a letter from Goethe to himself—a copy in characters which she could read, as well as the original. This greatly pleased the ambitious young girl. 'As written to Carlyle himself, it is highly complimentary,' she writes to Miss Stodart, 'and, coming from the man whom he honours almost to idolatry, must have gratified him beyond measure.'

Another yet more precious inclosure was a fragment of a letter from Byron, which affected Miss Welsh most powerfully. 'This, then,' she says, 'was *his* handwriting; *his*, whose image had haunted my imagination for years and years, whose wild, glorious spirit had tinctured all the poetry of my being.' This subject of Byron was one on which sympathetic utterances had been exchanged. When the fatal news had come from Missolonghi, Miss Welsh had written to Carlyle: 'I was told it all alone in a room full of people. If they had said the sun or the moon was gone out of the heavens, it could not have struck me with the idea of a more awful blank in the creation than the words, "Byron is dead!"' Carlyle had answered: 'Poor Byron! Alas! the news of his death came upon my heart like a mass of lead. . . . I dreamed of seeing him and knowing him, but the curtain of everlasting night has hid him from our eyes. We shall go to him; he shall not return to us. There is a blank in your heart and in mine since this man passed away.'

How exquisite must this sympathy, thus expressed by Thomas Carlyle, on this subject, have been to the enthusiastic young girl! What more perfect method could

Carlyle's good angel have suggested to him to ingratiate himself withal in this tenderly romantic heart? And the partaking of this sorrowful regret, taken in conjunction with the use of that charmed possessive pronoun, 'our,' certainly paved the way for nearer relations between these two isolated natures. Carlyle made a decided advance in Miss Welsh's good graces at this time.

In April 1825, Miss Welsh describes an amusing scene: Mr. Benjamin B—— called, bent on serious wooing, and found the field already occupied. Mr. Carlyle was there, a guest, in the drawing-room at Haddington. 'I kept talking,' says Miss Welsh; 'I just kept on talking away to Mr. Carlyle about the Peak of Teneriffe.' Benjamin B—— must have shown much patient perseverance, for it seems he subsequently 'talked for two hours, with a miraculous command of absurdity.' Such was the lady's verdict on his eloquence.

In the same letter to Miss Stodart occur the significant words: 'I do not go to London this season either, for reasons which I have not room to explain. It is not Mr. Irving's fault *this* time!' Mr. Froude tells us how it had been intended that Miss Welsh should visit Irving and his wife in London as soon as they were settled there, 'but Irving could not face the trial.' Brave and good Irving! he would not let *her* face the trial. He loved her better than he loved himself. Had she made that visit at that time, however, we cannot help thinking that the whole course of her own life might have been changed. For she would have gained some self-knowledge; it would have been forced on her—with a painful awakening, perhaps—but it would have prevented her, probably, from marrying as she did. Yet in saying this we are speaking in ignorance as to her having been happier either unwedded or otherwise wedded, since her nature was not easy to be made happy, and the causes which militated most strongly against her happiness were in her own nature, more than in circumstances. So, at least, we are led to think.

CHAPTER V

A. D. 1825

Carlyle in London—Thoughts of marriage—Difficulties—Mrs. Montagu—'Barry Cornwall'—Allan Cunningham—The breaking-off of the Buller engagement—Irving's hospitality—Serious reflections—Consultations with Miss Welsh—The idea of 'living on a farm'—Miss Welsh's very different project—Carlyle's independent spirit—Exceptional position of affairs—Miss Welsh's delicate health—The proposal to farm Craigenputtock—Final decision left to Miss Welsh—Suspense—Discussion—Modest wants of Carlyle—Miss Welsh demurs at the essential conditions, but still proffers friendship—Carlyle's renewed professions of attachment.

CARLYLE had sailed to London on June 5 of this same year, to continue his duties in the Buller family, and to see something of a new life. Irving had been sanguine that literary society would open its arms to a man of genius like his friend. Carlyle himself gravely doubted this, and had rather a hankering for some remote and undisturbed nook in Scotland, where he might possess his soul in peace, and devote himself to work, unmolested, at whatever the spirit might move him to do. Such rural paradise must, of course, contain some helpful and wholly unexacting human presence, which should attend to the 'cares of bread' without troubling him in any way, yet with strict attention to his simple but pronounced needs in this direction. This rendered the plan a difficult one to arrange. Meantime he would go to London, and await a summons from the Buller family. His own description of his reception in Irving's house is characteristic. It may be read in the 'Reminiscences.'

In a letter to Miss Welsh, dated a few days after his arrival, he sketches some of the people he has met; notably,

Mrs. Montagu, of whom his words are, possibly unintentionally, disparaging. It was she whom Irving always called the 'noble lady,' and to whom Carlyle, later on, addressed letters of the most affectionate cordiality; to whom, also, he was indebted for great kindness and hospitality. Carlyle speaks of Barry Cornwall, with 'the dreamy wildness in his eye;' of Allan Cunningham, 'my most dear, modest, kind, good-humoured Allan Cunningham;' and of many others.

The uncertainty of the Bullers' movements greatly annoyed and distracted Carlyle. It ended finally in the breaking-up of the engagement with that family. Carlyle now found himself free, and happier than he had been for some time. Irving's hospitality was immediately at his disposal.

One little trait may be quoted from a letter written to Miss Welsh in October of the same year, when Carlyle was visiting the Irvings at Dover. Carlyle found something hugely ridiculous in the interest Irving and his wife took in their firstborn, and quotes the 'Orator,' as he oftenest styled Irving, as having said on one occasion to his wife: 'Isabella, I think I would wash him with warm water to-night;' on which Carlyle's comment to the young mother, as reported by himself, was that he, were he in her place, would wash him with oil of vitriol if he pleased, and take no one's counsel.

It was, as we must remember, in absolute ignorance of the past that lay between Miss Welsh and Edward Irving, that Carlyle thus discoursed to her of the 'Orator.' 'Oh!' says he, 'that you but saw the giant, with his broad-brimmed hat, his sallow visage, and his sable fleece of hair, carrying the little pepper-box of a creature!' Yet, in the 'Reminiscences,' he adds how Irving said to him: 'Ah! Carlyle, this little creature has been sent to me to soften my hard heart.' And this utterance had evidently touched Carlyle's own heart, which was eminently *not* hard.

An unexpected excursion to Paris followed this holiday; after which Carlyle returned to London, and lived near

Irving, to finish his 'Life of Schiller.' He was still sick in body and perturbed in mind; he writes with intensified bitterness of the Irving family, but says, in a letter to John Carlyle in November: 'Yet were I a dog if I did not love him!' And here again the heart of Thomas Carlyle spoke.

The correspondence with Miss Welsh continued, and she must have been the main element in the dissatisfied and ambitious man's thoughts and schemes. He began to loathe London. He had saved a little money, even after his generous help to his brothers. He felt he must seriously consult her, whose opinion was almost all-in-all to him, and who he had some reason to think might consent to marry him when once he was able to offer her a tolerably comfortable home.

To such conclusion had Carlyle come after long and intimate correspondence with Miss Welsh. His own tastes were of the simplest; he concluded, with beautiful unconsciousness, that hers would also be so. His idea at this time was to take and stock a farm in Annandale, leaving his brother Alexander to manage it. Then he would have quietness to write and study, and the two sources of activity would surely realise a small but sufficient income to marry upon. It was a very simple Utopia, but as illusory as the wildest dreams of the dreamers.

He tells his plans to Miss Welsh, who had evidently thought, in her inexperience, that some ready-made 'pension' of 'sinecure' would be ready, lying at the feet of a man of such genius—something that, without effort on his part, should redeem him from the vulgar necessity of making a living.

A sinecure! (he says in reply). God bless thee, my darling! I could not touch a sinecure, though twenty of my friends should volunteer to offer! . . . For affection, or the faintest imitation of it, a man should feel obliged to his very dog; but for the gross assistance of patronage or purse, let him pause before accepting them from any one.

And these feelings were genuine, and expressed in manly language, such as Miss Welsh could not but admire.

The years during which this remarkable correspondence was going on must have been strange and unrestful years for Jane Welsh. The correspondence itself is as unlike the ordinary pre-matrimonial exchange of letters as the two writers were unlike the general run of people. There was, from the first, something altogether exceptional in the whole position of affairs—almost unprecedented.

Let us here draw attention for a moment to Miss Welsh's own account of her physical health, showing, as it does, the ominous foreshadowing of a highly sensitive and too finely balanced temperament, which was to develop such cruel forms of suffering in later life. In a letter dated Templand, August 1825, Miss Welsh writes to her friend, Miss Stodart:—

My life is passing on here in the usual alternating manner. One day I am ill and in bed; the next, in full puff at an entertainment. . . . What pains me most is, that between headaches and visiting my education is completely at a stand. . . . And, after all, I am not *very* blamable on the score of idleness; it is in vain to think of toiling up the steep of knowledge with a burden of sickness on one's shoulders, and hardly less difficult for a young person of my attractions to lead the life of a recluse.

We here see, plainly enough, that Jane Welsh was not strong and healthy, even in those early and comparatively untried days. She suffered at times, was restless, and ill at ease. Her strongest interest at the time was undoubtedly her friendship with Carlyle—that friendship bordering so closely on a deeper feeling.

There was more than mere ambition, we think, in the attraction she felt towards Carlyle. She admired and venerated him; she felt that he was superior to any man she had ever known: and he had sympathized with her, as we have already seen. She had certainly loved Edward Irving, but that love had not been destined to fill her life.

Would it ever have filled it? We can never know; and doubtless the scent of the rose-leaves clung round that early-closed page of her life, and possibly never quite left it. But what the actual result of the union would have been we cannot guess. How that keenly awakened, mocking spirit would have taken Irving's pious phraseology, and his whole mode of thought, is beyond our power to predict. The love-story was never dragged out to its end. Irving, bound in honour, had gone his way; and though Jane Welsh could not again give that passionate youthful love which was given to him, we need not conclude that therefore she could not love at all, and was bereft of all power or wish to make a good man happy. How many marriages, and happy marriages, too, are built on the second, rather than on the first deep, beautiful outpouring of the heart? Many a man would have preferred to marry Miss Welsh with the feeling she had for Thomas Carlyle than with that which she felt for Edward Irving. We are not speaking at random; we have heard it from the lips of a good man and true, who knew her long and intimately, and understood her as few have ever done. Probably she would not have found life perfect with any man, since her own eager, restless nature bore within it so many possibilities, almost necessities of pain.

Carlyle was nobly ready to relieve her from any promise to him. But she did not wish to be relieved. His proposal to farm Craigenputtock did not seem wild to *him*. His own recollections of Mainhill and the family life made it quite natural. His mother, whom he loved and venerated above all earthly beings, spent her life in a cottage, discharging the humblest of daily tasks. He saw nothing anomalous in the plan. It was merely an error in judgment, and a pardonable, and in some sense a natural one, that he should propose this solitary moorland life to Miss Welsh. He writes to her from London on January 9, 1825:—

. . . You bid me tell you how I have decided—what I mean to do. It is you that must decide. I will endeavour to explain to you what I wish; it must rest with you to say whether it can ever be attained.

You tell me you have land which needs improvement. Why not work on that? In one word, then, will you go with me? Will you be my own for ever? Say Yes, and I embrace the project with my whole heart. I send my brother Alick over to rent that Nithsdale farm for me without delay; I proceed to it the moment I am freed from my engagements here; I labour in arranging it, and fitting everything for your reception; and the instant it is ready I take you home to my hearth, never more to part from me, whatever fate betide us.

I fear you think this scheme a baseless vision; and yet it is the sober best among the many I have meditated—the best for me, and I think also, so far as I can judge of it, for yourself. . . . Depend upon it, Jane, this literature, which both of us are so bent on pursuing, will not constitute the sole nourishment of any true human spirit. . . . Literature is the wine of life; it will not, cannot be, its food.

. . . You, too, are unhappy, and I see the reason. You have a deep, earnest, and vehement spirit, and no earnest task has ever been assigned to it. You despise and ridicule the meanness of the things about you. To the things you honour you can only pay a fervent adoration, which issues in no practical effect. Oh that I saw you the mistress of a house, diffusing over human souls that loved you those clear faculties of order, judgment, elegance, which you are now reduced to spend on pictures and portfolios—blessing living hearts with that enthusiastic love which you must now direct to the distant and the dimly seen! All this is in you. You have a heart, and an intellect, and a resolute decision which might make you the model of wives, however widely your thoughts and your experience have hitherto wandered from that highest distinction of the noblest women. I, too, have wandered wide and far. Let us return; let us return together! Let us learn through one another what it is to live! . . .

The first, the lowest, but a most essential point, is that of funds. On this matter I have still little to tell you that you do not know. I feel, in general, that I have ordinary faculties in me, and an ordinary degree of diligence in using them, and that

thousands manage life in comfort with even slenderer resources.
. . . To my taste, cleanliness and order are far beyond gilding
and grandeur, which, without them, is an abomination; and for
displays, for festivals, and parties, I believe you are as indisposed
as myself. . . Two laws I have laid down to myself: that I
must and will recover health, without which to think, or even to
live, is burdensome or unprofitable; and that I will not degener-
ate into the wretched thing which calls itself an author, in our
capitals, and scribbles for the sake of lucre in the periodicals of
the day. . . I begin to entertain a certain degree of contempt
for the destiny which has so long persecuted me. I will be a
man in spite of it. Yet it lies with you whether I shall be a
right man, or only a hard and bitter Stoic ! . .
Speak, then! Think well of me, of yourself, of our circumstances, and determine! Dare you trust me? dare you trust
your fate with me, as I trust mine with you? Judge if I wait
your answer with impatience. I know you will not keep me
waiting. Of course, it will be necessary to explain all things to
your mother, and take her serious advice respecting them. For
your other friends, it is not worth while consulting one of them.
I know not that there is one among them that would give you as
disinterested advice as even I, judging in my own cause. May
God bless you and direct you! Decide as you will.

This was manly and true—sure to move a nature like
that of Jane Welsh. What woman could have read the letter
unmoved? But Miss Welsh was intensely practical, and
saw difficulties which Carlyle could not see. She was keenly
conscious of his total unfitness for the life he was proposing,
and doubtless felt its extreme unsuitability, at all points, to
herself. She answered his letter with a plain and unvarnished
truthfulness, which would have caused any ordinary man
and lover to throw up the whole project, and turn away for
ever from the terribly clear-sighted and deliberate young
lady. Here are passages from her reply, dated Haddington,
January 13, 1825:—

I little thought my joke about your farming Craigenputtock was
to be made the basis of such a serious and extraordinary project.

. . . You have sometimes asked me, Did I ever think? For once in my life, at least, I have thought myself into a vertigo, and without coming to any positive conclusion. However, my mind, such as it is, on the matter you have thus precipitately forced on my consideration, I will explain to you frankly and explicitly, as the happiness of us both requires. I love you, and I should be the most ungrateful and injudicious of mortals if I did not. But I am not *in love* with you; that is to say, my love for you is not a passion which overclouds *my* judgment, and absorbs all my regard for myself and others. It is a simple, honest, serene affection, made up of admiration and sympathy, and better, perhaps, to found domestic enjoyment on than any other. In short, it is a love which *influences*, does not *make*, the destiny of a life.

Such temperate sentiments lend no false colouring, no 'rosy light' to your project. I see it, such as it is, with all the arguments for and against it. I see that my consent, under existing circumstances, would, indeed, secure to *me* the only fellowship and support I have found in the world, and perhaps, too, shed some sunshine of joy on your existence, which has hitherto been sullen and cheerless; but, on the other hand, that it would involve you and myself in numberless cares and difficulties, and expose me to petty tribulations which I want fortitude to despise, and which, *not* despised, would embitter the peace of us both. I do not wish for fortune more than is sufficient for my wants—my natural wants, and the artificial ones, which habit has rendered nearly as importunate as the others. But I will not consent to live on less; because, in that case, every inconvenience I was subjected to would remind me of what I had quitted, and the idea of a sacrifice should have no place in a voluntary union. Neither have I any wish for grandeur: the glittering baits of titles and honours are only for children and fools. But I conceive it a duty which every one owes to society, not to throw up that station in it which Providence has assigned him; and, having this conviction, I could not marry into a station inferior to my own with the approval of my judgment, which alone could enable me to brave the censures of my acquaintance.

And now, let me ask you, have you any *certain* livelihood to maintain me in the manner I have been used to live in? any *fixed* place in the rank of society I have been born and bred in? No!

You have projects for attaining both, capabilities for attaining both, and much more. But as yet you have not attained them. Use the noble gifts which God has given you. You have prudence —though, by the way, this last proceeding is no great proof of it. Devise, then, how you may gain yourself a moderate but *settled* income. Think of some more promising plan than farming the most barren spot in the county of Dumfriesshire. What a thing that would be, to be sure—you and I keeping house at Craigenputtock! I would as soon think of building myself a nest on the Bass Rock. Nothing but your ignorance of the spot saves you from the imputation of insanity for admitting such a thought. Depend upon it, you could not exist there a twelvemonth. For my part, I could not spend a month at it with an angel. Think of something else, then. Apply your industry to carry it into effect; your talents to gild over the inequality of our births— and then we will talk of marrying. If all this were realised, I *think* I should have good sense enough to abate something of my romantic ideal, and to content myself with stopping short on this side idolatry. At all events, I will marry no one else. This is all the promise I can or will make. . . Write instantly, and tell me that you are content to leave the event to time and destiny, and, in the meanwhile, to continue my friend and guardian—which you have so long faithfully been—and *nothing more!*

It would be more agreeable to etiquette, and, perhaps, also to prudence, that I should adopt no middle course in an affair such as this; that I should not for another instant encourage an affection which I may never reward, and a hope I may never fulfil, but cast your heart away from me at once, since I cannot embrace the resolution which would give me a right to it for ever. This I would assuredly do if you were like the generality of lovers, or if it were still in my power to be happy independent of your affection. But, as it is, neither etiquette nor prudence can obtain this of me. If there is any change to be made in the terms on which we have so long lived with one another, it must be made by you, not by me.

This remarkable letter shows something of Jane Welsh's nature. It shows distinctly that she did not wish to give up Carlyle, or to give up the hope of being his wife. It shows that she was certainly attached to him, since she speaks of her friendship with him as the 'only fellowship and support' she had found in the world; and hers was a nature sorely needing both. One cannot doubt the sincerity of these words, so sacredly written—words which, were they not already before the public eye, would not have been here produced in print. The strong native Scotch prudence displayed in the letter would not be at all disenchanting to a man like Carlyle. First of all, he was too noble to consider anything in her as *mean;* secondly, he had been brought up in a hard school, and knew that some consideration for 'loaves and fishes' was inevitable in every human arrangement; thirdly, he loved her, and her ambitions for him were sweet in his ears. Then, had she not assured him that she would marry none other but himself? And had she not admitted that it was no longer possible for her to live happy, independent of his affection? This was much for any man to receive assurance of.

But the rejection of his definite proposition gave him pain. He replied, assuring her that selfishness had no place in his motives—that she had imperfectly understood him. He told her of the mighty voice within him urging him to work, 'to rebuild his destiny, not to die without ever having lived.'

In exploring the chaotic structure of my fortunes (he writes to Miss Welsh), I find my affection for you intertwined with every part of it; connected with whatever is holiest in my feelings or most imperative in my duties. It is necessary for me to understand completely how this matter stands; to investigate my own wishes and power in regard to it; to know of you both what you will do and what you will not do. These things once clearly settled, our line of conduct will be clear also.

Alluding to his proposition, he says:—

Had you accepted it, I should not by any means have thought the battle won. I should have hailed your assent, and the disposition of mind it bespoke, with a deep but serious joy;

with a solemn hope, as indicating the distinct possibility that two true hearts might be united and made happy through each other—might by their joint, unwearied efforts be transplanted from the barren wilderness, where both seemed out of place, into scenes of pure and wholesome activity, such as Nature fitted both of them to enjoy and adorn.

You have rejected it, I think wisely; with your actual purposes and views, we should both have been doubly wretched had you acted otherwise. Your love of me is completely under the control of judgment, and subordinated to other principles of duty or expediency. Your happiness is not by any means irretrievably connected with mine. Believe me, I am not hurt or angry. I merely wished to know. It was only in brief moments of enthusiasm that I ever looked for a different result.

And further on he says: ' Alas ! without great sacrifices on both sides the possibility of our union is an empty dream.'

Here one is tempted to ask what sacrifice Carlyle himself felt would be demanded of *him* in the contemplated marriage with Miss Welsh? It was not the utterance of selfish thoughtlessness. Had he gained some knowledge of the restless spirit with which he would be linking his own for all time? Did he realise that his part, if well and nobly played, would not be an easy one—that, possibly, the task of making this beautiful creature happy, would demand more than the spirit could give? It is clear that Miss Welsh, in her confidences with him, had taught him to regard hers as an isolated and detached nature, inharmoniously placed by circumstances. She must have given this impression very strongly to Carlyle, or the brave, simple man would never have dreamed of offering to fill the blank in her life. Of his own fitness to do so, of his power to carry out the wildly imaginative programme, *he* surely could never be expected to judge. But of mere selfishness he must be altogether acquitted.

Now this (he adds) is what I would do were it in my power. I would ask a generous spirit, one whose happiness depended on seeing me happy, and whose temper and purposes were kindred to my own—I would ask such a noble being to let us unite our resources; not her wealth and rank merely—for these were a small and unessential fraction of the prayer—but her judgment, her patience, prudence, her true affection, to mine, and let us try if, by neglecting what was not important, and striving with faithful and inseparable hearts after what *was*, we could not rise above the miserable obstructions that beset us both, into regions of serene dignity, living as became us in the sight of God and all reasonable men, happier than millions of our brethren, and each acknowledging with fervent gratitude that to the other he and she owed all. You are such a generous spirit. But your purposes and feelings are not such. Perhaps it is happier for you that they are not. . . .

I have thought of these things till my brain was like to crack. I do not pretend that my conclusions are indubitable. I am still open to better light. But this, at present, is the best I have. Do you also think of all this—not in any spirit of anger, but in the spirit of love and noble-mindedness which you have always shown me. If we must part, let us part in tenderness, and go forth upon our several paths, lost to the future, but in possession of the past!

No woman could be unmoved by such words as these. Supposing that Carlyle was deceived—self-deceived—it was yet in utter unconsciousness of the fact, that he thus tenderly, manfully pleaded. It is easy, looking back now on the strange and saddening history of his marriage, to say that he would have been better unmarried, left to wrestle out the mighty struggles and intellectual throes within him in absolute solitude. For his life was to be a convulsion, as it were, of spiritual forces, gathered to a climax in each of his wonderful books, and, after an interval of dissatisfied torpor, *not rest*—for he knew not rest—gathering again to gigantic effort and result. It is easy now, when all is over, to reason thus, with great show of truth and probability.

But Carlyle had tenderer yearnings. His love for his mother showed that he had a loving heart; and, had he not felt still stronger love for Miss Welsh, he would never have sought to marry her. He could have developed his great powers without contracting a tie so close as that of marriage. And truly selfish men, as a rule, *do not* marry.

Carlyle's ignorance of himself is touching, his action in the matter of his marriage based on the noblest integrity and good faith. It was impossible for him to view the matter otherwise than he did. If the hope of gaining a wife whose companionship would brighten life be selfish, then Carlyle's selfishness is shared by most men. As to his estimate of *love*, that was as God had given it to him. His pure life had left the shrine untouched and undesecrated. All that he had to offer, he offered out of an honest heart to Jane Welsh, and bade her accept or reject the gift as she would.

The reply to this last letter was still more outspoken on the lady's part:—

. . . I have refused my immediate consent to your wishes (she writes) because our mutual happiness seemed to require that I should refuse it. But for the rest, I have not slighted your wishes; on the contrary, I have expressed my willingness to fulfil them at the expense of everything but what I deem essential to our happiness. And, so far from undervaluing you, I have shown you, in declaring that I would marry no one else, not only that I esteem you above all the men I have ever seen, but also that I am persuaded I should esteem you above all the men I may ever see. What, then, have you to be hurt or angry at? . . . Yet I am prudent, I fear, only because I am not strongly tempted to be otherwise. My heart is capable (I feel it is) of a love to which *no* deprivation would be a sacrifice—a love which would overleap that reverence for opinion with which education and weakness have begirt my sex, would bear down all the restraints which duty and expediency might throw in the way, and carry every thought of my being impetuously along with it.

But the all-perfect mortal who could inspire me with a love so extravagant, is nowhere to be found—exists nowhere but in the romance of my own imagination. Perhaps it is better for me as it is. A passion like the torrent in the violence of its course might, perhaps, too, like the torrent, leave ruin and desolation behind. In the meantime, I should be mad to act as if from the influence of such a passion, while my affections are in a state of perfect tranquillity.

To an ordinary lover such language as this would be chilling in the extreme; but, after all, it must be admitted, that what Miss Welsh had to offer was very much what Carlyle professed to require. He did not desire a whirlwind of passionate love; he would not have known what to do with it. His own expressions of feeling were as moderate, as temperate, as those of Miss Welsh. And a young lady who could speak of a passionate love that might leave ruin and desolation behind, was presumably less entirely untried in the subject than her philosophic and simple-hearted lover, and more able to judge what she really was offering than was he to estimate it exactly as it deserved.

It needed Scotch people to enter so minutely and deliberately into the counting of the soul's pulse in an affair of the kind. Some writer speaks of being at a ball in Scotland when, on the sudden ceasing of the music, a fair maiden was heard to say to her partner in the dance: 'What you say, my lord, may be very true when spoken of love in the *abstract.*

This correspondence brings the matter to a very abstract position. Miss Welsh eagerly repudiates the notion that she should 'attain wealth and rank,' possibly, by an ambitious marriage.

I merely wish (she writes) to see you earning a certain livelihood, and exercising the profession of a gentleman. . . . Nor was it wholly with a view to improvement in your external circumstances that I have made their fulfilment a condition to our union, but also with a view to some improvement in my sentiments toward you, which might be brought about in the meantime. In withholding this matter in my former letter, I was guilty of a false and ill-timed reserve. My tenderness for your feelings betrayed me into an insincerity which is not natural to me. I thought that the most decided objection to your circumstances would pain you less than the least objection to yourself; while, in truth, it is in some measure grounded on *both*. I must be sincere, I find, at any cost.

It cannot be asserted, after reading this passage, that Miss Welsh *had* been quite fair and open with Thomas Carlyle. She herself pleads guilty to insincerity. No woman can quite honestly propose to herself to accept the addresses of a man to whom she feels a *personal* objection; and such is plainly acknowledged here. She was not forced to marry Carlyle; he himself left her, to the end, perfectly free to withdraw from the undertaking. She was frank enough in this letter, for she continues:—

As I have said, then, in requiring you to better your fortunes I had some view to an improvement in my sentiments. I am not sure that they are proper sentiments for a husband. They are proper for a brother, a father, a guardian-spirit; but a husband, it seems to me, should be dearer still. At the same time, from the change which my sentiments towards you have already undergone during the period of our acquaintance, I have little doubt but that in time I shall be perfectly satisfied with them. . . . My affection for you increases. Not many months ago I would have said it was *impossible* that I should ever be your wife. At present I consider this the most probable destiny for me. In a year or two I shall perhaps consider it the *only* one.

Let us for a moment consider Carlyle's position in this matter. He could not, obviously, deter Miss Welsh from her wish gradually to develop towards him sentiments that should render a marriage with him the only destiny possible for her, even had he felt, as he may have done, that the great master-passion was absent altogether from her feelings towards him. When he, in his doubts, spoke of their agreeing to part, she would not consent. She would not believe that he meant what he said. 'How could I,' she said, 'part from the only living one that understands me?' It was really she who would not set him free; and he desired no freedom from the sweet bonds which held him, save only if it were to end in a bondage no longer sweet for either of them, as he feared at times. He acted with simple loyalty and directness, following as best he could all Miss Welsh's tortuous reasonings, and arguments *pro* and *con*, and marking her one determination, which was—*not* to be set free, at any cost.

'Were you to will it,' she writes to him, 'parting would no longer be bitter. The bitterness would be in thinking you unworthy.' What wonder that Carlyle remained constant to his vows? She was the star to which he turned; yet would he manfully have faced the starless night without her, had she been willing. But, as we have seen, she was not willing.

I know not (she says in a subsequent letter) how your spirit has gained such a mastery over mine, in spite of my pride and stubbornness. But so it is. Though self-willed as a mule with others, I am tractable and submissive towards you. I hearken to your voice as to the dictates of a second Conscience, hardly less awful to me than that which Nature has implanted in my breast. How comes it, then, that you have this power over me? for it is not the effect of your genius and virtue merely. Sometimes, in my serious moods, I believe it is a charm with which my good angel has fortified my heart against evil.

Would any man desire a sweeter tribute from the woman he loves—a woman so eminent, too, for strength of will?

These letters, from which extracts have been given, show most convincingly how each of these people differed from the ordinary run of humanity. Had either one been wholly normal and natural, no marriage could possibly have resulted from such preliminaries. The wonderful thing is, that two such exceptional people should have *met*, and formed that tie—two people with so many points in common, so much that was almost identical in their natures. There were, indeed, startling points of resemblance existing from the beginning, but developed largely as time went on. Carlyle was instinctively drawn to her, whose great power was in many ways to mould his life; she, in her turn, was persistently attracted to the man of genius, through whose medium she was to be moulded, by mysterious methods, to the godlike proportions not clearly visible to the world's eye. Each was to be taught much, patiently and painfully, through the other. But noble ends, pure lives, endless strivings and hopings, consecrated the way. A stony path it was, but leading to the stars.

Carlyle's was essentially a lonely nature, separate from much that enters into the motives and actions of ordinary men. He felt his intense solitude, and craved for a gentle and intellectual companionship. It was all very natural; and if there was self-deception in the plan, it is but such as forms no unkindly part of many human impulses, without detracting from their sincerity.

As to the question whether Miss Welsh was happy in her choice, we must ask ourselves, first, whether she possessed the absolute requisites for happiness in her own nature and character, under any given circumstances and influences; and, secondly, whether we are to regard *happiness* as the acknowledged end and aim of life.

If this latter proposition be admitted, there opens a far wider question, obviously unsuitable for discussion here. We cannot regard as failures lives which serve to bring out the noblest and highest powers. We may deplore the painful methods though which alone, from causes hidden from us, those grand qualities and elevated courses of action can be drawn forth. And these two were both noble natures.

CHAPTER VI

A.D. 1825

Carlyle at Hoddam Hill—Miss Welsh's transference of Craigenputtock to her mother—Carlyle's personal appearance at this time—Miss Welsh's beauty—Letter from Mrs. Montagu to Miss Welsh—Reference to Edward Irving—An independent spirit—Second letter of Mrs. Montagu—Results—Miss Welsh informs Carlyle of her old attachment to Irving—A woman's appeal—Carlyle's reply—Imperfect understanding—Exciting correspondence—Engagement of Miss Welsh and Thomas Carlyle—Visits to Hoddam Hill and Mainhill—Difficulties as to future residence—Incompatibility between Carlyle and Mrs. Welsh—Misgivings—Correspondence with the Carlyle family—Their removal to Scotsbrig.

It was in March 1825 that Carlyle removed to Hoddam Hill, a farm leased for him by his father, and farmed by his brother, Alexander Carlyle. Here for a time he devoted himself to translating from the German, relieved by vigorous exercise on his Irish horse 'Larry,' and gave the rest of his time, no doubt, to love-dreams and long letters to Miss Welsh.

This time was spoken of in later years by Carlyle as 'a russet-coated idyl.' The position between the two was unusual; it was anomalous. So early as August 19, 1823, she had written to him: 'I owe you much: feelings and sentiments that ennoble my character, that give dignity, interest, and enjoyment to my life. In return, I can only love you, and *that* I do from the bottom of my heart.' Still, he was ready to resign the hope of marriage. Miss Welsh, however, as we have seen, began to think it her destiny. Proud and independent, she had caused a legal deed to be executed transferring to her mother, for the lifetime of the latter, the whole life-interest of Craigenputtock, some two hundred pounds a year. Determined she was that none should cast a slur on Thomas Carlyle's possible marriage with herself, and equally determined to secure the mother, whom she deeply loved, from want, whatever her own personal fate and fortunes were to be. This legal instrument, however, was supplemented by one leaving Craigenputtock to Carlyle after her own and her mother's death. It was well done, nobly done, showing the high opinion she had of Carlyle, and that she could not brook that others, in their ignorance, should think meanly of him.

Carlyle was now about thirty years of age: a tall, spare, angular man, with the rugged features and intense expression we know so well; his tint was ruddy, as of one much in the open air; his fine eyes a clear, deep blue—remarkable eyes, once seen, never to be forgotten; eyes that could flash forth indignation, but that could, and did, express much kindliness at times; a firm, dogged line of mouth, and an abundant shock of brown hair. Miss Welsh was something over twenty-four years of age, very beautiful, arch, and attractive, 5 feet 4 inches in height, slender, and singularly graceful, in the prime of womanhood. They must have been a goodly pair, and matters between them could hardly be expected to stand still indefinitely. A strange circumstance hastened the decisive step in this matter.

The impulsive Edward Irving, after first settling in London, had opened up the secrets of his heart to his valued friend, Mrs. Basil Montagu. Such confidences are critical, and though a man would naturally choose the wisest and best woman to whom to entrust them, still that same confidante may be romantic and imaginative. 'How some women love *love*,' says a great American writer—and so it is. The lady was profoundly interested, regarded Edward Irving as a noble martyr to duty—a sentiment we cannot endorse, as he had a good and loving wife in the lady whom, certainly, he had once desired to marry. Besides, the matter was all over and settled, and, had Irving thought fit, as a truly manly man *would* have thought fit, to keep silence on the story of his old love, all might have ended, if not well, at least otherwise than actually fell out.

For Mrs. Montagu, who corresponded occasionally with Carlyle, and had introduced herself by letter to Miss Welsh, felt irresistibly impelled to act the *Dea ex machinâ*, and administer some comfort to the beautiful young lady, whom she pictured to herself as pining in disappointed love for Edward Irving. But there was no balm to administer that a brave, loyal woman could take, and no wound complained of which should need such soothing. More than that, there was a proud and independent spirit, which would, in any case, have thrown aside such consolation.

Mrs. Montagu had acted on what proved to be, so far as Miss Welsh was concerned, 'a foregone conclusion'—a very unsafe thing, sure to lead to disaster. Actuated by this, and by a sincerely kind motive, she seems to have thought it politic and desirable to disparage Irving somewhat, and to paint him as one not deserving of such lifelong constancy as she, no doubt, believed Miss Welsh to retain with regard to him. She therefore dwelt on his having now other interests and other ambitions, and intimated that any woman who should concentrate her heart on him would find nothing but disappointment. But it is, as we have been told by a great poet, a delicate matter to meddle with souls; and Mrs. Montagu, with all her admirable motives and well-meant efforts, doing, probably, 'as she would be done by,' made a grievous mistake. Regarding Carlyle as simply an intimate of both the young people she was interested in, she wrote also to him on the subject, assuming, with beautiful unconsciousness, that he doubtless was aware of the circumstances; and thus Carlyle learned, for the first time, of the affection which had certainly existed at one time between Edward Irving and Miss Welsh; only he heard of it as still unextinguished, still living, and causing pain.

The fact that for two years past Miss Welsh had never

mentioned Edward Irving but with bitterness and mockery in speaking of him to Carlyle, might have made an ordinary man suspicious of the relations between them. But Carlyle was not like other men, and he believed in Miss Welsh. He believed in Irving—as, at least, a high-souled man of honour. So he was not troubled, and, when writing to Miss Welsh, merely mentioned Mrs. Montagu's eloquent statements as a strange delusion.

Mrs. Montagu, not feeling she had done her whole duty, was ready with a reply to Miss Welsh's assurance that she was in no way pining for Edward Irving, and, indeed, was about to marry Mr. Carlyle. Even this explicit statement did not quench Mrs. Montagu's determination to do her duty, and, in her quixotic attempt to set matters straight, and under the fatal idea that she understood the affairs of these people better than they did themselves, she, in true, kindly warm-heartedness, wrote again, adjuring Miss Welsh not to marry Carlyle if she were still attached to Irving—not, in fact, to allow a generous impulse to sway her, where only the heart's strongest feelings ought to be listened to.

After the first appeal, Miss Welsh had commented to Carlyle, some days later, on the well-meant interference: ' I had two sheets from Mrs. Montagu the other day, trying to prove to me that I did not know my own heart. Mercy! how romantic she is!'

This was a natural result of the letter. But after the second letter, Miss Welsh certainly wrote to Carlyle in a very different strain. She felt it honourably incumbent on her to tell Carlyle that she had indeed loved Edward Irving once—passionately loved him. There was neither shame nor reproach in the fact. If she had shown weakness in loving a man whom she knew to be engaged to another, she had at least made amends by helping to decide him to marry that other, and to save his honour from all reproach. What nobler part could a true woman take? What else can be the result where the man is good, and the woman is good, and where it *is* love, and not a lower feeling, which draws them together. No mystery is here that an honourable human heart cannot understand; nothing to blush for, though the angels might weep over it.

Jane Welsh keenly felt the necessity of showing Carlyle, who so intensely believed in her, that she had not been without disguise. If now his sternly upright nature turned from her, she could but bow the head; and very touchingly, with a woman's tenderness, she added, that he had never been so dear to her as now, when both his affection and his respect for her hung in the balance. 'Woe to me! then,' she says, ' if your reason be my judge, and not your love.' This is not the language of bitterness; it is calm, reasonable, and natural —sure to appeal to a man's generosity.

Carlyle replied after his own nature: 'You exaggerate this matter greatly,' he said; 'let it go to strengthen the schoolings of experience. You ask me to forgive you! *Forgiveness?*'... And again: ' Come and see, and determine. Let me hear you, and do you hear me. As I am, take or refuse me; but not as I am *not*, for this will not, and cannot come to good. God help us both, and show us both the way we ought to walk in!'

These are manly and honourable words, but they show unmistakably how little able Carlyle was to enter into and fully comprehend the ordinary feelings of human nature. He would have taken fright had he fully understood what Miss Welsh was telling him. It would have been *he*, and not Mrs. Montagu, who would have entreated the young girl to look well into her own heart before uniting her fate with his. All these people were blindly trying to do what was right. Mrs. Montagu, firmly believing that an impulsive, imaginative girl was about to make a mistaken and loveless marriage, tried to stave off what she felt could only end in disaster. Miss Welsh, after the fact of her attachment to Edward Irving had been told to Carlyle, in all good faith, by Mrs. Montagu, hastened honourably to admit that it *had* existed, but was now a thing of the past, and replaced by the strong influence of the man who understood and valued her, whose love was now all in all to her, as she believed; and Carlyle, in his honourable humility, lost no time in giving that young girl an opportunity of gravely reconsidering the whole position of affairs, and specially the step she was about to take, divesting it of all possible halo of false colouring by asking her to visit the farms of Hoddam Hill—where he was with his mother and his brother Alick—and Mainhill, where his sisters were keeping house for the father. Here Miss Welsh would see, with her quick eyes, the exact level and status of that family to which this genius, Thomas Carlyle, belonged. He was not ashamed of them. There was no cause for shame. He was proud of them and loved them truly. His relations with them were beautiful to the end. But it was a bold step to invite the elegant young lady to visit these humble homes, and Carlyle was brave and manly in taking it.

Miss Welsh had been staying for a time with her grandfather, Walter Welsh, at Templand, when the time came for her to pay this memorable visit. It had been preceded by an exciting correspondence, and at last, taking the opportunity of her comparative nearness, she determined to go over and bravely to face the whole position. She was ever energetic, decisive and thorough, in all she did, to the end. Carlyle's earnest wish that she should reconsider the matter, his expressed doubt as to whether he could make her happy—all went for nothing. In September 1825 she set forth by coach, expecting Carlyle to meet her on the road; but there had been a mistake. From Kelhead Kilns, the next morning, she sent him a characteristic little note, dated Friday, September 3, 1825:—

Good morning, sir,—I am not at all to blame for your disappointment last night. The fault was partly your own. . . . In the meantime I have billeted myself in a snug little house by the wayside, where I purpose remaining with all imaginable patience till you can make it convenient to come and fetch me, being afraid to proceed directly to Hoddam Hill, in case so sudden an apparition should throw the whole family into hysterics. If the pony has any prior engagement, never mind. I can make a shift to walk two miles in pleasant company. Any way, pray make all possible despatch, in case the owner of these premises should think I intend to make a regular settlement in them.

Yours, JANE.

The fact of the engagement was now known to the Carlyle family, and naturally was a source of pleasure and anxiety, as the new acquisition to the family circle was felt to be a lady of somewhat different upbringing to the homely and worthy circle she was about to enter. And though for a country surgeon's daughter to marry a man of genius whose father was a stonemason, possibly presents no incongruity, it yet remains that the cultivation and refinement in which Jane Welsh had been reared *had* created a different atmosphere from that in which she found herself with the excellent people at Hoddam Hill. 'She stayed with us about a week,' Carlyle writes, ' happy, as was very evident, and making happy. . . . From the first moment all embarrassment, even my mother's, tremulous and anxious as she naturally was, fled away without return.'

It seems that Carlyle's mother, who loved him so, was there to receive Miss Welsh in her son's home at Hoddam Hill, and afterwards accompanied her back to the family home at Mainhill, where were Carlyle's sisters and his father. The two farms seem to have been in occupation of the family at this time, the two sisters keeping home for the father at Mainhill, and the mother keeping house at Hoddam Hill for Thomas and Alexander.

We are prettily told of the reception given to the bright young lady by the family party at Mainhill, and how the father, called in from farmwork to give welcome to his son's intended wife, withdrew to wash and shave and don his Sunday clothes, before receiving the fair girl's dutiful salute. Carlyle says: 'She came to know us all, saw, face to face, *us*, and the peasant element and way of life we lead; and was *not* afraid of it, but recognized, like her noble self, what of intrinsic worth it might have, what of real human dignity. . . .' It was, perhaps, something like Marie Antoinette's idea of country life, as realised at the Petit Trianon—as unreal, in one way, as there was an unusual exaltation present which veiled the true nature and effect of such country life from the sensitive and delicate young lady, and she saw it all like a scene in a play in which she was an actress.

Carlyle was so impressed with the fact that the 'Haddington element had grown dreary and unfruitful' to Miss Welsh, that it is easily understood that he honestly believed he was offering her something better.

Supposing, however, that Miss Welsh were willing to enter on this method of existence, there was yet another person to think of, and that was Mrs. Welsh, delicately nurtured, sentimental in her ideas to the end, yet well aware that those youthful enthusiasms which run to 'love in a cottage' are apt to turn out most disastrously at times. Then, she knew her child: she had studied from early childhood that finely strung, nervous organisation, so brave, yet so apt to suffer; she knew that the wearing monotony of farm-life would *not* minister to health and peace in this delicate frame, and she viewed with dismay the final resolution of her beautiful Jeannie after the visit to Hoddam Hill.

It was a sad time to the two women. Miss Welsh told Carlyle of the painful interviews with her mother, and received all the comfort he could give in his answering letters. Mrs. Welsh was not attracted towards Carlyle, doubted his evenness of temper, disliked his strong governing disposition, being herself fond of ruling, and she naturally felt an anxiety about 'ways and means,' as any mother ought to do under the circumstances. She by no means shared her daughter's unbounded faith in Carlyle's genius. He seemed to her unfitted to fight the battle of life to practical advantage. No wonder she felt deeply concerned.

Carlyle writes very searchingly to Miss Welsh:—

If your mind have any wavering (he says) follow the truth fearlessly, not heeding me, for I am ready with alacrity to forward your anticipated happiness in any way. Or, was this your love of me no girlish whim, but the calm, deliberate self-offering of a woman to the man whom her reason and her heart had made choice of? Then is it a crime in you to love me, whose you are in the sight of God and man?

There is a touching earnestness in these words of Carlyle's. What, in truth, could he honourably do but hold fast to his engagement? That Miss Welsh considered her future as finally fixed, is amply demonstrated in a letter written to Carlyle's mother in November of the same year, from George Square, Edinburgh.

Indeed (she says), the more I am in the way of what is commonly called pleasure, the more I think of the calm days I spent under your roof. I have never been so happy since, though I have been at several fine entertainments, . . . and this is in no wise strange, since affection is the native element of my soul, and *that* I found in your cottage, warm and pure.

She was delicate, too, in those days, for she adds:—

All my impatience to see Haddington failed to make the journey hither agreeable, which was as devoid of 'Christian comfort' as anything you can suppose. Never was poor damsel reduced to such 'extremities of fate.' I was sick, woefully sick, and, notwithstanding that I had on four petticoats, benumbed with cold. To make my wretchedness as complete as possible we did not reach Edinburgh till many hours after dark. Sixteen miles more, and my wanderings for this season are at an end. Would that my trials were ended also! But no. Tell Mr. Carlyle my handsome cousin is coming to Haddington, with his sister Phœbe, and his valet Henley, and his great dog Toby, over and above Dash, Craigen, Fanny, and Frisk. My heart misgives me at the prospect of this inundation of company, for their ways are not my ways, and what is amusement to them is death to me. But I must just be patient, as usual. Verily I should need to be Job, instead of Jane Welsh, to bear these everlasting annoyances with any degree of composure.

I quote this letter to point out, first, that, even in these early days, Miss Welsh could not travel without serious bodily suffering; secondly, that she passionately disparages social entertainments and company; and, thirdly, that she writes with that strongly accentuated emphasis on ordinary matters, which, later in life, when she had, as the old nurses say, '*something to cry for*,' adds such painful intensity to her records of what befell her. It was a strongly dramatic gift, and Jane Welsh possessed it from the beginning, and would have manifested it under any circumstances. Carlyle possessed the same extraordinary power. It was often like using a steam-hammer to crack a hazel-nut; but, when once understood and recognized, the truth is less harmful than helpful in forming a just verdict of these very remarkable persons. In the letter here quoted, Miss Welsh continues:—

Mr. Carlyle must write next week without fail to Haddington, lest, in vexation of spirit, I curse God and die . . . (and she concludes), I am writing under many eyes, and in the noise of many tongues. God bless you!
I am, always affectionately yours,
JANE B. WELSH.

There is also a kind and graceful letter to Carlyle's little sister Jean, who, from her black eyes and hair, had the pet name of the 'Craw!' She was the only dark-complexioned member of the family, taking after the mother; all the rest being blonde.

After Miss Welsh's visit to Hoddam Hill, Carlyle continued his translating, smoking a pipe of an evening with his good mother, who never wearied in the effort to keep him spiritually in a satisfactory and orthodox condition. He felt himself happy at this time, master of 'his own four walls' and revelling in the thought, delighting to reflect on the devoted love which ever had surrounded him. 'There is no grumbling,' he says, 'at my habitudes and whims. If I choose to dine on fire-and-brimstone, they will cook it for me to their best skill.' It was perhaps not the best possible preparation for married life, this intense family adoration; but it was soothing, and Carlyle could value it. But changes were now impending. Differences with the landlord of the farm arose. Hoddam Hill was given up, and the lease of Mainhill, which fell in at the same time, was not renewed. The whole Carlyle family, therefore, returned to Scotsbrig—a substantial and well-sheltered farm near Ecclefechan, where in time both the parents died.

CHAPTER VII

A.D. 1825-1826

Loyalty of Miss Welsh—Her sense of being bound to the engagement with Carlyle—Proposal to live at Scotsbrig—The actual *versus* the ideal—Miss Welsh's mind made up—Carlyle's determination not to live in the house with Mrs. Welsh—A daughter's devotion and appeal—Renunciation of the cherished wish—The point yielded.

This change of plans affected the position of things between Carlyle and Miss Welsh: for he longed with a fierce longing for a home of his own, and with whom should that now be but with his promised wife? But there were obstacles.

We have seen what was Mrs. Welsh's attitude on the subject of the marriage. Mrs. Welsh, romantic in her ideas and passionately loving her child, would fain have restored the property and gone to live with her father, Walter Welsh, at Templand. But the high-spirited Jane Welsh would never hear of such a plan as this. She might herself consent to live in poverty, but her mother should be provided for; and she was inflexible. She had agreed to the visions of Carlyle of taking a small house in Edinburgh, so that Mrs. Welsh could live beside them. Even this was a change from the ideas of a year before, when it was a cottage in the country that had been held up to Miss Welsh as the only desirable home for her and him.

Surely (she writes to Carlyle), you are the most tantalising man in the world, and I the most tractable woman. This time twelve months, nothing would content you but to live in the country, and, though a country life never before attracted my desires, it nevertheless became my choice the instant it seemed to be yours... A change comes over the spirit of your dream. While the birds are yet humming, the roses blooming, and everything is in summer glory about our ideal cottage, I am called away to live *in prospectu* in the smoke and bustle and icy coldness of Edinburgh. Now this I call a trial of patience and obedience—and say! could I have complied more readily though I had been your wedded wife ten times over?

And in closing her letter, she says: ' But what am I talking about? As if we were not already married—married past redemption! God knows, in that case, what is to become of us! At times I am so disheartened that I sit down and weep.'

It seems almost as though these two people were talking in different languages, and without the intervention of an interpreter. It would, perhaps, have solved matters for the moment had the three lived together—Mrs. Welsh and her daughter and Carlyle. But it would have been but the beginning of new troubles, and, if even seriously proposed, was wisely abandoned. That it was contemplated seems pretty clear.

Meantime Carlyle's answer to the heart-breaking words of Miss Welsh amounted to a repetition of the offer to set her free. He is altogether enigmatical. 'If you judge it fit,' he writes, 'I will take you to my heart as my wedded wife this very week. If you judge it fit, I will this very week forswear you forever.' Surely these are hard terms to offer to a woman, when a lover leaves all decision to her in so matter-of-fact a way! Carlyle ends by assuring Miss Welsh that he is hers, at her own disposal, for ever and ever! Never, surely was such love-making—so bereft of that blessed *couleur de rose*, which makes many a young life glide so easily and gently into a safe and happy haven!

But now a new idea entered Carlyle's mind. It was that Miss Welsh should marry him and join the household at Scotsbrig. This, he thought, might answer. He 'would be a new man, the bitterness of life would pass away like a forgotten tempest;' and he and she 'would walk in bright weather thenceforward!' Here he deceived himself entirely, and lost sight of all the 'fitness of things'—a wilder dream was never dreamed! The whole letter is altogether remarkable, and might have been expected to deter any other woman than Jane Welsh from the thought of marrying this desperately plain-spoken lover:—

If (says he) my heart and my hand, with the barren and perplexed destiny which promises to attend them, shall, after all, appear the best this poor world can offer you, then take me, and be content with me, and do not vex yourself with struggling to alter what is unalterable—to make a man who is poor and sick, suddenly become rich and healthy. You tell me you often weep when you think what is to become of us. It is unwise in you to weep. If you are reconciled to be my wife (not the wife of an *ideal me*, but the simple, actual, prosaic *me*), there is nothing frightful in the future. I look into it with more and more confidence and composure, Alas! Jane, you do not know me. It is not the poor, rejected, unknown Thomas Carlyle that you know, but the prospective rich, known, and admired.

Such expressions would have caused a revulsion of feeling in any ordinary woman. That a future spent with the choice of his heart should simply escape the being called 'frightful,' is something out of all harmony with preconceived ideas and actual experience. These expressions, used at a time when merely to breathe the air breathed by the one beloved, when a chance touch even, fills the whole frame with joy—to view the fulfilling of these dear bonds with 'composure,' and assume it a virtue even to be able to do as much as that—casts a strange light on the whole circumstances of this marriage.

Carlyle, in the same letter, says: 'These are hard sayings, my beloved child, but I cannot spare them.' They were indeed 'hard sayings,' and none but a dauntless heart, true as steel, would ever have made the author of them her life-companion. Loyal, brave, and faithful as she was, small wonder that she wept!

But Miss Welsh had answered this last letter with the assurance that her mind was made up, and she would not alter it. Upon this Carlyle immediately replied that, since this was so, ' she had better wed her wild man of the woods at once, and come and live with him in his cavern in the hope of better days.' The 'cavern' so unattractive in contemplation was, of course, Scotsbrig, where the Carlyle family were now settled. It was not then the idea of two households living under one roof which repelled him, so long as one of those families was his own. Mrs. Welsh, though only one individual, was regarded as an insuperable difficulty when proposed as an inmate of the new home. Carlyle felt, perhaps, that, with that element, he would scarcely preserve the complete supremacy which he enjoyed with his own family, who truly loved him, and delighted to honour his wishes. He forgot that, into whatever inhabited or uninhabited home he should enter, he would take with him, inevitably, that feverous, restless nature, that spirit ill-at-ease, storm-tossed, dissatisfied, wrestling ever with unseen foes, which would effectually ban what is called peace from the threshold. He could not be expected to see this fact.

Miss Welsh was probably not blind to this aspect of things. Another thing she clearly saw was her duty to her widowed mother, and with much tenderness she tried to place the whole position before Carlyle, who also had a mother whom he truly loved. Miss Welsh pleaded for a united household; that Carlyle and she, after their marriage, should live in the same house with Mrs. Welsh, near Edinburgh, or where he wished; only she besought him not to ask her to forsake her mother, even though Mrs. Welsh's character was not one that ensured constant peace between the mother and daughter. Though she was at times 'difficult,' still she was the mother, and earnestly did her only child desire to be a good daughter.

Should I do well (she wrote) to go into Paradise myself, and leave the mother who bore me to break her heart? She is looking forward to my marriage with a more tranquil mind, in the hope that our separation is to be but nominal—that by living where my husband lives she may at least have every moment of my society which he can spare. And how would it be possible not to disappoint her of this hope, if I went to reside with your people in Annandale? . . . She would be the most wretched of mothers, the most desolate woman in the world. Oh! is it for me to make her so? who am so unspeakably dear to her, in spite of all her caprice? who am her only, only child, and she a widow? I love you, Mr. Carlyle—tenderly, devotedly. But I may not put my mother away from me, even for your sake. I cannot do it! . . . I see only one way to escape out of all these perplexities. Be patient with me while I tell you what it is. My mother, like myself, has ceased to feel any contentment in this hateful Haddington, and is bent on disposing of our house here as soon as may be, and hiring one elsewhere. Why should it not be the vicinity of Edinburgh after all? and why should not you live with your wife in your mother's house? . . . My mother would like you, assuredly she would, if you came to live with her as her son. . . . Her maternal affection, of which there is abundance at the bottom of her heart, would of necessity extend itself to him with whom I was become inseparably connected, and mere common-sense would prescribe a kind, motherly behaviour as the only expedient to make the best of what could no longer be helped.

Possibly the doubt of Mrs. Welsh's possessing this very quality, 'mere common-sense,' was one ingredient in Carlyle's determined rejection of the plan. Else, attached as he was to his own mother, it was to be expected that he would understand the love Miss Welsh bore to hers, and would have honoured her for it—and perhaps he did—whilst enabling her to act according to its dictates, which he decidedly did not. He knew he was not easy to live with, and had no idea of making conciliations which would surely be demanded of him were Mrs. Welsh a member of his household. He was too honest to profess a willingness to submit his will and his ways to a mother-in-law, so he held on to his own views in the face of the tender protest made by his intended wife. He stated his opinions most undisguisedly, in words which must forever 'overset the whole project.'

It may be stated in a word (he wrote). *The man shall bear rule in the house, and not the woman.* This is an eternal axiom, the law of nature which no mortal departs from unpunished. I have meditated on this many years, and every day it grows plainer to me. I must not, and I cannot, live in a house of which I am not head. I should be miserable myself, and make all about me miserable. Think not this comes of an imperious temper, that I shall be a harsh and tyrannical husband to thee. God forbid!

... Now think, Liebchen, whether your mother will consent to forget her own riches, and my poverty and uncertain—more probably my scanty—income, and consent, in the spirit of Christian meekness, to make me her guardian and director, and be a second wife to her daughter's husband.

Surely this was asking much—offering an unheard-of and impossible position! 'Second wife,' the terrible term, meant only, to Carlyle, a second being, who happened to be a woman, and who should, unquestioning, bend at all times to his imperious will. The word *wife* had, then, that one significance! The proposition was an astounding one, and was probably never communicated to Mrs. Welsh, certainly not in these terms. Carlyle continues:—

If she can, then I say she is a noble woman, and in the name of truth and affection let us all live together, and be one household and one heart, till death or her own choice part us. If she cannot, which will anything but surprise me, then also, the other thing cannot be, must not be; and for her sake, no less than for yours and mine, we must think of something else.

Carlyle, then, would not have been contented with one submissive woman, attending to every wish, and observing it as a law. If another woman be of the household, she must follow suit, and be called 'a noble woman' as her reward.

The matter was growing desperate. Miss Welsh, seeing the absolute impossibility of carrying out any plan which should include her mother, yielded the point and agreed to the other idea—to marry Carlyle and live at Scotsbrig.

CHAPTER VIII

A.D. 1826

Mrs. Welsh decides to further the marriage—Her decision to live with her father at Templand—The Carlyle parents see the impossibility of their son's bride living at Scotsbrig—A new home to be chosen—Impossible conditions—Blindness of Carlyle to the actual situation—Trying uncertainty—The idea of the home at Haddington as a residence for the newly-married pair—Painful objections—The idea abandoned—Recurring failure of plans—And a dissimilarity in ideas—The proposed cottage in Annandale.

MRS. WELSH, now in desperation, decided that the marriage should be celebrated without delay, and the long trying indecision brought to an end. She decided to live at Templand with her father, old Walter, and felt some comfort in the thought that here, at last, she would be within moderate distance of Scotsbrig, and could see her dear only child as often as she wished.

But alas! new difficulties arose. Carlyle, as it would seem, had not gone through the necessary formality of consulting his own father and mother on the proposed plan. They were fully aware of what quite escaped his perception—namely, of the extreme unsuitability of the arrangement. They well knew that their household arrangements were not such as a young lady, brought up as Miss Welsh had been, could easily accommodate herself to. 'Even in summer,' they said, 'it would be difficult for her to live at Scotsbrig, and in winter impossible.' And indeed this remote and humble farmhouse was not attractive.

Then, as to Mrs. Welsh coming occasionally, as she fondly hoped to do, on little visits to her daughter, it was universally felt by the Carlyle family as a thing out of the question—too wild an idea to be entertained. So, brick by brick the castle in the air crumbled and was demolished before the bright eyes of Jane Welsh.

You have misconceived (wrote Carlyle to her) the conditions of Scotsbrig, and your only possible means of existence there! You talk of your mother visiting us! By day and night it would astonish her to see this household. Oh! no! Your mother must not visit mine! What good were it? By an utmost exertion on the part of both they might learn, perhaps, to tolerate each other, more probably to pity, and partially dislike each other. . . The mere idea of such a visit argued too plainly that you *knew nothing* of the family circle, in which, for my sake, you were ready to take a place.

In all this Carlyle spoke without real understanding or knowledge. These two mothers had two strong bonds of union—a loved son and a loved daughter. And there was a basis of understanding and sympathy. Their best interest was to get on well together, and when actually brought into personal contact they respected each other, met kindly, and parted with an increasing and mutual regard. Carlyle did not understand the heart of woman, he never could, so we must pass over his extraordinary blindness as to the feelings of these two mothers, one of whom he loved better than all on earth.

Since, then, each plan was impossible, it was plainly necessary to look out for some alternative. What a time of trying uncertainty, almost of misery, must this have been to Jane Welsh, her heart torn with conflicting emotions incomprehensible to the man with whom she elected to spend the rest of her life! It could not be expected that Mrs. Welsh, after her daughter should have married and left her, would bear to live on in Haddington. The associations, already so sad, were rendered still more painful by the fact that the social circle in which she moved had but one opinion as to the marriage Miss Welsh was about to make. It was not approved, but regarded as offering uncertain worldly prospects, without compensating advantages. It would have been difficult, perhaps, to find a man deserving, in their eyes, of the admired and beloved Jeannie Welsh. In any case, Carlyle did not fit their preconceived idea of such a man, and no doubt they expressed what they felt. Their pity would have been intolerable, and Mrs. Welsh was proud, and did not desire their sympathy. Naturally, therefore, her one course was to leave Haddington immediately and permanently.

At this juncture it occurred to Carlyle that, in this case, the house at Haddington might do well for himself and his bride. There it was, comfortable, provided with all that was necessary, and with much more, in its sober elegance. And his mind turned away from the idea of Edinburgh—which was, after all, noisy and disagreeable—whilst Haddington was quiet, and already enriched with a thousand pleasant recollections. We might have supposed that the thought of Miss Welsh having to come there as a bride, and run the gauntlet of all her old friends known to regard her marriage as an entire mistake—to say nothing of the fact that, as her new home and yet her old home, there would be quite too many sad memories there to haunt her—we might surely have supposed that such considerations as these would at once have stamped the plan as impossible at the very outset. But a strange blindness seems to have possessed Carlyle. Those clear eyes which saw through the eternities, had limited vision in the little spot of earth on which he moved, and ears which were open to the great inarticulate cry of humanity, were unaccountably deaf, at times, to the distinct voice of pain in the utterance of the heart nearest his own.

What, indeed, would have been the result of a settling in the old home at Haddington? First of all, Carlyle would have cut off all intercourse with his wife's oldest friends, who would naturally have come constantly to see their dear companion, whom they loved so well, under the new auspices. 'To me,' he calmly wrote, ' among the many weightier evils and blessings of existence, the evil of impertinent visitors and so forth seems but a small drop of the bucket, and an exceedingly little thing. I have nerve in me to despatch that sort of deer, for ever, by dozens in the day.' No doubt he had, and the closed door would have shut out from the young wife all the old associations and friends of childhood.

Miss Welsh promptly and plainly negatived the plan of their living at Haddington. Yet once more the castle built up by hopes and wishes, fell to the earth in confusion and ruin. Strange that neither of these two hesitated—strange that each was not dimly aware that this marriage-scheme was not smiled upon by the Fates—the powers human or divine! The hardihood they displayed in rebuilding the still collapsing edifice is simply astounding. In any ordinary case the thing would have long since been laid aside as totally impracticable. One of the wisest of living women, illustrious as a writer, and the widow of one whose name is still fragrant amongst us, said once in our hearing: 'When you have made an attempt to carry out a reasonable plan, and find yourself unexpectedly foiled, it is well to try again, and even a third time; but it is well to take the *third* failure as an indication that, whatever it is you have been trying to compass, had best *not be;* and, if it is to be, it will come in its own way, and at its own time.'

But these remarkable people saw no omen in the continually recurring failure of their plans. Carlyle dropped the Haddington plan; but not without plainly showing Miss Welsh that he was disappointed at her want of judgment. He was annoyed and surprised.

The vacant home at Haddington (he said) occurred to my recollection as a sort of godsend, expressly suited to our purpose. It seemed so easy, and on other accounts so indispensable, to let it stand undisposed of for another year, that I doubted not a moment but the whole matter was arranged. If it turned out—which I reckon to be impossible, if you were not distracted in mind—that you really liked better to front the plashes and puddles, and the thousand inclemencies of Scotsbrig through winter, rather than stay another six months in the house where you had lived all your days, it was the simplest process imaginable to stay where we were. The loss was but of a few months' rent for your mother's house, and the certainty it gave us made it great gain. Even yet I cannot with the whole force of my vast intellect understand how my project has failed! I wish not to undervalue your objections to the place, or your opinion on any subject whatever; but I confess my inability, with my present knowledge, to reconcile this very peremptory distaste with your usual good sense.

It is to be feared that prompt acquiescence in any plan of his own, would have been regarded by Carlyle as ' good sense' in a woman.

Now a new plan must be made, and an Annandale cottage was once more proposed, but again the two minds went off at tangents and could by no means go in the same direction. If this was trying before marriage, what must it have been when the interests were absolutely *united*, or supposed to be so? Only between two noble and pure natures could such a marriage have held its ground, as it did, through forty years of pure and blameless conduct; but what suffering, what rending of human cords of Will and of Self, must be involved, to one or other of the parties to such a union, possibly in some degree to both! In one of Wendell Holmes's delightful books, the allegory is presented of a human soul as a musical-box, giving forth certain sweet melodies—

Life turns the winch, and fancy or accident pulls out the stops. I come under your windows some fine spring morning, and play you one of my adagio movements, and some of you say, ' This is good. Play us so always. . . .' ' How easily this tune flows!' you say. ' Ah! dear friends, I will open the poor machine for you, and you shall look. Every note marks where a spur of steel has been driven in! It is easy to grind out the song, but to plant these bristling points was the painful task of time.'

These words fit the case of Jane Welsh. Many a steel point was being planted during these days of uncertainty, and we hear the piercing melody in her later tones.

Carlyle could not understand Miss Welsh's distaste for his plans.

I should have 200*l.* to begin with (he said); many an honest couple has begun with less. I know that wives are supported, some in peace and dignity, others in contention and disgrace, according to their wisdom or their folly, on all incomes, from 14*l.* a year to 200,000*l.*, and I trusted in Jane Welsh, and still trust in her, for good sense enough to accommodate her wants to the means of the man she has chosen before all others, and to live with him contented on whatever it should please Providence to allot him.

Jane Welsh never failed any who trusted in her; she was loyal and faithful, but she had not parted with her reason.

Carlyle, in the letter just quoted from, describes the cottage and income of a labourer—Wightman—whose earnings of fifteen pence a day provided all that was needed to constitute one of the happiest and most enviable families on earth. But, as Mr. Froude most wisely observes—

If Carlyle had looked into the economics of the Wightman household, he would have seen that the wife made her own and her husband's and the child's clothes, swept and cleaned the house that was 'tidy as a cabinet,' washed the flannels and the linen, and weeded the garden when she required fresh air—that she worked, in fact, at severe bodily labour from sunrise to sunset.

And how was the delicate and sensitive young lady to view any existence that bordered on such possibilities as these?

CHAPTER IX

A. D. 1826

The home at Haddington broken up—Comely Bank furnished by Mrs. Welsh—Immediate difficulty over—Miss Welsh happier—Her pride in Carlyle's genius—Her estimate of him—The marriage at Templand—Natural cravings for the affection of Carlyle on the part of his bride-elect—Her unconventionality—State of mind as to the approaching ceremony—Miss Welsh prepares to put off her mourning for the occasion—The 'three cigars'—Good resolutions—White gowns—A post-chaise to Comely Bank.

THE long-protracted affair was at length arranged. The home at Haddington was broken up. Mrs. Welsh took a house in Edinburgh—at Comely Bank—and took her daughter with her, furnishing the new home with the contents of the Haddington house; and also undertaking to pay the rent. It was settled that she should remain with her daughter till near the date of the marriage, which was fixed for October. At that time Mrs. Welsh would remove to Templand, and finally settle with her father, in whose house the marriage would be solemnised. At Comely Bank Mrs. Welsh would be able to visit her daughter occasionally, and there was Carlyle's 200*l.* for immediate expenses, with such additions to it as he might be able to earn.

So things looked brighter, and the terribly long period of suspense was practically over. Miss Welsh was happier and took a cheerful view of her new home and surroundings. She wrote in June:—

It is by no means everything that one could wish, but it is by much the most suitable that could be got, particularly in situation, being within a few minutes' walk of the town, and at the same time well out of its smoke and bustle. Indeed, it would be quite country-looking, only that it is one of a range; for there is a real flower-garden in front, overshadowed by a fair spreading tree, while the windows look out on the greenest fields, with never a street to be seen. As for interior accommodation, there are a dining-room, and a drawing-room, three sleeping-rooms, a kitchen, and more closets than I can see the least occasion for, unless you design to be another Blue Beard. So you see we shall have apartments enough, on a small scale—indeed, almost laughably small; but, if this is no objection in your eyes, neither is it any in mine.

All was now in a fair way, and Carlyle was happy and deeply contented. The manifold difficulties had been surmounted. He was to have his own 'four walls,' and, within them, the being whose companionship he most desired. He wrote from Scotsbrig in July of that same year, 1826, congratulating himself on the solving of the great problem, and the near prospect of his new happiness.

Here are two swallows (he says) in the corner of my window that have taken a house (not at Comely Bank) this summer; and, in spite of drought and bad crops, are bringing up a family together with the highest contentment and unity of soul. Surely, surely, Jane Welsh and Thomas Carlyle, here as they stand, have in them conjointly the wisdom of many swallows! Let them exercise it then, in God's name, and live happy, as these birds of passage are doing.

As time went on perhaps Carlyle was dimly sensible of the loneliness of his home. 'Her little bit of a first chair,' writes the old man in his desolation forty years later, 'its wee, wee arms, &c., visible to me in the closet at this moment, is still here, and always was. I have looked at it hundreds of times, from of old, with many thoughts. No daughter or son of hers was to sit there; so it had been appointed us, my darling!'

Meantime the summer flew swiftly by, and Miss Welsh formally announced the approaching event to her relations, describing her intended husband to Mrs. George Welsh, the wife of her youngest uncle. She had unusual opportunities of knowing Carlyle, since he had never disguised his real character, had made no delusive professions, had almost aggressively presented himself as he was! There was, then, no blindness in Miss Welsh's estimate of him. He stood before her a good man, pure and stainless in life and honour, gifted with most magnificent mental powers.

A faithful and affectionate brother, an admirable son—in all private relations blamelessly innocent. He had splendid talents, which he rather felt than understood; only he was determined, in the same high spirit of duty which had governed his personal conduct, to use them well . . . never, never to sell his soul by travelling the primrose path to wealth and distinction. If honour came to him, it was to come unsought.

We quote Mr. Froude's words, the biographer to whom it would have been so easy to turn out from these facts a perfectly conventionalised and satisfactory portrait of Carlyle. With every line smoothed, every wrinkle filled up and every wilfulness ignored, such a portrait, could Mr. Froude have sacrificed his own integrity to produce it, would probably have called forth from some other quarter an exaggerated presentation of every flaw and every deficiency, and shown us a monster, who would indeed have borne scant resemblance to the great man whose inner life was so pure, and whose reputation, take him for all in all, would emerge so triumphantly from the innermost, most remorseless inspection.

The letter which the bride-elect sent in September, describing her intended husband to her aunt, came into his hands after her death in 1866. What thoughts must have risen in him while he read! 'It came to him,' he said, 'as a flash of radiance from above.' We give a brief extract:—

As much breath has been wasted on my situation, I have my own doubts whether they have given you any right idea of it. They would tell you, I suppose, first and foremost, that my intended is *poor* (for that, it requires no great depth of sagacity to discover); and, in the next place, most likely indulged in some criticisms scarce flattering on his birth, the more likely if their own birth happened to be mean or doubtful; and, if they happened to be vulgar fine people, with disputed pretensions to good looks, they would, to a certainty, set him down as unpolished and ill-looking. But a hundred chances to one they would not tell you he is among the cleverest men of his day—and not the cleverest only, but the most enlightened; that he possesses all the qualities I deem essential in my husband—a warm true heart to love me, a towering intellect to command me, and a spirit of fire to be the guiding star of my life. . . .

Such, then, is this future husband of mine—not a great man according to the most common sense of the word, but truly great, in its natural proper sense—a scholar, a poet, a philosopher, a wise and noble man, one who holds his patent of nobility from almighty God, and whose high stature of manhood is not to be measured by the inch-rule of Lilliputs! Will you like him? No matter whether you do or not, since I like him in the deepest part of my soul.

There is no mistaking the genuine ring of these glowing and sincere words.

We must always remember that, though in one sense Miss Welsh belonged to a superior class, and was accustomed to refinement and elegance of which the Carlyle family never dreamed, she yet received a certain promotion in marrying Thomas Carlyle, since his literary powers opened to her a far higher sphere of society than she could have entered as the wife of a man in such a position as her father had occupied—higher indeed than could easily have fallen to her lot through the acceptance of any suitor she had, or was likely to have had. And though her grace and brilliant gifts made her an addition to the best society, it must be doubted whether, save as Mrs. Carlyle, she would have had the opportunity of meeting constantly with the most intellectual and cultivated people in London.

The difficulties and prolonged suspense attending the carrying out of this marriage naturally took much of the bloom off its near contemplation. Everything had been dwelt on too long and too minutely, the reason had usurped the place of the heart, and hard, worldly facts had given a jaded aspect to Love's rosy wings. There was no beautiful haze of joy, and thrill of newness in the air. It seemed a worn-out story before it ever happened.

We cannot tell how the beautiful Jane Welsh felt as the time approached. Carlyle had nervous misgivings, felt that he was 'a perverse mortal to deal with,' and was manifestly depressed.

The betrothed pair felt it to be almost intolerable to have their names proclaimed in their respective churches, as custom in Scotland demanded. The marriage was to take place quietly at Templand, where Mrs. Welsh now lived with her father, and the newly-married pair were to go the same day to their new home at Comely Bank. Miss Welsh was cheerful and brave—

I am resolved in spirit (she said) and even joyful—joyful in the face of the dreaded ceremony, of starvation, and of every horrible fate. Oh! my dearest friend, be always so good to me, and I shall make the best and happiest wife. When I read in your looks and words that you love me, then I care not one straw for the whole universe besides. But when you fly from me to smoke tobacco, or speak of me as a mere circumstance of your lot, then, indeed, my heart is troubled about many things.

Prophetic words these. That the bright eager woman did come to be at times a mere circumstance in his lot was what Carlyle never knew until it was too late—never could realise until it was brought home to him in unmistakable language, when he read letters, never meant for his eye, in which the lonely woman had revealed to others something of what her life was. But in these early days it could only have been a passing cloud in her thoughts, for she loved him and craved to be loved by him—craved for it to the very end.

She, as well as Carlyle, had a strong disposition and fiery temper. When provoked, she showed a thoroughly unamiable side of her nature—inflexible she was—and her words cut

like knives. Another element in her blood, pointed out by
Dr. Japp, does much, in his idea (and I agree with him), to
account for many traits in her character. It has been somewhat overlooked, though told with some pride by Mrs. Carlyle
in speaking of her own ancestry, that she had a decided
strain of gipsy blood. That famous gipsy chieftain, Matthew
Baillie, who could steal a horse from under the owner if he
liked, was yet said to be a thorough gentleman in his way.
These inherited tendencies cling on in a remarkable way, and
the daring spirit of Jane Baillie Welsh was not unworthy of
her adventurous ancestor. The mystery of heredity is one
that has scarcely been touched, and I entirely endorse
Dr. Japp's remarks when he says, 'If Jane Welsh derived
from her father her serious thought, prudent decision, and
settled affection for place and person . . . she as certainly
derived from her mother's side a touch of waywardness, a
sudden variability of mood, a half-wild originality, a love of
primitive life, and a craving for the relief of fun and freedom and banter. ' One of her oldest friends now surviving
has spoken of her innate " trickiness," which showed itself in
many brilliant sallies; and there is no doubt that the fetters
of conventionality weighed heavily at times on her bright
spirit—more heavily when the spirit was no longer bright.'

She knew her own failings, and, at this momentous time,
made many good resolutions.

I am really going to be a very meek-tempered wife! (she wrote
to Carlyle). Indeed, I am begun to be meek-tempered already!
My aunt tells me she could live for ever with me without quarrelling, I am so reasonable and so equable in my humour. There
is something to gladden your heart withal! . . . Do you perceive,
my good sir, the fault will be wholly your own if we do not get
on most harmoniously together.

She evidently presaged storms. It is amusing, it would be
more amusing if it were less pathetic, to find these two people
striving to encourage each other, as if on the scaffold.

The wedding took place on October 17. On October 10

Miss Welsh had written from Templand to Carlyle—'You desired me to answer your letter on Thursday, but I have waited another post that I might do it better, if indeed any good thing is to be said under such horrid circumstances.' It must have been Carlyle himself who had caused Miss Welsh to regard the wedding preparations as 'horrid circumstances.' No girl would so have regarded them, unless the thought were forced upon her. It is generally felt as a joyful and beautiful time, and a loving word and assurance from Carlyle would have made all the difference. But if *he* so seriously deplored it, what could Miss Welsh do but follow suit?

Oh, *do* (she continues), for Heaven's sake, get into a more benignant humour! or the incident will not only 'wear a very original aspect,' but likewise a very heart-breaking one! I see not how I am to go through with it. . . .

I expected to know last night, when my mother is to come from Edinburgh, in which case I should have been able to name some day, though not so early a one as that proposed; but, alas! alas! my mother is dilatory and uncertain as ever, and the only satisfaction I can give you at this time is to promise I will soon write again. What has taken her to Edinburgh so inopportunely?—to set some fractions of women cutting out white gowns, a thing which might have been done with all convenience when we were there last month. But some people are wise, and some are otherwise, and I shall be glad to get the gowns anyway, for I should like ill to put you to charge in that article, for a very great while. Besides, you know it would be a bad omen to marry in mourning. When I first put it on, six years ago, I thought to wear it for ever; but I have found a second father, and it were ungrateful not to show, even externally, how much I rejoice in him.

These are strange expressions. We see that she had meant to wear perpetual black for that dearly loved father whom she had lost; but resolved to put it off, having now found 'a second father' in Thomas Carlyle. Few lovers would appreciate the title, however much they might like to see their brides in white, instead of mourning, garments.

Carlyle had evidently proposed to take the wedding journey in the coach from Dumfries—less perhaps from economy than from a general sense of protection; with the same idea he had wished his brother John to go part of the way with him and his bride. But a lady's wish at these times is law, and Miss Welsh absolutely declined the coach journey. She also adds, 'For the same reason I prohibit John from going with us an inch of the road; and he must not think there is any unkindness in this. I hope your mother is praying for me. Give her my affectionate regards. JANE WELSH.'

Carlyle, who had been striving to fortify himself against what Miss Welsh called 'the odious ceremony,' by reading Kant's 'Critique of Pure Reason,' had turned in despair to Scott's novels, which cheered him somewhat.

After all (he wrote), I believe we take this impending ceremony too much to heart! Bless me! have not many people been married before now? . . .

To your arrangements about the journey, and the other items of the how and when, I can only answer as becomes me. Be it as thou hast said! Let me know your will and it shall be my pleasure! And so, by the blessing of Heaven, we shall roll along side by side with the speed of post-horses, till we arrive at Comely Bank. I shall only stipulate that you will let me, by the road, as occasion serves, *smoke three cigars*, without criticism or reluctance, as things essential to my perfect contentment. Yet if you object to this article, think not that I will break off the match on that account, but rather, like a dutiful husband, submit to the everlasting ordinance of providence, and let my wife have her way. You are very kind, and more just than I have reason to expect, in imputing my ill-natured speeches (for which Heaven forgive me!) to their true cause—a disordered nervous system. Believe me, Jane, it is not I, but the Devil speaking out of me, which could utter one harsh word to a heart that so little deserves it. Oh! I were blind and wretched if I could make thee unhappy!

Strange words for an expectant bridegroom! uttered at that time in the history of betrothed pairs when, as a rule, every word is a caress; and, to quote from 'Sartor,' one might expect that the 'world lay all harmonious before them, like some fair royal champaign the sovereign and owner of which were Love alone!' Here it was not *all* harmony, though there was sincere affection.

As to the proclamation (he says), I protest I had rather be proclaimed in every church in the empire than miss the little bird I have in my eye, whom I see not how I am to do without. . . . (and, in conclusion, he says) Oh! we are two ungrateful wretches, or we should be happy. Write soon, and love me for ever; and so, good-night, *mein Herzenskind.* Thine, *auf ewig*,
T. CARLYLE.

The white gowns were made; the gloves were purchased; and the long, remarkable, and altogether unique preliminaries ended on October 17, 1826. Highly characteristic is the heading of Miss Welsh's final letter to Carlyle: '*The last speech and marrying words of that unfortunate young woman, Jane Baillie Welsh.*'

'Truly,' answered Carlyle, 'a most delightful and swan-like melody is in them; a tenderness and warm devoted trust worthy of such a maiden, bidding farewell to that unmarried earth of which she was the fairest ornament. Let us pray to God that our holy purpose is not frustrated. Let us trust in Him, and in each other, and fear no evil that can befall us.'

The quiet little ceremony being over, the minister and John Carlyle being the only persons present, except the bride's family and the 'high contracting parties,' Mr. and Mrs. Carlyle started in a post-chaise for Comely Bank. Whether the three cigars were found necessary to render the situation tolerable to the bridegroom is nowhere recorded. The deed was done.

It would be idle to speculate on the possibilities of fuller happiness for either of these truly exceptional natures, if married otherwise, to two other persons, less remarkable, and differently constituted. No romantic happiness was looked for by either of them. Thomas Carlyle was possessed of a feverish soul that struggled perpetually with minor problems—he had to wrestle with the demon within himself—as well as with dyspepsia and nervous irritability. These things could not be banished by the presence of the charming woman whose bright eyes now lighted up his new home. A little less intellect, a little more mere human lovingness, would have made things easier.

But we are not to dwell upon the '*might have been.*' The dainty, graceful girl, with something of Ariel, something of Puck in her nature, was now face to face with her difficult task, brave in her determination to make her husband's way smooth for him, to offer up the full service of a faithful devotion. She thought, no doubt, as women do think, that love would make the way plain. It certainly shewed the path—from which she never flinched—but the way was ever beset with thorns. She did not fear poverty—if she were rich in love; but what constituted that most precious treasure was imperfectly understood by Carlyle. And in all marriage the human element must ever be important, it cannot be overlooked. It is still there when the white-haired venerable pair sit on either side of the hearth, watching their greatgrandchild playing on the rug; or, if no such link carries them forward, it is still there when they recall golden days of youth, and the flush tints their faded cheeks, as they recount some fragments of the tale of their springtime, of no meaning to any one but themselves.

There would be no such tender memories to turn to in this case; but a correspondence, like a great legal case, a terrible dragging out of calculations and ponderings, a desperate resolve to take the final step, and many misgivings on both sides. There was, on each side, a power of severe speech, a clear insight into imperfections, hostile to perfect happiness. Then, again, there was much in common—keen intellectual sympathy, a certain likeness in views of life and its aims, a stern integrity and uprightness of character, a degree of contempt for the world's opinion. Valuable as a superstructure, provided the foundation were of the firmest, the most deeply laid, the true foundation of all lasting human ties—Love!

And here and now ended Jane Welsh's girlhood.

PART II

EARLY MARRIED LIFE

CHAPTER X

A. D. 1826

Comely Bank—Good resolutions—Social opportunities—A wifely letter—Narrow income—Visit of Dr. John Carlyle—The daily life—The little 'Wednesday evenings'—Friendship with Jeffrey—Brighter prospects—Household activities on Mrs. Carlyle's part—Renewed ideas of living at 'Craigenputtock'—Its unsuitability to Mrs. Carlyle's needs—Carlyle visits it with his brother Alick—The tenant about to leave—Letter from Mrs. Carlyle—Loving response.

THE home in which Mr. and Mrs. Carlyle began their new life was, according to Carlyle's own account to his mother, 'a perfect model, furnished with every accommodation that heart could desire.' The house was in Comely Bank, a row of houses to the north of Edinburgh; it then stood among open fields between the city and the sea. It had been beautifully fitted up by Mrs. Welsh, and must have offered every possibility that a mere house can offer for perfect happiness!

Mrs. Welsh was at this time settled at Templand with her father and her youngest sister, now a woman of about thirty, the 'Aunt Jeannie' of whom Carlyle speaks so tenderly in the 'Reminiscences'—the fair-haired gentle victim of that early love-tragedy which, as Carlyle said, 'closed her poor heart against hopes of that kind at an early period of her life.' Mrs. Carlyle was not anxious about her mother, to whom Haddington had become hateful, and who had a home with old Walter, and loving surroundings. She had done what she could to secure her mother's comfort, and now she turned her undivided loyal energy to the more difficult task of making Carlyle's life happy and peaceful.

It is difficult for people to realise that they inevitably bring the deep essentials of their happiness or unhappiness with them into whatever atmosphere they are transplanted. It is a trite saying that we can change the sky above us, but are apt to retain the spirit with which we regard it. So, although Carlyle had won his treasure, he was still himself—still tormented by the spirit within him, which did not come out of him under the beam of his wife's bright eyes. He says to his mother:—

For my wife, I may say in my heart that she is better than any wife, and loves me with a devotedness which it is a mystery to me how I have ever deserved. She is gay and happy as a lark, and looks with such soft cheerfulness into my gloomy countenance, that new hope passed into me every time I met her eye. In truth I was very sullen yesterday, sick with sleeplessness, nervous, bilious, splenetic, and all the rest of it.

The 'rest of it' was, we fear, a very irritable disposition, which showed itself even in those days of rosy hope.

Still, Carlyle vaguely hoped to be happier. He speaks of believing he shall get 'hefted to his new situation.' He wished his brother John to come and join him in his 'solitary wanderings by the sad autumnal sea.' But he was making good resolutions, and not forgetting the tender wish to please his old mother. 'Tell my mother,' he writes to John Carlyle, 'that by Jane's express request I am to read a sermon, and a chapter with commentary, at least every Sabbath day, to my household. Also that we are taking seats in church, and design to live soberly and devoutly, as beseems us.'

Comely Bank enabled the Carlyles to have some society, and it must have been a pretty sight when the dainty, gifted young wife entertained, in her own house, some of the choice spirits of Edinburgh, and was herself the light and the charm of the modest entertainments so rich in wit and intellectual surrounding. No invitation to Comely Bank was refused. These little tea-parties were an earnest of those held in later days in Cheyne Row—those never-to-be-forgotten evenings of which we have heard from those few now surviving who were privileged to attend them. Brewster (afterwards Sir David Brewster), De Quincey,* Sir William Hamilton, and many others were among the guests at Comely Bank.

If Carlyle at this time had been engaged in some congenial and remunerative employment the little home would have been brighter. Mrs. Carlyle wrote to her mother-in-law on December 9, 1826:—

My dear Mother,—I must not let the letter go without adding my 'Be of good cheer!' You would rejoice to see how much better my husband is since we came hither. And we are really very happy. When he falls on some work we shall be still happier. Indeed I should be very stupid or very thankless if I did not congratulate myself every hour of the day on the lot which it has pleased Providence to assign me. My husband is so kind, so in all respects after my own heart. I was sick one day, and he nursed me as well as my own mother could have done; and he never says a hard word to me unless I richly deserve it. We see great numbers of people, but are always most content alone. My husband reads then, and I read or work, or just sit and look at him, which I really find as profitable an employment as any other. God bless you and my little Jean, whom I hope to see at no very distant date.

This is a pretty and wifely letter. But money was not abundant, and work—which was almost more essential to Carlyle's well-being—kept aloof. Writing to his mother in January 1827, Carlyle mentions that Mrs. Welsh had sent sixty pounds in a letter. This was promptly returned, though the gift was felt to be both kind and handsome. The

* See Appendix IV.

good mother at Scotsbrig sent eggs from the farm and other home produce, and Mrs. Carlyle could turn her hand to the making of a dainty custard, pancakes, and the like.

John Carlyle came early in that first year to stay with the pair at Comely Bank, and in February Carlyle reports of the home-life very graphically to his brother Alexander.

Last week (he writes) I fairly began a book. Heaven only knows what it will turn to. . . . You would wonder how much happier steady occupation makes us, and how smoothly we all get along. Directly after breakfast the good wife and the doctor (John Carlyle) retire upstairs to the drawing-room, a little place all fitted up like a lady's work-box, where a spark of fire is lit for the forenoon; and I meanwhile sit scribbling and meditating, and wrestling with the powers of dullness till one or two o'clock, when I sally forth into the city or towards the seashore, taking care only to be at home for the important purpose of consuming my mutton chop at four.

Carlyle, then, in these early days did not as a rule spend any time with his wife between breakfast time and 4 P. M. 'After dinner,' he adds, 'we all read learned languages till coffee, and so on till bedtime.'

Carlyle speaks of the possibilities as to society, and of the limited degree to which they were utilised. 'Jane,' he says, 'has a circular, or rather two circulars—one for those she values, and one for those she does not value; and one or other of these she sends.' These were the replies to dinner-invitations. Thus no dinners were given or accepted. 'Only, to some three or four chosen people we give notice that on Wednesday nights we shall *always* be at home, and glad if they will call and talk for two hours with no other entertainment but a cordial welcome, and a cup of innocent tea.' The entertainment was truly a royal one—and was always felt to be so—by virtue of a banquet fit for the gods.

In this letter Carlyle mentions having in his pocket 'a

letter of introduction to Jeffrey of the "Edinburgh Review."'
'It was sent me,' he says, 'from Proctor of London.' That letter was the opening of a long and interesting friendship, which was most close and warm between Lord Jeffrey and Mrs. Carlyle, whom he came to regard with a chivalrous tenderness in which almost every man who knew her must have shared. Carlyle speaks in the 'Reminiscences' of striding off, with Proctor's introduction, one evening to George Square, where he had his first interview with Jeffrey, with whose personal appearance he had been familiar some fourteen years. The interview was a successful one, resulting not only in a return of the visit, but in much literary work for Carlyle in the shape of articles for the reviews, greatly to Mrs. Carlyle's delight and pride; for she admired her husband with all her heart, and, later on, in the sad days of her broken health and joyless conditions, was often heard to wind up one of her depressing accounts of him with—'But then, you know, he is *so clever!*'

A letter from Mrs. Cariyie *to* her mother-in-law, dated '21 Comely Bank, February 17, 1827,' gives some touching details of the life there. Speaking of the book Carlyle was engaged on—a novel, which was never finished—the young wife writes:—

More contented he certainly is since he applied himself to this task, for he was not born to be anything but miserable in idleness. Oh! that he were indeed well—well beside me, and occupied as he ought. How plain and clear life would then lie before us! . . . Within doors all is warm, is swept and garnished, and without, the country is no longer winter-like, but beginning to be gay and green. Many pleasant people come to see us. . . . *Alone* we are never weary. If I have not Jean's enviable gift of talking, I am at least among the best listeners in the kingdom, and my husband has always something interesting and instructive to say. Then we have books to read—all sorts of them, from Scott's Bible down to novels; and I have sewing-needles, and purse-needles, and all conceivable implements for ladies' work. There is a piano, too, for 'soothing the savage breast,' when one cares for its charms; but I am sorry to say neither my playing nor my singing seems to give Mr. C. much delight. I console myself, however, with imputing the blame to his want of taste, rather than my want of skill. . . . It is my husband's worst fault to me that I will not, or cannot, speak. Often when he has talked for an hour without answer, he will beg for some signs of life on my part, and the only sign I can give is a little kiss. . . .

Mrs. Carlyle's occupations at Comely Bank were by no means comprised in the small accomplishments she enumerates in this letter. Dainty in all her ways, the presence of one servant did not suffice to keep all things in the spotless order which she loved, without many little offices on her part, and her hand helped to give her dyspeptic husband a more delicate diet than an ordinary maid-of-all-work could provide. Her bright spirit and comparatively good health doubtless added a charm to these domesticities, and we can quite fancy her locking the kitchen door on herself, to essay her first pudding, which was to be something quite out of the common.

Had but Fortune smiled more kindly on these two people, and given them a comfortable income! But it was not so. Finances were ebbing—not fast, but surely—and the prospect was a dark one. It was natural, perhaps, that Carlyle's mind should revert at this time to his old scheme of living at Craigenputtock. His brother Alexander could farm it, and it would be a quiet, healthy, and cheap residence. Perhaps it was to some extent natural that he should forget to pause and consider whether this wild 'hill of the hawk' would be a fitting home for the fluttering dove that he had taken into his care. Perhaps he had become so entirely 'hefted to his new situation' that it seemed a matter of course. They twain being one, what was good for him must be good for her. Perhaps he thought—but it is less likely—'she will have *me*.' But a wilderness (and it was little better) needs very pronounced conditions of bliss before it will consent to 'rejoice and blossom as the rose.' She had told him she could not live a month at Craigenputtock 'with an angel;' but her faith and courage were to be put to a strong test. Writing of it afterwards, Carlyle said: 'To her it was a great sacrifice, if to me it was the reverse; but at no moment, even by a look, did she ever say so.' Brave Jane Welsh Carlyle! But Carlyle adds with great simplicity, 'Indeed I think she never felt so at all.'

One attraction this wild place presented: it was within fifteen miles of Templand, where Mrs. Welsh now lived; and the moment for the change seemed propitious, for the tenant of Craigenputtock was about to leave, and Mrs. Welsh anxiously desired to have the Carlyles there, and generously undertook much of the expense connected with the change.

In April, Carlyle, with his brother Alick, went on a visit of inspection, while Mrs Welsh joined her daughter at Comely Bank. The matter was quickly arranged, and the tenant was to leave almost immediately, Carlyle to follow his brother to Craigenputtock as soon after Whitsuntide as all was in order.

We must give a few sentences from the charming letter Mrs. Carlyle wrote to her husband during this, his first absence from her. The six-months wife begins with 'Dear, Dear, (Cheap! Cheap!)'—This being a little fun between them as Mr. Froude tells us, in a note, how 'Cheap! Cheap!' had evidently been an answer which Carlyle had made to some endearment of hers:—

I met the postman yesterday morning, and something bade me ask if there were any letters. Imagine my agitation when he gave me yours, four and twenty hours before the appointed time. I was so glad, and so frightened, so eager to know the whole contents, that I could hardly make out any part. . . . I did at length, with much heart-beating, get through the precious paper, and found that you still loved me pretty well, and that the Craig o' Putta was still a hope; as also that, if you come not back to poor 'Goody' on Saturday, it will not be for want of will. Ah! nor yet will it be for the want of the most fervent prayers to Heaven that a longing Goody can put up; for I am sick—sick to the heart—of this absence, which indeed I can only bear in the faith of its being brief. . . My head has ached more continuously than any time these six months. But health and spirits will come back when my husband comes back with good news—or rather, when he comes back at all, whether his news be good or bad. . . . To be separated from you one week is frightful as a foretaste of what it might be; but I will not think of that, if I can help it; and, after all, why should I think of life without you?

Plainly, she thought of her father, of the wrench that death had made when she lost *him*. It would be idle to say Mrs. Carlyle did not love her husband—ay, to the end the love was not killed, and it would, it *might*, have blossomed forth in the last years, had time been granted. The letter goes on: 'Is not my being interwoven with yours so close that it can have no separate existence? . . . But you will be calling this "French sentimentality," I fear; and even the style of mockery is better than that. . .'

Later in life Carlyle heard much of this latter style, but it was the fruit of bitterness and suffering, and did not rise to the heart of the young wife in these early, untried days.

This letter contains a curious little touch of that 'trickiness' which was characteristic of Mrs. Carlyle. Speaking of visitors who had called at Comely Bank during Carlyle's absence, she mentions several names; then an evening's engagement to the house of a Mrs. Bruce. Being disinclined to go, she evaded it with great adroitness. 'I wrapped a piece of flannel about my throat, and *made my mother carry an apology of cold.*' The italics are our own.

To this letter came a loving and worthy reply, ending with :—

Oh Jeannie! Oh my wife! we will never part—never through eternity itself; but I will love thee, and keep thee in my heart of hearts!—that is, unless I grow a very great fool—which, indeed, this talk doth somewhat betoken. God bless thee!

Ever thine,   T. CARLYLE.

CHAPTER XI

A.D. 1827

Alexander Carlyle and his sister Mary go to live at Craigenputtock—The visit of the Carlyles to Templand, Scotsbrig, &c.—Prospect of some professorship for Carlyle—Disappointment—Decision for Craigenputtock—A sacrifice—Bleak and barren situation of the new home—Jeffrey's disapproval of the plan—Mrs. Carlyle's courage—House-moving—Carlyle's despair—Correspondence of Mrs. Carlyle with her old friend, Miss Eliza Stodart—Ideals of married life relinquished—Carlyle's frequent depression and absorption in his work—The wife's isolation.

In the summer of 1827, Alexander Carlyle and his sister Mary entered into occupation of Craigenputtock, as had been arranged; but the Carlyles were loth to leave Edinburgh quite so soon as they had at first intended. For the prospect was somewhat brighter for Carlyle. Jeffrey could appreciate his uncommon powers, and an admission into the 'Edinburgh Review' gave him congenial work, and hope therewith of yet wider scope of literary prosperity. There was not quite the same sympathy between Carlyle and Jeffrey as existed between Mrs. Carlyle and the 'clever little gentleman;' but the introduction was a memorable event in many ways.

The literary work now offered to Carlyle kept him in Edinburgh. But during the summer he and his wife spent a short holiday with the family at Scotsbrig, a few days at Templand, and took a look at the 'Hill of the Hawk.' In August they were again settled in Comely Bank.

It was at this time that Carlyle began to look forward to the possibility of some permanent and honourable appointment—some professorship, maybe—that should be a literary haven to him. He consulted Edward Irving as to some opening in the London University, and comments on his reply in a letter to his brother John in September. Irving, he said, had written 'in a strange, austere, puritanical, yet on the whole, honest and friendly-looking style. He advises me to proceed and make the attempt.'

The plan never came to fruition. The Carlyles dined with the Jeffreys to talk the chances over. If the plan succeeded, it would at least do away with the necessity for living on the wild, bleak moors, which must have been depressing to contemplate. But the appointment was given to someone else.

Other hopes, including one of a professorship in St. Andrews University, also failed, and the idea of living at Craigenputtock returned with renewed insistence, and finally shaped itself into a definite intention. The house was placed under repair, and with the early spring these remarkable people were to leave the world—as represented by the social refinement and attractions of Edinburgh—and bury themselves in the wild Dunscore moors, at a farm sixteen miles from the nearest town and the nearest doctor, in a spot where, through long months, winter would hold his iron reign, and almost cut off access to the outer cheerfulness of life. With a giant's stock of strength, with a help-mate strong also, and gentle and responsive, with a great share of the sweet double life which marriage sometimes brings, there is no doubt that a happy, though not a luxurious, existence might have been realised at Craigenputtock by Mrs. Carlyle. But these conditions were imperfectly fulfilled. No giant's strength was hers. Never robust, she had already shown absolute delicacy of health; and her help-mate was dyspeptic, restless, troubled with sleeplessness, nervous, and possessed by some inner struggle which often made his own days hard to endure, and left him little power to make a woman's life attractive and harmonious.

The house at Comely Bank was held only by the year. They must now decide whether it should be taken for another twelve months, and they determined to see Craigenputtock once more together, before taking a final step. The impression made on their minds cannot have been very attractive. March is a bleak month in the North, and there may have been misgivings in the minds of both husband and wife as to the severing of themselves from all the warmth and pleasantness of their pretty home in Edinburgh.

But the decision was taken out of their hands in a manner, for, on their return from this visit, they found their landlord had actually let the house at Comely Bank to another tenant, so that at Whitsuntide they must certainly leave it, and so the question settled itself rather unexpectedly, and immediate steps were taken to render the Craig o' Putta comfortable and habitable. Carlyle wrote to his brother: 'I anticipate, with confidence, a friendly and rather comfortable arrangement at the Craig, in which, not in idleness, yet in peace, and more self-selected occupations, I may find more health, and, what I reckon weightier, more scope to improve and worthily employ myself, which either here or there I reckon to be the great end of existence and the only happiness.' There may be other forms of happiness known to other human beings, but it would be idle to dwell on the point. Whether this ideal of happiness included and insured the happiness of that other human being so closely linked with his life, is a question to which the answer will not tarry long.

Mr. Froude's description of Craigenputtock gives a vivid idea of it:—

. . . . The dreariest spot in all the British dominions. The nearest cottage is more than a mile from it; the elevation, 700 feet above the sea, stunts the trees, and limits the garden produce to the hardiest vegetables. The house is gaunt and hungry-looking. It stands, with the scanty fields attached, as an island in a sea of morass. The landscape is unredeemed either by grace or grandeur, —mere undulating hills of grass and heather, with peat bogs in the hollows between them.

An ungentle home for the delicate woman.

Carlyle, in a letter to Goethe, describes it in much the same terms, as being,

Among the granite hills and the bleak morasses which stretch westward through Galloway almost to the Irish Sea. . . . The roses, indeed, are still in part to be planted. . . . Two ponies, which carry us everywhere, and the mountain air, are the best medicine for weak nerves. . . . I came thither solely with the design to simplify my way of life, and to secure the independence through which I could be enabled to remain true to myself.

There must have been some sinking of Mrs. Carlyle's dauntless spirit at the prospect of this remote and lonely existence. Some such feelings on her part were evident to some of her friends. The kind-hearted Jeffrey felt really alarmed, but trusted that the experience of life in the wilderness would bring about a prompt return to the amenities of Edinburgh. Whether this attached and considerate friend foresaw anything of the disastrous consequences of the step, we do not know; but, finding it inevitable, he did all he could to make it easy for Mrs. Carlyle, inviting her with her husband to visit him in Moray Place, while the carts conveyed the Lares and Penates of Comely Bank into the wilds of the Dunscore moors.

This change of residence was a turning-point in Mrs. Carlyle's life. Before going further, we will cite a charming passage from one of Prof. Masson's articles in 'Macmillan,' December 1881. It calls to mind the words often quoted by Mrs. Carlyle in later life—

> And my youth was left behind
> For someone else to find.

An old Haddington nurse, speaking to Prof. Masson of Mrs. Carlyle before her marriage, said:

Ah! when she was young, she was a fleein', dancin', lightheartit thing, Jeanie Welsh, that naething would hae dauntit. But she grew grave a' at ance. There was Maister Irving, ye ken, that had been her teacher; and he cam aboot her. Then there was Maister—— (this name, possibly that of Irving's successor in the Haddington School, is not given). Then there was Maister Carlyle himsel'; and *he* cam to finish her off like. . . .

This bright creature was not yet 'dauntit,' but bravely, cheerfully set to her new task, for already it became something of a task to fulfil all that the conditions demanded.

The actual day came for the married pair to enter their new home. That the cottage where Alexander Carlyle was to live was attached to the premises, was a comfort to Carlyle, and, as Mr. Froude tells us, 'the outdoor establishment of field, stall, and dairy servants was common to both households.'

House-moving is never pleasant. Even the completeness of modern arrangements fails to redeem it from the reproach of intense discomfort attaching to it. But this must have been quite a unique 'flitting.' Carlyle's despair, as witnessed by his letter to his brother John, written a week or two after the arrival at Craigenputtock, is tragic and yet amusing. He speaks of the 'chaotic uproar' of dismantling the modest house at Comely Bank, and adds: 'From all packers and carpenters and flitting by night or day, Good Lord deliver us!' We may be sure that the clear-headed lady at the head of affairs would reduce chaos into cosmos at the earliest possible date, and in due time the Carlyles settled in the intense solitude of their new home. They had entered it about the last week in May, before the year wears its real spring smile in these northern districts.

The 'cares of bread' soon made themselves felt. On July 29 we find Mrs. Carlyle appealing once more to her 'dear, dear angel Bessy!' with a request that she would order for her, tea, coffee, sugar, &c., in Edinburgh, to be sent by carrier to Craigenputtock; all her groceries, she says, are done, and without a fresh supply she fears 'her husband would soon be done also.'

In this letter she addresses Miss Stodart as 'thou archangel Bessy,' and wrote cheerfully enough. 'Dear Edinburgh!' she says, 'I was very happy there, and shall always love it, and hope to see it again often before I die.' The servant, Grace Macdonald, is spoken of as excellent, and even in such desolate surroundings there was no absolute barrier to a very happy life.

Here and now, however, we feel as if Mrs. Carlyle silently relinquished her ideal of married life, or at least of life with Carlyle. As in his wooing there had ever been more of the intellectual sympathy than of the passion of a lover, and as Mrs. Carlyle, who knew how a man loves, was well able to discern the tone of the attachment offered to her, it had never been expected by her that this sternly-absorbed, spirit-tormented man would be content to lie at her feet on the heather at Craigenputtock and look into her eyes for his inspirations. What she probably did expect, was—what the union naturally seemed to promise—a close intellectual companionship. She would fain have set her little foot on each round of the ladder beside his, and gone with him in his spirit-flights; but here the fulfilment seemed strikingly imperfect.

Carlyle, often depressed or irritable from ill health and mental absorption, needed much solitude. His nervous wakefulness necessitated his sleeping in a room alone, as the least sound drove sleep from him. He could not write to any purpose unless he were alone, and, as time went on, would even eat his dinner alone. So that his wife often saw only the lurid reflection, as it were, of what had been passing in his mind, without the interest of sharing his thoughts. In the days at Comely Bank she speaks of sometimes just sitting and looking at him; but she soon found, perhaps, that it was best to leave him to forge his thunderbolts alone, with no spectator of the fierce war of elements in his distracted mind.

The marriage certainly presented some features of what the French call a *solitude à deux*. Doubtless the heavier share of that solitude fell on Mrs. Carlyle; but Carlyle often expressed in his journals, &c., a loneliness and isolation that could be felt—a separation not only from her, but from much of the living, breathing world around him.

If, then, there was an element of disappointment in the lives of these two, we must remember that many very commonplace marriages are not wholly free from that element. It may pass unnoticed by the outer world. In this case, however, we are drawn inevitably to consider it.

CHAPTER XII

A. D. 1827-1829

'Cares of bread'—The first loaf—Visit of the Jeffreys to Craigenputtock—Mrs. Carlyle's preparatory ride to Dumfries—Friendly advice of Jeffrey to Carlyle—Invitation to Moray Place—The two mountain ponies—Mrs. Carlyle's loneliness—'Brother Alick'—A visit to Templand—Letter from the wife to the husband—Visit of the Carlyles to Edinburgh—22 George Square—Return to 'The Desert'—Serious illness of Mrs. Carlyle—Visit of Mrs. Welsh—Permanently weakened health.

AMONG the sorest of Mrs. Carlyle's efforts at Craigenputtock was the difficulty of propitiating her husband's digestion, bad at all times. At Comely Bank he could eat the baker's bread. Here, the bread manufactured by the 'active maid' who had come with the pair from Edinburgh quite failed to meet Carlyle's requirements, and Mrs. Carlyle determined to bake some herself. It sounds simple enough, but bread-making really *is* a matter requiring much nicety. Mr. Froude quotes Mrs. Carlyle's own account, written nearly thirty years later, to a Miss Smith of Carlisle. The narrative is given characteristically, with that intensity of language which was natural to the writer, inevitable, and also admirable, if we are careful to remember that, though not the language of exaggeration, it certainly gives more emphasis than bare facts will always fully bear out. She wrote as she felt, absolutely, and as things presented themselves to her.

So many talents are wasted (she writes), so many enthusiasms turned to smoke, so many lives spoilt, . . . for want of recognising that it is not the greatness or littleness of the duty nearest hand, but the spirit in which one does it, that make one's doing noble or mean. I can't think how people who have any natural ambition, and any sense of power in them, escape going *mad* in a world like this, without the recognition of that. . . . I had gone with my husband to live on a little estate of *peat-bog*, that had descended to me all the way down from John Welsh, the Covenanter who married a daughter of John Knox. *That* didn't, I am ashamed to say, make me feel Craigenputtock a whit less of a peat-bog, and a most dreary, untoward place to live in. . . . Further, we were *very* poor, and, further and worst, being an only child, and brought up to 'great prospects,' I was sublimely ignorant of every branch of useful knowledge, though a capital Latin scholar and a very fair mathematician. It behoved me, in these astonishing circumstances, to learn to sew ! Husbands, I was shocked to find, wore their stockings into holes, and were always losing buttons; and *I* was expected to 'look to all that.' Also it behoved me to learn to *cook!*—no capable servant choosing to live at such an out-of-the-way place. . . . It was plainly my duty as a Christian wife to bake at home! So I sent for Cobbett's 'Cottage Economy,' and fell to work at a loaf of bread.

But, knowing nothing about the process of fermentation, or the heat of ovens, it came to pass that my loaf got put into the oven at the time that myself ought to have been put into bed. And I remained the only person not asleep in a house in the middle of a desert. One o'clock struck, and then two, and then three, and still I was sitting there, in an immense solitude, my whole body aching with weariness, my heart aching with a sense of forlornness and *degradation* that I, who had been so petted at home, whose comfort had been studied by everybody in the house, who had never been required to *do* anything but cultivate my mind, should have to pass all those hours of the night in watching a *loaf* of *bread*—which might not turn out bread after all ! Such thoughts maddened me, till I laid down my head on the table and sobbed aloud. It was then that somehow the idea of Benvenuto Cellini sitting up all night watching his ' Perseus ' in the furnace came into my head, and suddenly I asked myself —' After all, in the sight of the Upper Powers, what is the mighty difference between a statue of Perseus, and a loaf of bread, so that each be the thing one's hand has found to do ! . . . .' *

* See Appendix V.

No doubt Mrs. Carlyle was thoroughly tired and disheartened on the occasion referred to. But the 'prospects' to which she alludes could hardly have promised an immunity from all household cares. Many a clergyman's wife, many a barrister's wife placidly darns the socks of her husband and children, and, though not actually making bread, attends actively to culinary operations now and then, should occasion require. If any 'only child' is made the first study of all the inmates of a household, that child is ill-prepared for the realities of life; and no wife would expect to go on after marriage with the cultivation of her mind as her 'sole care.'

Few wives, however, pursue their domestic activities in an atmosphere so barren of life's best charm as did Mrs. Carlyle, and few were less physically able for the exertions which come lightly and pleasantly to women of more robust temperament. If she felt everything with the acuteness which this letter displays—and it is to be feared she *did*—then was her outlook into life indeed a dark one.*

An event much looked for was the promised visit of the Jeffreys to Craigenputtock, which took place in October of the same year, 1828. We can fancy the big carriage standing in the humble farmyard, and the altogether unwonted elements introduced on the scene. Short notice had been given to the Lady of Craigenputtock—only a day, seemingly. Carlyle speaks in the 'Reminiscences' of his wife's gallop to Dumfries and back, on this occasion, to make her preparations—'thirty good miles of swift canter, at least,' he calls it. Carlyle himself was at Scotsbrig, and no time to be lost. Mounted on 'Harry,' her 'well-broken, loyal little horse,' she made this flying journey, ' laid her plans while galloping, ordered everything at Dumfries,' says Carlyle—' sent word to me express, and galloped home, and stood victoriously prepared at all points to receive the Jeffreys.

The party consisted of Jeffrey, his wife and daughter, and a servant. Well might the guests learn with surprise that

* See Appendix V.

their hostess's fair hands had cooked the excellent dinner. But such violent exertion was fatally wrong for Mrs. Carlyle's health; and after those physical efforts to be for two days 'on duty' as hostess was a strain, no doubt, though no complaint would be made.

Jeffrey was not blind to the state of things at Craigenputtock, and felt a genuine alarm on account of Mrs. Carlyle, whose health and well-being were always so dear to him. But Carlyle could not see through his friend's eyes, and was absorbed in quite other lines of thought. Writing from Edinburgh after his visit, Jeffrey says to Carlyle:—

Take care of the fair creature who has trusted herself so entirely to you. Do not let her ride about in the wet, nor expose herself to the wintry winds that will, by-and-by, visit your lofty retreat; and think seriously of taking shelter in Moray Place [Jeffrey's house in Edinburgh] for a month or two; and in the meantime be gay and playful and foolish with her, at least as often as you require her to be wise and heroic with you. You have no *mission* upon earth, whatever you may fancy, half so important as to be innocently happy. . . .

Jeffrey was wise and kind, and well understood how things were at Craigenputtock; but such advice was useless.

The first winter at the 'Devil's Den,' as Carlyle had called his home, must have been a new experience to Mrs. Carlyle. A carrier's cart made its way weekly from Dumfries, when weather permitted; thus, the solace of letters was only an occasional one. Happily, Carlyle was well employed on paying work for the Reviews. Flour and oatmeal were supplied from Scotsbrig; the farm yielded milk, eggs, hams, and poultry; groceries and tobacco were almost the only requisites to be bought. Sometimes the husband and wife rode out together on the two ponies, 'Larry' and 'Harry;' but Carlyle's rides were too often solitary, indifferent as he was to wet and cold, courting fatigue in every weather.

In November, Mrs. Carlyle writes to Miss Stodart, and speaks of 'sitting here, companionless, "like owl in desert,"' and says she is feeding poultry, galloping on a bay horse, baking bread, improving her mind, eating, sleeping, making, and mending. She writes cheerfully, and had not yet really lost her quick energy and freshness. She speaks of the Jeffrey visit, and assures her friend that never did she (Mrs. Carlyle) assist at such a talking since she came into the world. No doubt Carlyle did his share on this occasion.

Mrs. Carlyle, probably, hoped to be in Edinburgh during some part of the winter. It would have been easy, had Jeffrey's invitation been accepted. But the visit did not take place. Now and then she would gallop off alone to Templand—fifteen miles—to see her mother, who was seldom able to leave the house now, in consequence, probably, of her father's ill-health.

In December, Mrs. Carlyle again writes to Miss Stodart on the subject of 'groceries,' adding pens and paper to the list of purchases to be made, to say nothing of sealing-wax, and a certain brown earthenware coffee-pot; the latter needful because the servant, Grace Macdonald, had, in excitement at receiving a letter from her lover, dashed the existing coffee-pot to pieces by her sudden movement. Truly Mrs. Carlyle did her utmost to turn the desert to an earthly paradise. But was there not much loneliness in the life—loneliness by no means to be cured by tending pigs and poultry?

By Carlyle's own account, he wrote hard all day, in his little library, with a clear fire and green curtains to cheer him. Spanish they read between dinner and tea—a chapter of 'Don Quixote.' After tea, he sometimes wrote again, and then not unfrequently went over to his brother Alick's cottage to smoke his last pipe; whether accompanied by Mrs. Carlyle or not is left unstated. He sometimes strolled in the plantations with his axe, and when not writing was generally reading. But his wife was contented so that she felt she had spared him an anxiety or an attack of indigestion.

At the end of that year she spent a few days with her own people at Templand, but her heart was with her husband at Craigenputtock. A beautiful letter is given by Mr. Froude, from which I must quote a few sentences, it is so womanly, and so tender in expression.

      Templand: December 30, 1828.

 Goody, Goody, dear Goody,—You said you would weary, and I do hope in my heart you are wearying. It will be so sweet to make it all up to you in kisses when I return. You will *take me*, and hear all my bits of experiences, and your heart will beat when you find how I have longed to return to you. Darling, dearest, loveliest—'The Lord bless you!' I think of you every hour, every moment.

 As to the blessing here given, Carlyle, annotating the letter in the sad days of his bereavement, says: 'Poor Edward Irving's practice and locution; suspect of being somewhat too solemn.' Ending her letter, she says :—

 Dearest, I wonder if you are getting any victual. . . I have many an anxious thought about you, and I wonder if you sleep at nights, or if you are wandering about—on—on—smoking and killing mice. Oh! if I was there, I could put my arms so close about your neck, and hush you into the softest sleep you have had since I went away. Good-night! Dream of me!

      I am, ever,
       Your own GOODY.

And so, tenderly, harmoniously, ended the year 1828.

 Little is recorded of the year that followed. The spirit of beauty which attended on the dainty lady of Craigenputtock showed ever-new manifestations. A rose-garden was laid out, and many graceful home arrangements perfected. Carlyle added a gig to the establishment, and many long drives were taken in it. A visit from Margaret, Carlyle's sister, was a welcome change for Mrs. Carlyle. It was in the summer of 1829. Margaret was a most interesting and lovable woman. Carlyle was much attached to her, and deeply mourned her death, which took place in June 1830 of consumption.

It was in November of 1829 that the Carlyles visited Edinburgh for a short time, on a visit, we conclude, to Mr. John Bradfute, at 22 George Square. It would seem that the return to the solitude of Craigenputtock was felt to be very trying by Mrs. Carlyle. She tells Miss Stodart how she had wept at leaving Edinburgh, yet assures her that, after her first affright at returning to the 'desert,' she was again contented. What best reconciles her to the return to the wilds, is that Carlyle always likes her best 'at home'—a pretty reason, and a good one. She assures her old friend that she never loved her more dearly than now, and adds: 'And Carlyle loves you, too, more than you are aware!'

So the life at Craigenputtock went on in the old groove. But the second winter there proved calamitous. It was near New Year's time, a season much celebrated in Scotland.

A fat goose had been killed for the New Year's feast, when the snow fell, and the frost came, and Mrs. Carlyle caught a violent sore throat, which threatened to end in diphtheria. There was no doctor nearer than Dumfries, and the road from the valley was hardly passable. Mrs. Welsh struggled up from Templand through the snowdrifts. Care and nursing kept the enemy off, and the immediate danger in a few days was over, but the shock had left behind it a sense of insecurity, and the unsuitableness of such a home for so frail a frame became more than ever apparent.

These words of Mr. Froude's give the whole state of the case very clearly. Jeffrey had seen it when he visited the Carlyles, but his counsels had been rejected. Carlyle, of course, *could not* see it. Perhaps it was hardly to be expected that he should do so. The rigid simplicity and laborious economy of his father's household inclined him rather to consider Mrs. Carlyle's position at Craigenputtock as one of ease, if not of affluence. So there was no help for it. The wife's stern sense of duty caused her to hide her real sufferings from her husband, and her love for him was not of that wholly absorbing and overpowering nature which could make such silent martyrdom a glory, or could withhold her from telling her sad tale to others as time went on, and receiving such heart-sympathy as seems the due of such overweighted and suffering humanity—the more so when the sufferer is a woman. We should doubt if Mrs. Carlyle was ever quite the same after this severe illness. Her spirits began to weary in the solitude, and the gleams of light from without were few.

One memorable episode occurring in the winter of 1829-30 was the correspondence with Goethe, to whom Mrs. Carlyle sent 'an incomparable black ringlet'—'*eine unvergleichliche schwarze Haar-locke*,' to quote Goethe's own words. He regretted that he could not send her a lock of his own in return.

CHAPTER XIII

A. D. 1830-31

Alexander Carlyle leaves Craigenputtock—Second visit of the Jeffreys to the Carlyles in their solitude—Mrs. Carlyle confesses her unhappiness to Jeffrey—The eventless life again sets in—The Jeffreys go to London—Carlyle's generosity to his brothers—He accepts help from Jeffrey, and goes to London to push his literary enterprises—A hard and sad time for Mrs. Carlyle—Ill-health and anxiety—Her verdict on 'Sartor'—Letters from Carlyle to his wife—Irving in the region of the supernatural—Caution of publishers—Good appointment for Dr. John Carlyle—Thoughts of living in London—Tender letters from Carlyle—Solitude doing its work on the delicate constitution of Mrs. Carlyle—Kindness of Carlyle's mother—Mrs. Carlyle's determination to join her husband in London—Encouragement.

THE year 1830 opened somewhat ominously. Alick's farming of Craigenputtock had turned out ill—another tenant must be found; and so the little family party was robbed of a bright and wholesome element. Carlyle felt his brother's absence much, and was more gloomy than before. In vain the kind Jeffrey urged the Carlyles, with every cordial expression, to come and visit him at Craigcrook. He besought Carlyle to bring 'his blooming Eve out of his "blasted paradise," and seek shelter in the lower world.' To Mrs. Carlyle he promised 'roses, and a blue sea, and broad shadows stretching over the fields.'

As it might not be, the Jeffreys again came to Craigenputtock to see their friends. Carlyle was again at Scotsbrig at the critical moment.

Returning (he said, September 18, 1830) late in the evening from a long ride, I found an express from Dumfries that the Jeffreys would be all at Craigenputtock that night. Of the riding and running, the scouring and scraping, and Caleb-Balderstone-arranging my unfortunate but shifty and invincible Goody must have had, I say nothing. I set out next morning, and, on arriving here, actually found the Dean of the Faculty, with his adherents, sitting comfortably, in a house swept and garnished, awaiting my arrival.

Again Jeffrey felt the pain of Mrs. Carlyle's position—it shocked and distressed him. He saw, only too well, what might come of it all, and had the double pain of feeling his own helplessness in the matter. Mrs. Carlyle had, naturally, confessed to him her unhappiness at Craigenputtock. No such admission was needed to one who was able to feel for the delicate woman, cut off from so much that made life pleasant, and facing another frightful winter. The Jeffreys reluctantly departed, and again the eventless life set in for Mrs. Carlyle. It was in October that Carlyle wrote to his mother: 'The wife and I are very quiet here, and accustoming ourselves as fast as we can to the stillness of winter, which is just coming on. These are the greyest and most silent days I ever saw. My broom, as I sweep up the withered leaves, might be heard at a furlong's distance.'

So, drearily, silently the third winter at the Desert set in, and the year 1831 began. It was marked by an important change for the Jeffreys. The Dean of Faculty went into Parliament, and was taken into the new Government, as Lord Advocate. His duties now took him to London, and his letters to Mrs. Carlyle were full of details of his new life—a contrast indeed to that of his friends at Craigenputtock.

Carlyle had made up his mind, if by utmost economy the sum of 50*l*. could be raised, to go to London and find a publisher for 'Sartor,' or, failing that, possibly to give lectures. His generosity to his brothers had left his own finances very low. It was a hard and a sad time for the Carlyles—hardest of all for her.

And now begins the record of severe headache, which

recurs so often in the sad letters she was yet to write. In a letter dated Spring 1831 to Jean Carlyle, Mrs Carlyle says: 'I was meaning to write you a long letter by Alick, but I have been in bed all day with a headache, and am risen so confused and dull that, for your sake, as well as my own, I shall keep my speculations—news I have none—till another opportunity. . . .'

The financial difficulty pressed heavily. The warm, dry, summer days brought no cheering. Even Carlyle's heart failed him.

The kind Jeffrey, presenting to him a list of all possible situations, asked him which he would detest the least, that he might know before applying for it. But the end of it all was his unwilling acceptance of a loan of 50*l.* from Jeffrey to try the fate of 'Sartor' in London. Mrs. Carlyle's verdict, 'It is a work of genius, dear,' might cheer him on his lonely way. He wrote in 1866, speaking of that journey:—

Night before going—how I still remember it! I was lying on my back, on the sofa in the drawing-room. She sitting by the table late at night—packing all done, I suppose. Her words had a guise of sport, but were profoundly plaintive in meaning. 'About to part; and who knows for how long, and what may have come in the interim.' This was her thought, and she was evidently much out of spirits. 'Courage, dear! Only for a month!'

Here are a few sentences from the letter he wrote her on August 11, 1831, a week after his departure:—

6 Woburn Buildings, Tavistock Square.

Dearest, and Wife,—I have got a frank for you, and will write from the heart whatever is in the heart. A blessing it was that you made me give such a promise, for I feel that an hour's speech, in speaking with my own, will do me infinite good. It is very sweet, in the midst of this soul-confusing phantasmagoria, to know that I have a fixed possession elsewhere; that my own Jeannie is thinking of me, loving me; that her heart is no dream, like all the rest of it. Oh! love me, my dearest—always love me. I am richer with thee than the whole world could make me otherwise.

Delightful it was . . . on opening my trunk, to find everywhere traces of my good 'coagitor's' care and love! The very jujube-box, with its worsted and darning needle, did not escape me; it was so beautiful I could almost have cried over it.

And again, on August 15, he writes:—

Your kind, precious letter came to me on Friday like a cup of water in the hot desert. It is all like yourself, so clear, so precise, loving, and true to the death. I *see* poor Craigenputtock through it, and the best little Goodykin sitting there, hourly meditating on me, and watching my return. Oh, I am very rich, were I without a penny in the world! But the Herzen's Goody must not fret herself, and torment her poor sick head. I will be back to her; not an hour will I lose. Heaven knows the sun shines not on the spot that could be pleasant to me where she were not. So be of comfort, my Jeannie! . . .

Again, August 22, he addresses her as 'My dearest little comforter,' with many other tender expressions:—

Compose thyself, my darling (he writes)—we *shall* not be separated, come of it what may. And how should we do, thinkst thou, with an eternal separation? O God! it is fearful, fearful! But is not a little temporary separation like this needful to manifest what *daily* mercy is in our lot, which otherwise we might forget, or esteem as a thing of course? Understand, however, once more, that I have yet taken up with no other woman . . . there has no one yet fronted me whom, even to look at, I would exchange with my own. 'Ach, Gott!' Yes, proud as I am grown (for, the more the Devil pecks at me, the more vehemently do I wring his nose), and standing on a kind of basis which I feel to be of adamant, I perceive that, of all women, my own Jeannie is the wife for me; that in her true bosom (once she were a mystic) a man's head is worthy to lie. Be a mystic, dearest; that is, stand with me on this everlasting basis, and keep thy arms around me; through life I fear nothing.

It was well that Carlyle dwelt thus fondly on the remembrance of his absent wife, for his London visit gave him little pleasure. His old friend Irving was in the 'region of the supernatural'—very uncongenial quarters for Carlyle; Badams (another old friend), hovering on the verge of ruin from intemperance; another Craigenputtock neighbour having come out as a 'wonder-worker, and speaker with tongues.' And, on the whole, Carlyle felt that the Devil was busier than ever, and turned for healing thoughts to his wise and beautiful little Jeannie, in the lonely house on the Dunscore moors. There lay sympathy for him, and a loving heart, as he well knew; and he needed such.

Publishers were cautious, and the MS. of 'Teufelsdröckh' hung fire unaccountably. But an unexpectedly good appointment for Dr. John Carlyle made things easier, as Carlyle was now repaid the money he had so generously advanced to that well-loved brother; and thus Mrs. Carlyle was able, without help from Mrs. Montagu, which had been offered and declined, to join her husband in London, and leave her snowy solitude, as it would be in a few months' time. She hailed the prospect with joy.

Carlyle again wrote tender words on August 29: 'In this spectre-crowded desert I have a living person whose heart I can clasp to mine, and so feel that I, too, am alive. Do you not love me better than ever now? I feel in my own soul that thou dost and must. Therefore, let us never mourn over this little separation, which is but to make the reunion blessed and entire.'

It would seem that Mrs. Carlyle, in these lonely days, could not await the weekly carrier as postman, but took to riding to Dumfries herself, in her impatience, and calling for letters—thirty-two miles hard riding in the month of August; and Carlyle says: 'Bless thee, my darling! I could almost wish thee the pain of a ride to Dumfries weekly for the sake of such a letter. But *had* you actually to faint all the way up? Heaven forbid!'

It is plain that the return from these frantic rides after letters were made in exhaustion, probably more than once. But we can understand the feverish eagerness after letters from her husband, for Alick Carlyle and his sister were no longer at the farm. Strangers occupied it, and the solitude was crushing—'often, for hours, the only sound, the sheep nibbling the short grass a quarter of a mile away.' The conditions, not realised by Carlyle, were truly almost intolerable to his wife, and absolutely harmful to an extent which can never be estimated.

The kind old mother at Scotsbrig had sent Jean and Alick to the rescue, and Mrs. Carlyle thanked her for this loving care, 'without which' she says,—

I think I must soon have worked myself into a fever or other violent disorder; for my talent for fancying things . . . had so entirely got the upper hand of me, that I could neither sleep by night nor rest by day. I have slept more since they came. . . . I have news: I am going to my husband, and as soon as I can get ready for leaving. Now, do not grieve that he is not to return so soon as we expected. I am sure it is for his good, and therefore for all our goods. . . . Jean is going with me to Templand to-day, as a sort of protection against my mother's agitations.

Mrs. Carlyle evidently dreaded the excitability of Mrs. Welsh, and possible outbursts, and she was ill able to cope with such elements.

Carlyle was becoming restless and dissatisfied in London. He wrote on September 11: 'One should actually, as Irving advises, "pray to the Lord:" if one did but know how to do it!' He winds up a bitter reflection of his incompatibilities with Jeffrey in the words: 'Why should a man, though bilious, never so nervous, impoverished, bug-bitten and bedevilled, let Satan have dominion over him? Save me! save me, my Goody. . . .'

It was no ordinary mission that the delicate lady of Craigenputtock undertook in this visit to London, no mere pleasure-trip, so to speak. It was not easy to face it all, and carry it out with high courage and spirits. She had shown signs of flagging in her letters, and no wonder.

Carlyle wrote on September 23:—

You are agitated, and provoked, which is almost the worst way of the two. Alas! and I have no soft Aladdin's palace here, to bid you hasten and take repose in—nothing but a noisy, untoward lodging-house, and no better shelter than my own bosom. Yet, is not this the best of all shelters for you?—the only safe place in this wide, wide world. Thank God, this still is yours, and I can receive you there without distrust, and wrap you close with the solacements of a true heart's love! Hasten thither, then, my own wife. . . .

CHAPTER XIV

A. D. 1831

Mrs. Carlyle's arrival in London—Ampton Street—The Irvings—Ill-health of Mrs. Carlyle—Position with Mrs. Montagu—Meetings with congenial spirits—Carlyle still restless—Death of his father—Impending return to Craigenputtock—Misgivings—A sad return—Solitary habits—Realisation of the actual by Mrs. Carlyle—Jeffrey's anxiety about Mrs. Carlyle.

It was on October 1, 1831, that Mrs. Carlyle arrived in London, tired with her journey, and charged with the care, not only of her personal belongings, but with substantial reinforcements from the generous folk at Scotsbrig—oatmeal, hams, butter, &c.—towards the living-expenses of the coming winter. Comfortable rooms were found in Ampton Street, out of Gray's Inn Road, in the house of an excellent family named Miles, members of Irving's congregation. Eliza Miles was a devoted admirer of Mrs. Carlyle from the first. Friends began to flock around the gifted pair, and London society was open to them in several directions. Mrs. Carlyle was a great attraction; her light, no longer hid under a bushel, made itself apparent on all sides.

The latest developments in the Irvingite congregation distressed the Carlyles sadly. Urged to go into the house while a 'meeting' was going on, the sounds they heard shocked and disgusted them both, reducing Mrs. Carlyle to the verge of fainting. Carlyle could not drag Irving back from what seemed an awful precipice, and, after one effort, tragical in its circumstances and failure, the matter was left alone. There could be no real intercourse or sympathy any more between the friends.

Writing to her aunt, in Maryland Street, Liverpool, in December of this year, Mrs. Carlyle says, speaking of London:—

Nowhere have I found more worth, more talent, or more kindness; and I doubly regret the ill-health I have been suffering under, since it has so curtailed my enjoyment of all this. Nevertheless, though I dare seldom accept an invitation out, I have the pleasantest evenings at home. . . . I have seen most of the literary people here, and, as Edward Irving said after his first interview with Wordsworth, 'I think not of them so highly as I was wont.'

In a letter of the same date, to 'ean Carlyle, she writes:—

I do not forget you in London, as you predicted. . . Often, when I have been lying ill here among strangers, it has been my pleasantest thought that there were kind hearts at home to whom my sickness would not be a weariness; to whom I could return, out of all this hubbub, with affection and trust. Not that I am not kindly used here—from the 'noble lady,' down to the mistress of the lodging, I have everywhere found unlooked-for civility, and at least the show of kindness. With the 'noble lady,' however, I may mention my intercourse seems to be dying an easy, natural death. Now that we *know* each other, the 'fine en-thu-si-asm' cannot be kept alive without more hypocrisy than one of us, at least, can bring to bear on it.

These hard words came not from the heart of Jane Welsh Carlyle; they welled up from a bitter fountain, due to the influence of physical suffering, perhaps, which tinctured many utterances of one who was naturally loyal, generous, and kind. Such harsh judgments must be looked on with gentleness, and largely discounted, as we consider the intense nervous suffering of the speaker, her eagle eye, and quick wit, which rendered such cutting speeches so easy to make; and, above all, when we remember the deep kindliness of heart that lay beneath the sarcastic expression.

It was to Mrs. Montagu that Carlyle wrote: 'Indeed, indeed, my dear Madam, I am not mad enough to forget you.

The more I see of the world and myself, the less tendency have I that way; the more do I feel that in this, my wilderness-journey, I have found but *one* Mrs. Montagu!' This was written on Christmas Day, 1826, and as late as 1830 Carlyle was writing in most cordial terms to this dear, valued friend, assuring her that he was 'in nowise of the forgetting species,' but with a heart whereon 'the love-charm and think-of-me, once written, stood ineffaceable, defying all time and weather!' And these words were written *after* the episode of Mrs. Montagu's unwise but kindly-meant interference in the Edward Irving affair.

Evidently Mrs. Montagu, in her kindness of heart, finding Carlyle lonely in London during the visit he was making, had, not unnaturally, offered pecuniary help to make it easy for Mrs. Carlyle to join him. It was not easy to offer such help to the Carlyles—impossible to do it without giving pain —but surely not unnatural to offer it under the circumstances. We are left to imagine how the offer was received, but Carlyle thus alludes to it in his letter to his wife dated August 22, 1831: 'On the whole, my original impression of that "noble lady" was the true one. . . . She goes upon words—words. . . . For trust or friendship it is now more clearly than ever a chimera. I smiled . . . at her offer of "giving you money" to come hither. *Jane Welsh Carlyle* a taker of money in this era of the "gigmen"—*nimmer und nimmermehr!*'

Friendship could not easily stand such a strain as this was on either side. But Carlyle owed much to Mrs. Montagu; and her title of 'noble lady' remains to her intact through all time. Extreme sensitiveness causes many sad perversions in human judgment.

There are pleasant records of visits from Jeffrey—often in an afternoon—quick, lively, and light; of dinner with Fraser; meetings with Allan Cunningham, Hogg (the Ettrick Shepherd), Galt, Lockhart, and others; and by-and-by the Bullers came to town, and Charles Buller, Carlyle's former pupil, a most brilliant and lovable young man, renewed intercourse with his gifted friend. It should have been a congenial time for Carlyle. But he continued 'hag-ridden' here, as on the lonely moors. He spoke of London as 'a wild, wondrous, chaotic den of discord,' but doubts not there is 'a deep, Divine meaning in it, and God in the midst of it'—this to his father, in one of the last letters he ever wrote to the old man, dated December 13, 1831. The father's death took place in January 1832, and though unable to be present at the funeral, Carlyle wrote tenderly to his good mother—beautifully and piously, in a way that gave certain comfort to her.

And now there remained but a few weeks of the London visit, and the prospect of a return to Craigenputtock loomed up on the horizon. Hope of fixed employment or literary appointment there seemed none; but editors of magazines were anxious to employ Carlyle, and, with the anxiety of his brother John quite relieved, he felt that he could look to a modest competence, and with indifference, not unmixed with scorn, he prepared for a return to the 'wilderness.' Carlyle felt it a blessing to have the place to go to; but Mrs. Carlyle must have dreaded the renewal of many of the conditions inseparable from it. Travelling from Liverpool by the Annan steamer was a real martyrdom to the delicate woman. Her health was low, and the dreary shadow fell on her spirit. It was on March 25, 1832, that the homeward journey was begun, and in a few days the vision of the brilliant bit of life in London had come to look quite unreal—all was as before.

Carlyle's account of this memorable London visit, as given in the 'Reminiscences,' may be quoted here. He tells how he wished to 'give our brave little Jeannie a sight of this big Babel,' adding:—

She came right willingly, and had—in spite of her ill-health, which did not abate, but the contrary—an interesting, cheery, and, in spite of our poor arrangements, really pleasant winter here. . . . Visitors, &c., she had in plenty: John Mill one of the most interesting, so modest, ardent, ingenuous, ingenious, and so very fond of me, at that time. Mrs. Basil Montagu (already a correspondent of hers), now accurately seen, was another of the distinguished. Jeffrey, Lord Advocate, often came on an afternoon. . . . In the evening, miscellany, of hers and mine. . . . News of my father's death came here. Oh, how good and tender she was, and consolatory by every kind of art in those black days! I remember our walk along Holborn forward into the city, and the bleeding mood I was in, she wrapping me like the softest of bandages. . . . Nothing was wanting in her sympathy, or in the manner of it, as even from sincere people there often is. How poor we were, and yet how rich!

It was not a cheering beginning of the home-coming that Mrs. Carlyle should suffer from sea-sickness, so frightfully as she did, in the steamer which conveyed them from Liverpool to Annan. There had been a few days of pleasant rest by the way at Maryland Street, with uncle John and the kindly cousins, but the voyage was a martyrdom to Mrs. Carlyle. In the 'Reminiscences,' Carlyle says, 'Sick, sick, my poor woman must have been—but she retired out of sight, and would suffer with her best grace in silence;' and again:—

At Whinniery I remember brother Alick and others of them were waiting to receive us; there were tears among us (my father gone when we returned); she wept bitterly, I recollect, her sympathetic heart girdled in much sickness and dispiritment of her own withal. . . . We returned in some days to Craigenputtock, and were again at peace there. . . . Our summers and winters for the future (1832–1834) were lonelier than ever.

The loneliness must have been overwhelming, and more terrible from contrast with the bit of social life in London. Carlyle's intense pre-occupation, of the stormy and often gloomy type, rendered him unable to endure the presence of a second person while he wrote, or wrestled with his spiritual demon. He sat alone, therefore, he also walked alone; nor could any delicate woman have tramped beside him, or after him, with benefit to her health. He often rode alone, in the same environment of stormy thought. What he did need, now and then, was a listener; but as his style was the monologue, it hardly offered the attractions of what is called conversation, and was rather a violent and drastic outpouring from his own overcharged spirit, leading to no blessed response of sympathy and wifely understanding—for it was susceptible of none! It was not as when the tired man of business or of letters tells, in his own brief way, the causes of an anxious day, and is soothed by sympathy and understanding—in his wife's few words and clasp of the hand, or silent caress.

Carlyle, fevered, hag-ridden, fiercely self-involved, was able only for such solitary relief as we have described, and his wife quietly settled into what she now felt to be her place beside him. Her courage enabled her to hide her own sufferings from him, but her heart must have been heavy. Possibly she felt some comfort in the correspondence with Jeffrey, to whom she wrote more freely than to any one else, for he understood, and was man enough to sympathise without pitying.

Mr. Froude's estimate of a certain peculiarity in Carlyle's character is so trenchant, so intensely true, that we quote it as containing volumes. 'If matters went well with himself, it never occurred to him that they could be going ill with any one else; and, on the other hand, if he was uncomfortable, he required everybody to be uncomfortable along with him.' This is perfect as a sketch of character. And as Carlyle was so much oftener *un*comfortable than comfortable, some idea can be formed of Mrs. Carlyle's position on the Dunscore moor; some idea can also be formed of the agony of regret and pain with which, after her death, her husband, who really loved her in his own way, read the letters and records of the profound anguish and deep discouragement which he had never known or ministered to.

Meantime, he writes in May 1832 to his mother: 'Jane is far heartier now that she has got to work—to bake.' He himself was vigorous—working with a 'dock-spade' and riding on horseback; but the two sides of the picture did not correspond.

Carlyle was now cutting out an original intellectual path for himself; and, but for his indigestion, which weighed perhaps more heavily on others than on himself, was well and tolerably satisfied, though never a cheerful companion. His wife, on the other hand, was realising the intense trial of solitude and shattered nerves. Resolved as she was to be a help and not a hindrance to her husband, she *manfully*, we use the word advisedly, in its best sense, set herself to endure in silence if not in patience, and to make Carlyle's path as smooth as she could, in the only way open to her.

The daughter of the London landlady, Miss Eliza Miles, had formed quite a romantic attachment to her mother's charming lodger, and wished to go to Craigenputtock as servant to the dainty, delicate lady. But Mrs. Carlyle knew that would be a mistake and a sacrifice. Mrs. Carlyle wrote kindly to her admiring friend in June 1832:—

. . . I never forgot my gentle Ariel in Ampton Street; it were positive sin to forget her—so helpful she, so trustful, so kind, so good! Besides, this is the place of all others for thinking of absent friends, where one has so seldom any present to think of. It is the stillest, solitariest place that it ever entered your imagination to conceive, where one has the strangest, shadowy existence. Nothing is actual in it but the food we eat, the bed one sleeps on, and, praised be Heaven, the fine air one breathes. The rest is all a dream of the absent and distant, of things past and to come. . . .

For my part I am very content. I have everything here my heart desires that I could have anywhere else, except society, and even that deprivation is not to be considered wholly an evil. If people we like and take pleasure in do not come about us here as in London, it is thankfully to be remembered that here 'the wicked cease from troubling and the weary are at rest.' If the knocker make no sound for weeks together, it is so much the better for my nerves. My husband is as good company as reasonable mortal could desire. Every fair morning we ride on horseback for an hour before breakfast .... and then we eat such a surprising breakfast of home-baked bread and eggs, &c., as might incite anyone that had breakfasted so long in London to write a pastoral. Then Carlyle takes to his writing, while I, like Eve, 'studious of household good,' inspect my house, my garden, my live stock, gather flowers for my drawing-room, and lapfuls of eggs, and finally betake myself to writing, or reading, or mending, or making, or whatever work seems fittest. After dinner, and only then, I lie on the sofa (to my shame be it spoken) sometimes sleep, but oftenest dream waking. In the evening I walk on the moor. . . .

Brave Jane Welsh Carlyle! she drew a 'fair picture,' of which the reverse side looked very differently.

Some touching lines, written by her at this period, dated from 'The Desert,' and sent with rose-leaves along with them in a letter to Jeffrey, tell a different tale, and, we fear a truer one! The verses are 'To a swallow building under our eaves.' The last stanza is as follows:—

> God speed thee, pretty bird; may thy small nest
> With little ones all in good time be blest.
>   I love thee much;
> For well thou managest that life of thine,
> While I! Oh, ask not what I do with mine!
>   Would I were such!

It was not to be wondered at if Jeffrey's kind heart ached now and then, as he thought of his delicate and beloved cousin's helplessness, and his own helplessness, to alter the conditions of her life!

CHAPTER XV

A. D. 1832-1834

Carlyle's letter to his mother—Mrs. Carlyle's overstrained nerves and failing strength—Her letter to Eliza Stodart—Mrs. Welsh's delicate health—Death of Walter Welsh of Templand—The Carlyles plan a long visit to Edinburgh—The home at 18 Carlton Street, Stockbridge—The 'disgraceful home march'—An angel's visit at Craigenputtock—Meeting of Emerson and the Carlyles—The relapse into solitude—Living in London seriously contemplated—Preparations.

CARLYLE wrote to his brother John in July 1832:—

As to Craigenputtock, it is, as formerly, the scene of scribble—scribbling. Jane is in a weakly state still, but I think clearly gathering strength. Her life beside me, constantly writing here, is but a dull one; however, she seems to desire no other; has in many things, pronounced the word *entsagen*, and looks with a brave, if with no joyful, heart into the present and the future.

August in this year was marked by household trouble. the valued maid-servant had misconducted herself, and was sent away at an hour's notice. Her place could not immediately be filled, and all the work fell on Mrs. Carlyle. 'Oh, mother, mother!' exclaimed Carlyle, in telling her the story, 'what trouble the devil does give us! . . ' In this case, no doubt the heaviest share of the trouble fell on the delicate frame of Mrs. Carlyle. For accounts more or less 'mythical' as to her active occupations during the residence at Craigenputtock, the reader is referred to Miss Jewsbury's 'In Memoriam' notice of Mrs. Carlyle in the 'Reminiscences' and Carlyle's own commentary thereon. That Mrs. Carlyle overtaxed her physical strength and powers of endurance is beyond all doubt, and the actual cause of the over-exertion cannot be exactly set down in black and white. There was habitual over-strain, and a deficiency in the elements that her sensitive, and always tender, health needed for well-being. It is idle to dispute as to the detail of such deficiency.

The autumn wore on, a servant was found, and things went on much as before. In a letter written to Miss Stodart early in October 1832, Mrs. Carlyle says:—

In prolonged bad health, and worse spirits, I judged there could be small call upon me to be sending letters out, as it were, into infinite space, no sounds of them ever more heard. Still vainer seemed it to apply for sympathy to one who was apparently nowise concerning herself whether I remained behind in a nice flower-potted London churchyard, or returned in a state of total wreck to my own country. . . . Does your uncle ever make the *smallest* mention of me? ever inquire if the mischievous creature who broke his ' folder ' is still working deviltry on this planet? Alas, no? She is sober enough now; a long succession of bad days and sleepless nights have effectually tamed her. O, Bess! for one good laugh with you, for the sake of old times !

Mrs. Welsh's health was giving her daughter uneasiness at this time, and, after a brief visit to Templand, Mrs. Carlyle went back to assure herself all was well at Craigenputtock, and again prepared to go to Templand, deploring at the same time the weak and nervous state of body which caused her to suffer for days after her so short a journey.

It was towards the end of November 1832 that Walter Welsh died, and again there was need of settling on a home for Mrs. Welsh, whose own strength had visibly failed her. There was a plan for the Carlyles to spend the coming winter in Edinburgh, and inquiries had already been made as to a positive house, which must be subject to three limitations: ' First, it must be free of bugs; secondly, of *extraordinary* noises; and lastly, of a high rent.' Such had been Mrs. Carlyle's instructions to her old friend a few weeks before the death of Walter Welsh.

The question now arose whether Mrs. Welsh would

come and live with her daughter, could a suitable home be found; but it seemed unlikely, and Mrs. Welsh probably felt that the atmosphere would be overcharged with elements not soothing to her in her overwrought and nervous state. Mrs. Carlyle, too, was keenly conscious of the difficulties all round, and dreaded their own little flitting, grieved over her mother's loneliness, and was acutely sensible of her *own*, and ends her letter of December 5, to Miss Stodart, with significant words : 'In the meantime God help her and all of us !

Mrs. Carlyle had the comfort of having helped her mother in the nursing of good old Walter, who, as Carlyle said in a letter to his brother John, 'had the gentlest death, and had numbered four score years !' But for his daughter, the cessation by death of her long and tender cares, was a dreary blank, admitting scant consolation.

It was determined once more to try a residence in Edinburgh, and a small furnished house was found in Stockbridge, a part of the city lying in the valley of the Water of Leith, 18 Carlton street. Miss Stodart was to find some honest woman to put on a fire and have a kettle boiling to receive the travellers, and Mrs. Carlyle was to bring a small maidservant with her. Mrs. Welsh, weak and depressed, would not accompany the Carlyles, but was to join them later, but it is not clear that she ever did so.

This second residence in Edinburgh was not a success. Carlyle was, according to his own account, 'languid, bilious, not very open to kindness.' A wretched state for him, and no less so for his wife; solitude had wearied him and palled on him. Society was barren enough to him. He was ill at ease. Neither he nor his wife could sleep for street noises after the deadly silence of Craigenputtock. Both of them suffered from catarrh. Jane in particular. 'We have society enough,' says Carlyle. 'The best the ground yields. The time for returning to Puttock will *too soon* be here. I have not abated in my dislike for that residence, in the conviction that it is no longer good for me.' It was certainly no longer good for his wife—it had never been good for *her;* but Carlyle did not think of that just then! Attached to the letter from which we are quoting, a letter to John Carlyle, is a postscript in Mrs. Carlyle's hand. Excusing herself for delay in replying to her brother-in-law's letter, she says: 'In truth I am always so sick now and so heartless that I cannot apply myself to any mental effort without a push from Necessity. . . .'

Carlyle became more and more embittered with Edinburgh: 'One of the dullest, and poorest, and, on the whole, paltriest places for me.' Those last two words, 'for me,' strike the key-note of so much of Mrs. Carlyle's unhappiness. What was it for *her*, and to what could the nervous, shrinking, delicate woman look if Edinburgh failed?

At the end of March Carlyle writes to his brother John: 'She (Jane) bears up with fixed resolution, appears even to enjoy many things in Edinburgh, yet has grown no stronger of late.'

It is during this month of March 1833 that Mrs. Carlyle speaks of such intense pain in her head that she became quite unconscious, and on the return journey to Craigenputtock, which Mrs. Carlyle terms 'the disgraceful home-march!' she could get no further than Templand, suffering such misery by the way as she could not describe, and there she lay for a week, ill and helpless with a species of influenza, which also attacked Mrs. Welsh. But at last the weary pilgrimage was over and Mrs. Carlyle was again in her solitude and found all well, save for the accidental burning of a plantation of trees which had been planted by Dr. Welsh, and this misfortune gave sharp pain to the loving daughter, who could have cried over it, in the pain of seeing the work of that beloved hand destroyed.

A characteristic letter, written in July 1833, to Eliza Miles, shows something of the real state of Mrs. Carlyle's mind and health at this time. We can only give a brief extract:—

... What is it, then, you will ask, that makes me fail in so simple a duty of friendship as the writing of a letter? ... My first impulse, after reading your letter, was to sit down and answer it by the very next post. Then I thought, I will wait till the Lord Advocate's return, that he may frank it! Then troubles thickened round me : my mother's illness, my grandfather's death, gave me much fatigue of body and mind. That, again, increased to cruel height my own persevering ailments. ... I wrote to no one; had enough to do in striving with the tempter ever present with me in the shape of headaches, heartache, and all kinds of aches, that I might not break out into fiery indignation over my own destiny and all the earth's. ...

So wrote the wife, while the husband was confiding to the pages of his private journal that he was 'the solitariest, stranded, most helpless creature.' Distinctly, then, it was a *solitude à deux*, as we have said before.

But Craigenputtock was about to receive an angel's visit. An entry in Carlyle's Journal gives hint of a new-comer, a new voice, a new step on the stair. In another handwriting stand the words 'Ralph Waldo Emerson.'

Emerson's health had failed him in 1832, and conscientious scruples also led to his resigning his pastorate of the Unitarian church of Boston. Advised to try a sea voyage, he embarked for Europe in 1833, and made delightful pilgrimages to classic spots on the Continent, as well as in England. In Edinburgh he made the acquaintance of Mr. Alexander Ireland, with whom he rambled about for a few days. He spoke much of Carlyle and some of his essays which had appeared in 'The Edinburgh Review' and 'Foreign Review.' He expressed an ardent desire to see Carlyle face to face. He also wished to meet Wordsworth. 'Am I,' he said to Mr. Ireland, 'who have hung over their works in my chamber at home, not to see these men in the flesh and thank them, when I am passing their very door?' He had great difficulty in finding out exactly where Carlyle lived. Mr. Ireland was able to obtain the information, and at last Emerson found his way, after many hindrances, to Craigenputtock. He had the grand American indifference as to our petty distances, in these insignificant quarters of the world, and would not be deterred by a score or so of barren miles of moorland. It may here be mentioned that Mr. Ireland's acquaintance with Emerson in Edinburgh in 1833 led to the honour and privilege of a life-long friendship with the latter. One result of the intimacy was Mr. Emerson's memorable lecturing visit to England in 1847-48 which was arranged by Mr. Ireland. It is pleasant also to recall that final visit to England in 1873, when Emerson, with his daughter Ellen, spent his last two days on British ground in Mr. Ireland's home at Bowdon.

In faithful fulfilment of his promise, Emerson wrote a long and deeply interesting letter to Mr. Ireland, on August 30, 1833, with details of his visit. He had, indeed, found his way, after many hindrances, to the centre of desolation, where lived Carlyle with his bright and accomplished wife. Twenty-four hours he spent there, and, in the walks over the barren moors, the pleasure of joyful acquaintance ripened quickly but surely into a deep friendship of such loyalty and beauty as were worthy of the two noble men who were parties to it. 'The Carlyles were sitting alone at dinner,' Mr. Froude tells us, 'on a Sunday afternoon at the end of August, when a Dumfries carriage drove to the door, and there stepped out of it a young American, then unknown to fame, but whose influence in his own country equals that of Carlyle in ours, and whose name stands connected with his wherever the English language is spoken.'

A few sentences from Emerson's letter to Mr. Ireland may be quoted. Speaking of Carlyle he says :—

I found him one of the most simple and frank of men, and became acquainted with him at once. . . . The comfort of meeting a man of genius is that he speaks sincerely; that he feels himself to be so rich, that he is above the meanness of pretending to knowledge which he has not, and Carlyle does not pretend to have solved the great problems. . . . He is, as you might guess from his papers, the most catholic of philosophers; he forgives and loves everybody, and wishes each to struggle on in his own place and arrive at his own ends. . . . He talks finely—seems to love the broad Scotch, and I loved him very much at once. I am afraid he finds his entire solitude tedious, but I could not help congratulating him on his treasure in his wife, and I hope he will not leave the moors. . . .

In Emerson's 'English Traits' (not published until 1856), he speaks much of this visit, and says, 'Carlyle was already turning his eyes towards London.'

Years later, when Carlyle was writing to Emerson in acknowledgment of some of the never-failing kindnesses of that unselfish friend, Mrs. Carlyle adds a little postscript. '*Forgotten you?*' she says.—'O no indeed! If there were nothing else to remember you by, I should never forget the visitor who, years ago in the desert, descended on us, out of the clouds as it were, and made one day there look like enchantment for us, and left me weeping that it was only *one* day. . .

The bright ray of Emerson's visit was again sunk into darkness, and the old monotony and cloud returned. Mrs. Welsh, with a mother's anxiety, took her daughter away for a few days of change and rest, during which Carlyle wrote tenderly solicitous, saying, 'Take a little amusement, dear Goody, if thou canst get it! God knows little comes to thee with me, and thou art right patient under it.' This was in September 1833. At the end of a fortnight Mrs. Carlyle returned from Moffat to Craigenputtock. That autumn witnessed the marriage of Carlyle's youngest sister, the 'Craw,' to Mr. James Aitken. His youngest brother also married, but the good old mother remained on in the homestead, loved and honoured to the end of her days.

We must quote a few lines of the letter Carlyle wrote the intending bridegroom, to contrast its suggestions with the course actually followed by Carlyle himself in the matter of Mrs. Welsh; not his own mother, certainly, but the mother of his wife. Remonstrating against what he thought James's haste to marry, he says:—

I understand what wonderful felicities young men like you expect from marriage; I know, too (for it is a truth as old as the world), that such expectations hold out but for a little while. I shall rejoice much (such is my experience of the world) if in your new situation you feel *as* happy as in the old; say nothing of happier. But, in any case, do I not know that you will never (whatever happens) venture on any such solemn engagement with a direct duty to fly in the face of?—the duty, namely, of doing to your dear mother and your dear sisters *as you would wish that they should do to you.* . . .

These undoubtedly sincere expressions point inexorably to the conclusion that Carlyle, like many of us, was absolutely blind at times to his own actions, while so clear-sighted in respect of the duties of others in similar situations. And there is something almost pathetic in this eclipse of judgment.

That winter seems to have been unusually severe—Carlyle speaks of the ' winter grimness and winter seclusion,' and says, ' nothing could exceed the violence of the December weather.'

The year 1834 opened discouragingly. Jeffrey had written of late in a ' frosty ' tone. The Lord Advocate genuinely wished to help Carlyle to a professorship, and two such had offered themselves, either of which Carlyle *believed* Jeffrey could have procured for him. But this was not so, and there was inevitable misunderstanding between the two men, who each resented what appeared coldness and almost ingratitude in the other. Mrs. Carlyle was in no mood to quarrel with her friend, and had given Jeffrey ' a soft answer.' Jeffrey, in return, had cordially asked the Carlyles to visit him at Craigcrook; but a harsh expression of candid opinion on the Advocate's part to Carlyle, chilled and checked any real friendship between the two, so unlike in mental and moral characteristics.

The final idea of leaving Craigenputtock for London was taking shape rapidly at this time, and soon was a determination. It is amusing to find Carlyle writing to his brother John of *bolting* out of 'all these sooty despicabilities .... lying draggle-tails of byre-women, and peat-moss and isolation, and exasperation and confusion.'

If this was *his* view, what must have been that of Mrs. Carlyle? She adds a P. S. to this same letter, which is of ominous significance.

Here is a new prospect (she writes) opened up to us with a vengeance! Am I frightened? Not a bit. I almost wish that I felt more anxiety about our future; for this composure is not *courage*, but *diseased indifference*. There is a sort of incrustation about the inward *me*, that renders it alike insensible to fear and to hope. . . . It seems as if the problem of living would be immensely simplified to me if I had health. It does require such an effort to keep oneself from growing quite wicked, while that weary weaver's shuttle is plying between my temples!

We feel that already the brave woman had lost much of her slender stock of health, and was but ill-equipped for future unknown storms and exigencies.

And now came the winding-up of affairs at Craigenputtock, two months of what the French call *déménagement*. While friends in London looked out for suitable houses for the Carlyles, who had an idea that in London, as in Edinburgh and Scotland generally, houses could only be let at the Whitsuntide or Martinmas term, Carlyle, unable to bear the uncertainty, rushed off to London to see about a house himself, leaving his wife to pack and arrange, and to join him in town when the new habitation should have been decided on.

Thus the exile on the Dunscore moors was practically at an end. What had it left behind? To Mrs. Carlyle remained an undermining of physical strength, a failing of many a bright hope. Contact with the almost pessimistic views of Carlyle had shaken much of the simple faith in which Mrs. Carlyle had been brought up. Yet she could not embrace the negative views in which some men, but fewer women, find satisfaction. A dull apathy began to overspread her keen spirit, and the efforts that she made were now felt to be efforts, and lacked the sweet spontaneity of earlier days. She could not accustom herself to a loneliness for which her past had ill-prepared her. She needed a brother's tenderness to tide her over the rough places, and a man's consideration and tenderness to give her courage to go forth and face the unknown and the untried world before her. As Mr. Froude says: 'Carlyle himself recognised occasionally that she was not happy.' But that was not enough! Such glimpses of so sad a truth did not avail towards removing the causes and conditions of the unhappiness. The recognition of the pain was transient, the pain itself permanent. With Mrs. Carlyle, the keen knowledge of the suffering of others was constant, and ever woke her to kindly deeds. One of the touching records of life at Craigenputtock tells of her gentle ministrations to 'old Esther,' which took place early in the Carlyles' stay on the moors. Carlyle says:—

Poor old Esther sank to bed—death-bed, as my Jane, who had a quick and sure eye in these things, well judged it would be. Sickness did not last above ten days: my poor wife, zealously assiduous, and with a minimum of fuss and noise. I remember those few poor days so full of human interest to her, and through her to me, and of a human pity, not painful, but sweet and genuine. She went walking every morning, especially every night, to arrange the poor bed, &c. . . .

It was the impulse of a kind and tender heart towards the poor old creature, who would rest the softer and the sweeter for it. The instances are numerous, and we probably shall never know half of them, in which both Mr. and Mrs. Carlyle befriended and solaced those in heavy need. But they did it quietly, unostentatiously, without drums and trumpets, and without even telling each other at times, and their liberal actions ceased only with their breath.

The special failure of the marriage prospect, as felt by Mrs. Carlyle, was *not* poverty; *not* forced retirement from the world; *not* a want of affection on Carlyle's part. It was the total loss of that close intellectual companionship of which she had so confidently dreamed, and for which she was so unusually fitted. Mere love and passion she had thought transitory and unfruitful; the thorn had pierced her hand in leaning on these. But in Carlyle she saw a man whose qualities would last and ripen to giant stature. Here, she thought, was no illusion, and she justly felt herself his mate.

Carlyle, too, thought perhaps, ' Here is a woman unlike others, one who can value me for what I am, love the things I love, be contented with what shall content *me*, and, above all, spread around me a soft domestic calm, in which my spirit may wrestle undisturbed by the pettiness and friction of daily life.' A natural thought perhaps, this, but events did not justify the hopeful forecast.

The position was impracticable. Each married partner remained lonely, but with an intensity of loneliness of which they had separately never dreamed, and the years at Craigenputtock left Mrs. Carlyle with only the fixed determination of doing all she could for her husband's comfort, of providing to her utmost power for his physical well-being, as she always nobly did. Things being as they were, could love do more? It was always something for *him* that sufficed her. Had he but shown sign of recognition, had he manifested some of the 'small sweet courtesies of life,' all had been well. But Carlyle could not show such signs. Brought up in a family where demonstration and caresses were almost unknown, he was absolutely incapable of adding the vital ingredient of personal tenderness to the life so closely linked with his own, unless, indeed, when parted from his wife, he wrote letters of truest love and regard; telling of those depths within him which found no vent in actual intercourse with the one he loved so well. When they were together, it never occurred to him to show these feelings, and thus his sensitive and highly-strung wife, who passionately longed for notice, with that in-born longing which is the very root of some women's natures, was left constantly unsatisfied.

The leaving of Craigenputtock offered, at least, an escape from the pressing personal loneliness under which she suffered. It recommended itself to Mrs. Carlyle as a measure favourable to her husband's literary prospects, and she believed in him with genuine wifely pride. It also promised some improvement in the way of congenial friends, sorely needed by them both.

The experiment was to be tried. Carlyle went first, on May 19, 1834, taking up his old quarters in Ampton Street, and Mrs. Carlyle followed by steamer from Annan and coach from Liverpool, arriving on June 10 at the house, 5 Cheyne Row, Chelsea, where the remainder of their life was to be passed. Carlyle, writing at the time to his brother, says:—

A hackney coach, loaded to the roof and beyond it with luggage and the passengers, tumbled us all down here at eleven in the morning. By *all*, I mean my dame and myself, Bessy Barnet (the servant), who had come the night before, and little Chico, the canary bird, who, *multum jactatus*, did nevertheless arrive living and well from Puttock, and even sang violently all the way by sea and land, nay! struck up his lilt in the very London streets, whenever he could see green leaves and feel the free air. . . .

So the new life began with the cheer of a bird's song, and in the quiet precincts of the densely-populated vast city the new order of things was now fairly inaugurated.

PART III

LIFE IN LONDON

CHAPTER XVI

A. D. 1834-1836

The new, yet old life—Unalterable conditions—The removal to London—Leigh Hunt—John Stuart Mill—Allan Cunningham—The circle of friends—Edward Irving's visit—George Rennie and his sister—Eliza Miles—Burning of the MS. of Vol. I. of 'French Revolution'—Wifely sympathy—'The Sterlings'—Sprinklings of foreigners—Domestic difficulties—Visit of Mrs. Welsh—Maternal counsels from Scotsbrig—Godefroi de Cavaignac.

And now the experiment of living in London was really to be tried, and the Carlyles took possession of their roomy house in Cheyne Row, with their 'romantic maid,' Bessy Barnet. The removal was soon accomplished, the few days of ' quasi-camp-life ' were soon over, all too soon perhaps, and the ' settling-down ' began, much harder to bear for Mrs. Carlyle, weary as she was, for now the old realities came in, also, with their fixed and inexorable shapes.

The frequent visits of the gentle and cheerful Leigh Hunt were among the earliest welcomes. John Stuart Mill, too, would often come and discuss Carlyle's great subject with him, namely, 'The French Revolution,' with the first stormy conceptions of which he was now grappling. Allan Cunningham, with his fine, picturesque figure and unmistakable Scottish tongue, would ' drop in' of an evening, bringing, as it were, a veritable breath from the moors into that city drawing-room. Such visits as his must have ministered somewhat to that deep, unquenchable love of Scotland and the old days, which lay so close to Mrs. Carlyle's heart. Mrs.

Austin and Mrs. Buller kept up a kindly intercourse with Mrs. Carlyle, but the passionate attachment to her old home clung to her, to the very end, saddening, yet sustaining.

Meantime the demonstrations of this tender nature grew sharp and cold, as was inevitable. Take a mountain stream, cut a channel for it, straight and even, and turn it into that, and the water will flow, it is true, but you must not expect the wild tangle of flowers, and rushes, and grasses, nor the nameless charm of nature.

Novelty, gaiety, and some hopefulness may have marked these early days in Chelsea, but nothing more. Mrs. Carlyle's impressions of the London ladies whom she knew were not altogether flattering. She acknowledges thinking, 'with a chastened vanity,' of the difference between the Scotch and the English housewives, of the superiority of Scotch thrift over the English careless way of managing, and points her moral by instances of Mrs. Leigh Hunt's unbelievable 'borrowings' to meet daily needs.

It was in November of this year that Edward Irving made his one call on these old friends, but a few weeks before his own death. He had ridden to Cheyne Row, his strength fast failing him, and Carlyle briefly describes his visit. There was his old love, her thorny path not mercifully shortened as his was to be. Perhaps he still saw in her what others now failed to see—the gay, bright girl of those old Haddington days. He looked round the room, 'Ah, yes,' he said, ' you are like an Eve: make every place you live in beautiful!' And so she did. And here this tall, gaunt figure of the noble, pure-minded Edward Irving vanishes from these pages. No mention of his name occurs in the letters of Mrs. Carlyle written about the time of the visit.

The cold weather is complained of in a letter to old Mrs. Carlyle, but two friends are spoken of as living quite near, 'a brother and sister, the most intimate friends I ever had in East Lothian,' says Mrs. Carlyle. This must have been a redeeming circumstance; for the brother was George Rennie, then a sculptor, and afterwards member of Parliament, of whom we shall have more to say in the later days. Eliza Miles, too, the daughter of the Ampton Street landlady, kept up her loving devotion to Mrs. Carlyle, and gave cheer and attachment.

Still Carlyle himself did not seem to have gained much in those early times, meeting little favour from editors who *had* tried him, and receiving a wide berth from those who did not wish to engage him. And this told on the home atmosphere, causing clouds and convulsions, not to be done away with by the rapid opening up of social opportunities.

The great dinners to which the Carlyles were now invited, gave but scanty satisfaction to either of them. In February 1835, in a postscript to Carlyle's letter to Dr. John Carlyle, his brother, Mrs. Carlyle writes: 'Dearest of created doctors. . . . I went the other day, distracted that I was, to a great, modern, fashionable, horrible dinner. . . . There was huge venison to be eaten, and new service of plate to be displayed; Mrs. —— talked about the *Aarts* (arts)—and the great Sir John R—— favoured us with " idears " on the Peel Administration. . . .'

We cannot help thinking that the gipsy blood which undoubtedly ran in Mrs. Carlyle's veins was answerable for much of her wandering spirit and impatience with social amenities and town life. There seemed in her a sort of silent rebellion against many trifling restraints and limitations, and we are not alone in this opinion of her. Dr. Alex. H. Japp, author of a very admirable brief sketch of Mrs. Carlyle in ' True and Noble Women,' touching on this particular point, thinks, that much of the fate of this remarkable woman's life lay in that strain of gipsy blood, combined, as it was, with undoubted genius and altogether unusual circumstances. She was certainly a 'Baillie' and not a 'Welsh' in her character and disposition, and those who study the strange laws of heredity, may see more deeply into the matter than we ourselves can pretend to do. Certain it is that the gods did not smile propitiously on the pair at Cheyne Row.

The catastrophe of the burning of the manuscript of the completed first volume of 'The French Revolution,' was more than an ordinary misfortune. This nervous, highly wrought man, Carlyle, saw in a moment the hard brain-work of many months irretrievably torn from him and annihilated. It is an old story how, on March 6, 1835, John Stuart Mill was ushered in, deadly pale and tottering with fear. A careless housemaid had lighted her fires with the all-precious manuscript, entrusted to Mill for a first reading. The thing was hopeless, and, as Carlyle says in the 'Reminiscences,'

It was like half-sentence of death to us both, and we had to pretend to take it lightly, so dismal and ghastly was his horror at it: and try to talk of other matters. He stayed three mortal hours or so: his departure quite a relief to us. Oh, the burst of sympathy my poor darling then gave me, flinging her arms round my neck and openly lamenting, condoling, and encouraging like a nobler second self.

And again, when the pen was taken up, such reparation made by the generous Mill as Carlyle would accept, and the book at length finished, he speaks of going forth to walk in the evening 'with her dear blessing upon me.' This great trouble certainly drew the two nearer together, though it wrung from Carlyle the bitter cry: 'Oh ! that I had faith ! Oh ! that I had !'

It was in May of 1835 that Mrs. Carlyle, writing to her mother-in-law of an interview 'with an old rejected lover,' whose attachment and *thousands* had had no effect on her, says: 'I continue quite content with my bargain.' She adds: 'I could wish him a little *less yellow* and a little more *peaceable*, but that is all.'

The memorable friendship with the Sterlings began in this summer of 1835, and in the first letter printed in the collection of Mrs. Carlyle's correspondence, as addressed to John Sterling, is a singularly frank manifestation of one of her eminently womanly characteristics, betraying one of the intangible causes of her undoubted lack of happiness; we mean that longing for notice and approbation and appreciation which underlay all her daring and spirited ways. She speaks to this new-made friend of her honest efforts to annihilate her *Iety* or *Ego*, or merge it in what the world doubtless considered her '*better half*,' and she laments that she still finds herself 'a very self-subsisting, and, alas! self-seeking *me*.' It was this craving which was more or less starved in her marriage, and which was at the root of much of the bitter railing, in which she undoubtedly indulged at times, against the seeming insensibility of a husband, who yet thought her peerless among women and ever held her to be so. In time she learned to scoff at demonstration of every kind, in her anguish of loneliness, but this sense of isolation was only now truly waking up; not in the solitudes of Craigenputtock, where she felt, at least, that all she did was for her husband, but in this wider world, where understanding and sympathy came to her in every form, came even dangerously near at times. Then she began to look into her own life with different eyes.

Old Mrs. Sterling and her husband were frequent visitors now, as well as the younger branches of the family,—Henry Taylor, the Wilsons, Rev. F. D. Maurice, James Spedding, and many others, with what Carlyle vaguely calls, 'sprinklings of foreigners;' amongst whom, by-and-by, were the never-to-be-forgotten Mazzini, and Godefroi Cavaignac, brother to General Cavaignac, a singularly attractive and noble man, described by Carlyle as 'A fine Bayard soul, with figure to correspond.' The friendship between him and Mrs. Carlyle was a deep one—how could it be otherwise ?—his gentle breeding and refined courtesy ministered to her natural tendencies. It was not, however, till some years after the Carlyles came to Cheyne Row that the aquaintance was made, and death soon ended it—about 1846 we believe.

But we must return to 1835, when the first mention of those endless and inexplicable domestic difficulties at Cheyne Row occurs in a letter from Mrs. Carlyle to Miss Hunter of Edmonton. Here Mrs. Carlyle speaks of that 'valley of the shadow of char-woman,' which entered so largely into her very uncomfortable *ménage* during succeeding years, and coupled with it, is an allusion to one of the terrible nervous headaches to which she was now too often subject.

A mystery would attach to these unending household discomforts, were we to forget that the highly-wrought imagination and cruelly overstrained nervous system of the sufferer partly created, and distinctly, though all-unconsciously, exaggerated, many of them; and this was the state of things to the very end, and must be borne in mind, by no means to the exclusion of thorough sympathy that such things should be so heavy a cause of suffering, nor with an incredulity as to their being recounted exactly as they appeared to Mrs. Carlyle herself.

When Carlyle speaks of these domestic troubles, after his wife's death, with praise of her reticence in not irritating him with them, and speaks of 'results quasi-perfect,' we must remember that these words were written when all was quiet for ever, and that, as a fact, there was by no means even a 'quasi-perfect' calm in that small household during many long years—however the retrospect showed the matter forth.

Writing to her sister-in-law in August of this same year, Mrs. Carlyle was joyful in anticipation of a visit from her mother, and in tune with many of her surroundings. 'The people here,' she writes, 'are extravagantly kind to me,'—and speaking of the conclusion of the 'French Revolution,' or rather of the 'second *first* volume,' she says: 'Then we shall sing a *Te Deum* and get drunk.' She also recounts the names of pleasant new acquaintances: the Rev. Mr. Dunn, an Irish clergyman who had 'refused two bishopricks in the course of his life, for conscience' sake,' and sundry delightful Italian exiles, not forgetting her old lover and countryman, George Rennie.

There was a gleam of sunshine in this letter, shadowed over, as most things were for her, by six weeks of continual illness following immediately, ending in a short visit to her kind friends, the Sterlings (Mrs. Sterling's brother): 'a perfect Paradise of a place, peopled, as every Paradise ought to be, with angels.' But she fell ill again the very day after her return, and admitted that, neither 'man nor woman lives by bread alone, nor warm milk, nor any of these things.'

But her mother was now with her, and Carlyle on the eve of his departure for Scotland. During this absence of his, the mother and daughter were together, in the varying and unequal happiness of two natures that did not respond harmoniously the one to the other.

It was during the latter part of this visit, probably after Carlyle's return, that a small evening party was given by Mrs. Carlyle, when Mrs. Welsh had placed more wax lights on the supper table than her thrifty daughter approved, with other arrangements thought extravagant by Mrs. Carlyle, who made alterations and took away two of the candles. According to Miss Jewsbury's account, who had it from Mrs. Carlyle, the mother was much hurt, and shed tears over the matter; and in her remorse for having pained that dearly loved mother, Mrs. Carlyle put away the candles with instructions that when she herself should lie in death, they were to be lighted and burned, all of which most sadly came to pass in time. We cannot wonder that Carlyle should say in a letter to his brother John, written during Mrs. Welsh's second visit to Cheyne Row: 'Quiet observation forces on me the conclusion that Jane and her mother *cannot* live together.'

Mr. Froude says: 'They loved each other dearly, even passionately. They quarrelled daily and made it up again.' The two excitable women could not jog on together in the common-place 'hum-drum' of much happier and simpler natures. Mrs. Carlyle learned Italian and accomplished numberless useful and elegant tasks. Carlyle, in his contentment with *his* mother, looked perhaps with a certain feeling of anxious dismay on the domestic life awaiting him in Cheyne Row, where that too eager, broken spirit was still chafing at the inevitable. The servant-trouble constantly haunted her, and Carlyle was looking out for a suitable girl and thought he had found one. To his description of the servant, his wife replied: 'Fetch her then, in God's name, and I will make the best I can of her: after all, we fret ourselves too much about little things; much that might be laughed off, if *one were well and cheerful.*' (The italics are our own.)

It was on October 26, 1835, that Mrs. Carlyle penned the pretty letter, half in her newly learned Italian, to her husband at Scotsbrig, beginning—' Caro e rispettabile il mio Marito' —and we feel that his response on November 2 must have struck coldly on that warm spirit, when he says, in reply to her graceful badinage, 'And thou, my poor Goody, depending on cheerful looks of *mine* for thy cheerfulness! For God's sake do not, or do as little as possible,' but in the same letter he says: 'My poor Goody. It seems as if she could so easily be happy, and the easy means are so seldom there.' And again in the same letter he adds a few tender words in German, entreating her not to quarrel with her mother, reminding how soon the visit will be over, and he ends with: 'God bless thee, my poor little darling; I think we shall be happier some time.'

The holiday ended, Mrs. Welsh went to her brother in Liverpool, Carlyle returned, and still happiness held aloof.

Sad letters mark the coming on of that winter of 1835. Carlyle felt ' sick of soul,' and wrote in the pages of his Journal on December 23: 'Be silent, be calm, at least not mad;' and Mrs. Carlyle, on the same day, writing to the good old mother at Scotsbrig, speaks bitterly of her suffering health, of the blood all frozen in her brains, and her brains turned to a solid mass of ice. Her vitality failed her, and, but for the kindness of friends, notably Mrs. Sterling, Count Pepoli, and others, she would have lost heart.

Meantime the mother at Scotsbrig was carefully writing her pious exhortations to her son Thomas, whose lot she must have felt was not all of roses, telling him in quaint phrase to 'wait on the Lord and be strong.' That was all very well, but the worldly prospect was pressingly discouraging, and as the true obstacle to literary success lay in Carlyle's own strange and impracticable nature, the hope grew faint and ever fainter that this great genius would accept the conditions which could alone promise prosperity. Patronage was intolerable to him, and a situation that was offered him by his good friend Basil Montagu—a situation which would have provided a sure and sufficient income, whilst allowing him ample time for his own literary labours—was rejected as an injury.

Thus the year 1836 found matters far from cheerful at 5 Cheyne Row. It was in April of that year that Mrs. Carlyle, writing to her cousin Helen Welsh, of Liverpool, describes her husband as 'anything but well, nor likely to be better, until he have finished his "French Revolution,"' and adds, with a caustic touch, 'I myself have been abominably, though not writing, so far as I know, for the press.'

Worse days were at hand, however; for, soon after this date, Mrs. Carlyle became extremely ill, and felt that, 'unless she could get out of London, she would surely die.' As Mr. Froude tells us, she fled to Scotland, to her mother, who met her at Dumfries with embraces and tears, and took her on to Templand, where love and care were with her. But she remained the victim of sleeplessness, cough, and headache, and after two months' trial, despairing of everything here below she returned to Cheyne Row in August, 'a sadder and a wiser woman' as she herself said, to find recovered health at home.

It was during the freshness of these new feelings that Mrs. Carlyle mentions Godefroi de Cavaignac, of whom we have already spoken. It was the dead season in London, but this French Republican was in town, and was often in Cheyne Row. Mrs. Carlyle speaks of him as 'one who has had the glory of meriting to be imprisoned and nearly losing his head: a man with that sort of dark, half-savage beauty with which one paints a fallen angel . . . who defies all men and honours all women, and whose name is Cavaignac.'

CHAPTER XVII

A. D. 1836—1840

Retrospect on the Scotch journey—Return to Chelsea—Mrs. Carlyle's letter to Sterling—Carlyle's supposed 'lady admirers'—The lectures—Success and congratulations—Second visit of Mrs. Welsh—Flight of Carlyle into Annandale—'The bird and the watch'—Regrets and ill-health of Mrs. Carlyle—Cheque from Emerson, being proceeds of 'French Revolution'—John Sterling's health—Reflections thereon—Carlyle again in Scotland—Letter to John Forster: 'Why do women marry?'—The 'Lion's wife!'

THE journey to Scotland had been a mistake; and no wonder. 'Cœlum non animam mutant'—change of place could do little for Mrs. Carlyle.

We go back to quote a few words written to her by Carlyle during her absence:—'No rest for the poor wearied one! In her mother's house, too, she must wake "at four in the morning," and have fretting and annoyances! . . . The world is so wide. And for my poor Jane, no place where she can find shelter in it! . . . Oh, my poor lassie, what a life thou hast led! and I could not make it other. It was to be that and not another.'

And again, on August 24, he wrote:—'Oh, my poor bairn, be not faithless, but believing! Do not fling away life as insupportable, despicable; but let us work it out and rest it out together, like a true *two*, though under some obstructions.'

Here the difficulty of Mrs. Carlyle's life is laid bare. It was not as *two*, but as *one*, that his wife wished to live with him, and no tender words in letters could alter that inevitable sorrow. The pain that was given was truly such as can only exist where love exists, in some shape. But two faithful, loyal natures, learning, side by side, yet in loneliness, to compass the hard struggle of life ; two individuals bound together, yet unable to share completely the scarce comprehended burden; two human souls painfully moulded by adverse conditions to the god-like form destined for them— these images touch our imagination with reverence and pity: but the condition described hardly fits our ideal of *marriage*.

'Happy,' says Renan, 'are the children who only sleep and dream !' Of these two remarkable natures one awoke too early and too fully to sharp realities, and the other, in some senses, awoke too late. To Mrs. Carlyle the awakening was a stern one. The 'wind was not tempered' to her sensitive nature. Her keen pain caused bitterness and caustic speech; which truly returns so often with added sharpness into the heart of the speaker. Then that inseparable companion, the body, added its ceaseless sufferings to the incurable mental ones, and she began that long course of languishing, so sad to read of, so almost *impossible* to bear. Yet it was borne ! She could only turn to one quarter and another for a brief respite, and was glad to return to Chelsea, with a vague hope of some alleviation. And, after all, it was *home* she was hastening back to, with a quickened sense of possibilities of some comfort and rest therein.

It is pretty to note how she saw Carlyle trying to join her in the Chelsea omnibus, ' his face, beautifully set off by a broad-brimmed white hat, gazing in at the door like the Peri, who

'At the Gate of Heaven stood disconsolate.'

He had recognized her *trunk*, 'one of the most indubitable marks of genius,' she adds, 'which he ever manifested,' and thus hastened to shorten the time of separation. The trouble seemed to be that when re-united, so little heart-happiness attended the pair who wrote with so much affection to each other, who really *felt* it when absence removed the inexorable difficulties of personal contact.

In February 1837, writing to John Sterling, then in Bordeaux, Mrs. Carlyle strangely illustrates this. Apologising for long silence, she says :—' It has proceeded from some "crook in the lot," and not in the mind.' In the same letter, after pleading that she has become 'too sick and dispirited' for letter-writing, she announces the conclusion of the 'French Revolution,' adding :—' *Quelle vie!* let no woman who values peace of soul ever dream of marrying an author.' But the next lines show an admirably womanly jealousy of all Carlyle's supposed lady admirers—from Harriet Martineau, who 'presents him with her ear-trumpet with a pretty blushing air of coquetry'—to other lesser lights and attractions.

The lectures on German literature which were arranged for the month of May furnished Mrs. Carlyle with a fruitful topic. 'The exhibition,' as she terms it, caused her no little anxiety, and she looked to his following up the effort by a long holiday in Scotland, 'to rest himself,' adding :—' For my part, having neither published nor lectured, I feel no call to refresh myself. . . .' The lectures were a great success, though Carlyle pitied himself :—' Agitated, terrified, driven desperate and furious' (to use his own words), the financial result was satisfactory, and the enterprise, to any other than Carlyle, was a matter of congratulation.

A second visit from Mrs. Welsh marked the close of the lectures, and Carlyle's own departure for Annandale, in his blind desire for 'Silence! silence!' The graceful and clever dialogue of 'The Bird and the Watch' was written for John Sterling about this time, with the pathetic 'Remonstrance of my old Watch'—each needless to give here but for their remarkable brilliancy, and the light they cast on the character and powers of the writer. Much can be read 'between the lines.' We extract them from 'Letters and Memorials :'—

To the Rev. John Sterling, Blackheath.

Chelsea: Sept.–Oct., 1837.

My dear Friend,—Being a sending of more dialogue, it were downright extravagance to send a letter as well. So I shall merely say (your father being sitting impatiently beating with his stick) that you are on no account to understand that by either of these dialogians I mean to shadow forth my own personality. I think it is not superfluous to give you this warning, because I remember you talked of Chico's philosophy of life as my philosophy of life. which was a horrible calumny.

You can fancy how one must be hurried when your father is in the case.

God bless you!

Always yours,

JANE W. CARLYLE.

DIALOGUE.

The Bird and the Watch.

Watch. 'Chirp, chirp, chirp;' what a weariness thou art with thy chirping! Does it never occur to thee, frivolous thing, that life is too short for being chirped away at this rate?

Bird. Never. I am no philosopher, but just a plain canary-bird.

Watch. At all events, thou art a creature of time that hast been hatched, and that will surely die. And, such being the case, methinks thou art imperatively called upon to think more and to chirp less.

Bird. I 'called upon to think!' How do you make that out? Will you be kind enough to specify how my condition would be improved by thought? Could thought procure me one grain of seed or one drop of water beyond what my mistress is pleased to give? Could it procure me one eighth of an inch, one hair's-breadth more room to move about in, or could it procure me to be hatched over again with better auspices, in fair green wood beneath the blue free sky? I imagine not. Certainly I never yet betook myself to thinking instead of singing, that I did not end in dashing wildly against the wires of my cage, with sure loss of feathers and at the peril of limb and life. No, no, Madam Gravity, in this very conditional world, depend upon it, he that thinks least will live the longest, and song is better than sense for carrying one handsomely along.

Watch. You confess, then, without a blush, that you have no other aim in existence than to kill time?

Bird. Just so. If I were not always a killing of time, time, I can tell you, would speedily kill me. Heigh ho! I wish you had not interrupted me in my singing.

Watch. Thou sighest, 'Chico;' there is a drop of bitterness at the bottom of this froth of levity. Confess the truth: thou art not without compunction as to thy course of life.

Bird. Indeed, but I am, though. It is for the Power that made me and placed me here to feel compunction, if any is to be felt. For me, I do but fulfil my destiny: in the appointing of it, I had no hand. It was with no consent of mine that I ever was hatched; for the blind instinct that led me to chip the shell, and so exchange my natural prison for one made with hands, can hardly be imputed to me as an act of volition; it was with no consent of mine that I was fated to live and move within the wires of a cage, where a fractured skull and broken wings are the result of all endeavour towards the blue infinite, nor yet was it with consent of mine that I was made to depend for subsistence, not on my own faculties and exertions, but on the bounty of a fickle mistress, who starves me at one time and surfeits me at another. Deeply from my inmost soul I have protested, and do and will protest against all this. If, then, the chirping with which I stave off sorrow and *ennui* be an offence to the would-be-wise, it is not I but Providence should bear the blame, having placed me in a condition where there is no alternative but to chirp or die, and at the same time made self-preservation the first instinct of all living things.

Watch. 'Unhappy Chico! not in thy circumstances, but in thyself lies the mean impediment over which thou canst not gain the mastery.'* The lot thou complainest of so petulantly is, with slight variation, the lot of all. Thou are not free? Tell me who is! Alas, my bird! Here sit prisoners; there also do prisoners sit. This world is all prison, the only difference for those who inhabit it being in the size and aspect of the cells; while some of these stand revealed in cold strong nakedness for

---

* Goethe's *Wilhelm Meister*.

what they really are, others are painted to look like sky overhead, and open country all around, but the bare and the painted walls are alike impassable, and fall away only at the coming of the Angel of Death.

Bird. With all due reverence for thy universal insight, picked up Heaven knows how, in spending thy days at the bottom of a dark fob, I must continue to think that the birds of the air, for example, are tolerably free; at least, they lead a stirring pleasurable sort of life, which may well be called freedom in comparison with this of mine. Oh that, like them, I might skim the azure and hop among the boughs; that, like them, I might have a nest I could call my own, and a wife of my own choosing, that I might fly away from the instant she wearied me! Would that the egg I was hatched from had been addled, or that I had perished while yet unfledged! I am weary of my life, especially since thou hast constituted thyself my spiritual adviser. *Ay de mi!* But enough of this; it shall never be told that I died the death of Jenkin's hen. 'Chico, *point de faiblesse!*'

Watch. It were more like a Christian to say, 'Heaven be my strength.'

Bird. And pray what is a Christian? I have seen poets, philosophers, politicians, bluestockings, philanthropists, all sorts of notable people about my mistress; but no Christian so far as I am aware.

Watch. Bird! thy spiritual darkness exceeds belief. What can I say to thee? I wish I could make thee wiser, better!

Bird. If wishes were saws, I should request you to saw me a passage through those wires; but wishes being simply wishes, I desire to be let alone of them.

Watch. Good counsel at least is not to be rejected, and I give the best, wouldst thou but lay it to heart. Look around thee, Chico—around and within. Ascertain, if thou canst, the main source of thy discontent, and towards the removal of that direct thy whole faculties and energies. Even should thy success prove incomplete, the very struggle will be productive of good. 'An evil,' says a great German thinker, 'ceases to be an evil from the moment in which we begin to combat it.' Is it what you call loss of liberty that flings the darkest shadow over your soul? If so, you have only to take a correct and philosophical view of the subject instead of a democratic sentimental one, and you will find, as other captives have done, that there is more real freedom within the walls of a prison than in the distracting tumult without. Ah, Chico, in pining for the pleasures and excitements which lie beyond these wires, take also into account the perils and hardships. Think what the bird of the air has to suffer from the weather, from boys and beasts, and even from other birds. Storms and snares and unknown woes beset it at every turn, from all which you have been mercifully delivered in being once for all cooped up here.

Bird. There is one known woe, however, from which I have not been delivered in being cooped up here, and that is your absolute wisdom and impertinent interference, from which same I pray Heaven to take me with all convenient speed. If ever I attain to freedom, trust me, the very first use I shall make of it will be to fly where your solemn prosy tick shall not reach me any more for ever. Evil befall the hour when my mistress and your master took it into their heads to ' swear eternal friendship,' and so occasion a juxtaposition betwixt us two which nature could never have meant.

Watch. My ' master?' Thou imbecile. I own no master; rather am I his mistress, of whom thou speakest. Nothing can he do without appealing to me as to a second better conscience, and it is I who decide for him when he is incapable of deciding for himself. I say to him, ' It is time to go,' and he goeth; or, ' There is time to stay,' and he stayeth. Hardly is he awake of a morning when I tick authoritatively into his ear, ' *Levez-vous, monsieur ! Vous avez de grandes choses à faire;* ' * and forthwith he gathers himself together to enjoy the light of a new day —if no better may be. And is not every triumph he ever gained over natural indolence to be attributed to my often repeated remonstrance, ' Work, for the night cometh?' Ay, and when the night is come, and he lays himself down, I take my place at his bed-head, and, like the tenderest nurse, tick him to repose.

Bird. And suppose he neglected to wind thee up, or that thy main-spring chanced to snap? What would follow then? Would the world stand still in consequence? Would thy master

* St. Simon (he of 1825, n. b. l).

—for such he is to all intents and purposes—lie for ever in bed expecting thy '*Levez-vous?*' Would there be nothing in the wide universe besides thee to tell him what o'clock it was? Impudent piece of mechanism! Thing of springs and wheels, in which flows no life-blood, beats no heart! Depend upon it, for all so much as thou thinkest of thyself, thou couldst be done without. *Il n'y a point de montre nécessaire!* The artisan who made thee with files and pincers could make a thousand of thee to order. Cease, then, to deem thyself a fit critic and lawgiver for any living soul. Complete of thy kind, tick on, with infallible accuracy, sixty ticks to the minute, through all eternity if thou wilt and canst; but do not expect such as have hearts in their breasts to keep time with thee. A heart is a spontaneous, impulsive thing, which cannot, I would have thee know, be made to beat always at one measured rate for the good pleasure of any time-piece that ever was put together. And so good day to thee, for here comes one who, thank Heaven, will put thee into his fob, and so end our *tête-à-tête.*

Watch. (With a sigh.) 'The living on earth have much to bear!' J. W. C.

(Mrs. Carlyle had evidently contemplated providing herself with a new watch; her own, which had been her mother's, getting rather venerable, and perhaps not keeping such good time.)

Remonstrance of my Old Watch.

What have I done to you, that you should dream of 'tearing out my inside' and selling me away for an old song? Is your heart become hard as the nether millstone, that you overlook long familiarity and faithful service, to take up with the new-fangled gimcracks of the day? Did I ever play thee false? I have been driven with you, been galloped with you, over the roughest roads; have been jolted as never watch was; and all this without 'sticking up' a single time, or so much as lagging behind! Nay, once I remember (the devil surely possessed you at that moment!) you pitched me out of your hand as though I had been a worthless pin-cushion; and even that unprecedented shock I sustained with unshaken nerves! Try any of your new favourites as you have tried me; send the little wretch you at present wear within your waist-band smack against a deal floor, and if ever it stirred more in this world, I should think it little less than a miracle.

Bethink you, then, misguided woman, while it is yet time ! If not for my sake, for your own, do not complete your barbarous purpose. Let not a passing womanish fancy lead you from what has been the ruling principle of your life—a detestation of shams and humbug. For, believe me, these little watches are arrant shams, if ever there was one. They are not watches so much as lockets with watch-faces. The least rough handling puts them out of sorts; a jolt is fatal; they cost as much in repairs every year as their original price; and when they in their turn come to have their insides torn out, what have you left? Hardly gold enough to make a good-sized thimble.

But if you are deaf to all suggestions of common-sense, let sentiment plead for me in your breast. Remember how daintily you played with me in your childhood, deriving from my gold shine your first ideas of worldly splendour. Remember how, at a more advanced age, you longed for the possession of me and of a riding-habit and whip, as comprising all that was most desirable in life! And when at length your mother made me over to you, remember how feelingly (so feelingly that you shed tears) I brought home to your bosom the maxim of your favourite Goethe, ' The wished-for comes too late.' And oh! for the sake of all these touching remembrances, cast me not off, to be dealt with in that shocking manner; but if, through the caprice of fashion, I am deemed no longer fit to be seen, make me a little pouch inside your dress, and I am a much mistaken watch if you do not admit in the long run that my solid merit is far above that of any half-dozen of these lilliputian upstarts.

And so, betwixt hope and fear, I remain,
Your dreadfully agitated
WATCH.

I find so much reason as well as pathos and natural eloquence in the above that I shall proceed no further with the proposed exchange.
JANE.

The spring of 1838 found Carlyle miserable and restless, having as yet fallen on no new work; the domestic pressure was heavy, and Mrs. Carlyle speaks plainly of her own suffering—reflected, in some measure, from the state of her husband's mind, though indeed *health* had long become an impossibility to her. 'So much to bear, for a long, long time back!' she writes her cousin Helen at Liverpool. It was now the time when Carlyle was delivering the second course of lectures, and Mrs. Carlyle adds:

If he could get sleep at nights, while the lecturing goes forward, and if I could look on without being perpetually reminded by the pain in my head, or some devilry or other, that I am a mere woman . . . we should find this new trade rather agreeable. . . . A single woman (by your leave be it said) may be laid up with comparative ease of mind; but in a country where a man is allowed only one wife, and needs that one for other purposes than mere show, it is a singular hardship for all parties.

In August of this year Carlyle was in Kirkcaldy, and his wife wrote him poor accounts of her health. Sleep was beginning to forsake her—three hours one night, forty minutes the next, then none at all; showing a steady decline in the healthy nervous balance so desirable to maintain. Society did little to ameliorate Mrs. Carlyle's condition, and, though she speaks of 'tea-shines,' at one of which Mr. and Mrs. Crawford, George Rennie and his wife, Mrs. Sterling, Count Pepoli, Erasmus Darwin, and Robert Barker attended, the result was apparently mere weariness of spirit and body. The first money, sent in a bill of exchange by Emerson, that came in from an American edition of the 'French Revolution' cheered her somewhat, though it brought 'a sort of tears' into her eyes. Perhaps there were too many painful memories connected, for her, with that book.

And now the good, gentle John Sterling was ordered off to Italy for his health, and came to take his leave. We note that Mrs. Carlyle makes one of her rare exceptions in saying, 'He looked as Edward Irving used to do.' She *had*, then, marked the fading life and strength of that old and attached friend, though all in silence. But the passage, so pregnant with pathos, loses its effect when she adds: 'Woe to him, if he fall into the net of any beautiful Italian. People who are so dreadfully devoted to their wives are so apt, from mere habit, to get devoted to other people's wives as well.' These words may prove a key to much that happened later on.

Meantime the spring of 1838, which found Carlyle busy preparing for his third course of lectures, had left Mrs. Carlyle weakened and shaken in mind and body. No influence seemed able to lift her from the growing suffering of her condition and its hopeless outlook; while her husband was confiding to the pages of his journal that he is 'tortured to death,' and feeling he must rush away from all his surroundings! 'Be still, wild weak heart,' he says, 'convulsively bursting up against the bars!' And surely Mrs. Carlyle might have said the same, though hers was an inarticulate cry for a long time yet; when at length it, too, struggled into expression.

A natural question for ordinary people to ask, is, What *was* this crushing and deeply-felt grief in these two hearts? And the answer, honest and disappointing as it is, must be, that the grief which can openly be spoken of is *not* the unbearable grief. So the sorrow of these isolated hearts must be held sacred.

The close of Carlyle's Scotch visit found his wife somewhat improved, and soon an idea of Cromwell as a subject for his next work interested him, and Mill's suggestion, that he should write an article, developed into his great undertaking. Thus his uneasy spirit found some sort of repose in work. Jeffrey was still the kindest of friends, and joined the chorus of those who openly and heartily admired Carlyle's genius.

Mrs. Carlyle, in a letter to her mother-in-law, had gaily

hazarded the idea that she, too, was a genius as well as her husband. She had charmed noisy neighbors into quietude —had done away with an obstreperous parrot whose shrieks had caused her husband to cry out that he ' could neither think nor live,' and in a hundred ways had made the path smooth for him. It was not 'genius' she lacked.

It was during the second course of lectures that Mrs. Carlyle had seen the widowed Mrs. Edward Irving sitting opposite to her, and spoke of the coincidence with true womanly tenderness.

In July the Carlyles had been in Scotland, he with his people, she partly with her mother at Templand; but the unfavourable winter spent by Mrs. Carlyle, with her ' violent chronic cold, and fiercely torturing, nervous headache, continuous sometimes for three days and nights,' was a gloomy preparation for the strain of home-life in Chelsea. Her ' little Fifeshire maid,' Kirkcaldy Helen, as Carlyle calls her, was no small solace to her in these suffering days. Writing to Mrs. Aitken she says: ' When I am very bad she bends over me in my bed as if I were a little child . . . one might think one's maid's tears could do little for a tearing headache, but they do comfort a little.'

A significant passage, also given by Mr. Froude, occurs in a letter to John Forster, written about this date. ' Why do women marry?' she wrote; 'God knows, unless it be that, like the great Wallenstein, they do not find scope enough for their genius and qualities in an easy life.' It would, perhaps, not be easy for us to predict what would have been *an easy life* for one whose highly-strung nervous temperament would have required the physique of an ox to make ordinary life bearable and pleasant.

Carlyle had been mixed up with an annoying trial by jury —' a Manchester case of patents,' as he describes it in his note on the letter from which we are about to quote—and had been in ' intolerable suffering, rage, almost despair, and resolution to quit London, in consequence of these jury-summonses,' and it is in reference to this that Mrs. Carlyle writes to John Sterling in October 1840:—

My poor man of genius had to sit on a jury two days, to the ruin of his whole being, physical, moral and intellectual. . . . While I, *poverina*, have been reacting against his reaction, till that malady called by the cockneys 'mental worry' fairly took me by the throat, and threw me on my bed for a good many days. And now I am but recovering, white as the paper I write upon, and carrying my head as one who has been making a failed attempt at suicide. . . .

The next special burden reported as dragging down Mrs. Carlyle's weakened frame, is dated by her husband as falling in the autumn of the same year, 1840, when, excusing herself for seldom writing to her mother-in-law at Scotsbrig, she says: 'I should be glad enough to write a letter now and then, just to keep the devil from my elbow,' and goes on to describe the downfall of the Fifeshire maidservant, from a giving way to intemperance. She says: 'I am really much attached to the poor wretch, who has no fault under heaven but this one.' The matter ended as was inevitable; but not till after a first, second, and third forgiveness and chance to do better had been granted.

Carlyle, meantime, was 'reading voraciously' in preparation for his 'Cromwell,' and growling away in the old style, to which his wife professes a certain wholesome indifference. But *indifference* was not in her nature, helpful as it would often have been: and the year closed in more or less of disquiet.

The bitter tone which made itself felt in later days, crops up in a letter written to her friend Susan Hunter, now Mrs. Sterling, by Mrs. Carlyle, in January 1841, in words which show how little real satisfaction or happiness came to her in her new sphere of life. Her character of 'Lion's Wife,' she says, gives her enough compulsory writing to disgust even a Duchess of Orleans: 'applications from young ladies for autographs; passionate invitations to dine; announcements of inexpressible longing to drink tea with me.' All these were a weariness to her, and she began to look on the world with a cynical distrust of its favours, and perhaps many a secret longing after that old, quiet time, when she was herself the centre of her little world, loved and watched and petted. It was not her nature to play the part of 'Lion's Wife,' small blame to her! It would have been almost impossible to find a man to whom she *could* have been *second;* but that man did exist, and she did marry him, and there entered into her a deep and suffering dissatisfaction, traceable in all she ever wrote to those she loved and trusted, and wholly uncomprehended by the one nearest to her. She was a woman, tender and excitable, and her burst of unaccountable tears over some trifling gift from John Sterling shows a spirit pent up and ready to come forth at a touch. But that touch, to bring peace, could only come from the one man in the world; and from him, spite of a faithful attachment, it did not come.

What more severe ordeal to a woman such as Jane Carlyle than life with a husband who writes to his brother John in 1840: 'The absence of ill-fare and semi-delirium is possible for me in solitude only. Solitude indeed is sad as Golgotha, but it is not mad like Bedlam.' That 'solitude' was a term strictly applied, and meant an absolute severance from the close contact of domestic life, no less than a freedom from the galling fetters of society.

Carlyle was, as Mr. Froude tells us, unable to keep his discomforts to himself, and passionately dilated on them to his wife, blindly unaware of her own heavy burden of pain, so that the time they spent together was often the hardest bit of all, and her keen disposition and sharp, caustic tongue made matters no better. There was no remedy. And when we find Carlyle writing in his journal in April 1840: 'If I were a little healthier—ah me! all were well'—we feel that only one side of the question is touched upon.

CHAPTER XVIII

A. D. 1841-1846

Trouble at Templand—Sudden Alarm—Summons too late—Mrs. Carlyle receives the news of her mother's death when on her way to nurse her—Carlyle goes to Templand to wind up the estate—Mrs. Welsh buried at Crawford—Heart-stricken letter to Mrs. Russell of Thornhill—Troston Rectory and the Bullers—Lady Harriet Baring—Mrs. Carlyle's return to Cheyne Row—First meeting with Miss Jewsbury and the Paulets—'The three-cornered alliance '—Household ' earthquaking' in Cheyne Row—Mrs. Carlyle's first expressed judgment of Lady Harriet Baring—Stay at Ryde—Father Mathew—Loss of Strength—Need of a quiet place for Carlyle to write in—Failure of the attempt—Letter to John Welsh of Liverpool—Carlyle's hopefulness of his wife's health—Her visit to Liverpool and Seaforth (the Paulets)—Visit to the Grange—Painful thoughts—' Cromwell' concluded.

THERE is little to mark the year 1841, but some charming letters to John Sterling, now at Falmouth. There had been some slight misunderstanding between the two friends, and Mrs. Carlyle writes : ' Had I loved you little, I should not have minded; but loving you much, I regarded myself as a *femme incomprise* and, what was still worse, maltreated. . . .' The matter which caused the temporary coolness was purely a literary one, unnecessary to dwell on here; but Mrs. Carlyle ends with, 'I care little what comes of John Sterling the poet, so long as John Sterling the *man* is all that my heart wishes him to be,' and no cloud ever came between them again.

But a far deeper trouble was near. Mrs. Welsh's health, never strong, gave way. Some allusion, not meant as serious, in a letter from Templand had roused anxiety, and after Carlyle had written confidentially to Dr. Russell, and received a cautious though hopeful answer, the blow fell, and 'on

February 23 or 21,' Carlyle tells us, 'came tidings of "a stroke," apoplectic, paralytic; immediate danger now over, but future danger fatally evident.'

Carlyle tells, in touching words, how his stricken wife hurried off by night train for Liverpool, on her way to her mother; he tells of the violent pain in which she started, 'her beautiful eyes full of sorrowful affection;' of the sad greeting at Liverpool: 'All is over at Templand, cousin; *gone, gone!*' and how with all tenderness, the pitying hands laid the bereaved woman to rest, as best she could rest in her sorrow and utter weariness.

It was on Feb. 26, 1842, that Mrs. Welsh breathed her last, 'that first stroke, mercifully the last one.' Mr. Carlyle immediately went to Templand to settle affairs there, and two months passed in this sad and lonely manner, but, as he says, 'not unhappy.' The unhappiness was at Cheyne Row, where the blow that struck the quick-responsive heart of Mrs. Carlyle, stifled the powers of life.

Mrs. Welsh was laid in Crawford churchyard, twenty miles from Templand. It was long before the stricken woman at Chelsea could write on the subject—we give an extract from a letter.

To Mrs. Russell, Thornhill.

5 Cheyne Row, Chelsea : Tuesday, April 1842.

My dear Mrs. Russell,—I sit down to write to you at last! But how to put into written words what lies for you in my heart! If I were beside you, I feel as if I should throw myself on your neck, and cry myself to rest like a sick child. At this distance, to ask in cold writing all the heart-breaking things I would know of you, and to say all the kind things I would say for her and myself, is indeed quite impossible for me. You will come and see me, will you not, before very long? I can never go there again; but you will come to me? traveling is made so easy now! And I should feel such gratification in receiving into my own house one who was ever so dearly welcome in hers, and who, of all who loved her, was, by one sad chance and another, the only one whose love was any help to her when she most needed our love ! She blessed you for the comfort you gave her, and you shall be blessed for it here and hereafter. The dying blessings of such a pure fervent heart as hers cannot have been pronounced on you in vain ; and take my blessing also, 'kind, sweet woman !' a less holy one, but not less sincerely given !

It was not until early in May that Carlyle was able to return to his home in Chelsea,

where (he says) my poor, sorrow-stricken darling, with Jeannie, her Liverpool cousin, had been all this while. . . . I found her looking pale, thin, weak ; she did not complain of health, but was evidently suffering that way too ; what she did feel was of the mind, of the heart sunk in heaviness ; and of this also she said little, even to me not much. Words could not avail; a mother and mother's love were gone, irrevocably. . . .

There was also in Mrs. Carlyle's heart the bitterness of vehement and fruitless self-reproach as to real or fancied shortcomings in her conduct as a daughter—a shadow which falls on the most blameless hearts, when once the object of love and duty is taken from them for ever; and Carlyle, in his own loneliness, reproached himself in his turn, possibly equally groundlessly, with an impatience of his wife's reiterated expressions of pain on this very subject.

Mrs. Carlyle's letters to Mrs. Russell, of Thornhill, one of her best-loved friends, and wife of the physician who had attended Mrs. Welsh, are most touching in their abandonment of sorrow. 'Think of me—pray for me !' she says, out of her depth of depression. The first anniversary of her birthday, in July of that year, was naturally a sad one; but Carlyle made a little gift of a smelling-bottle to his wife on that day, and never again omitted the thoughtful attention of some memento after the mother's death.

The month of August was spent by Mrs. Carlyle at Troston Rectory, Suffolk, where the Rev. Reginald Buller held the living, with his father and mother as guests also. Carlyle was on the eve of a short trip to the Continent—a few days merely, with Spring Rice, on public business. Here in the peaceful country village was no peace for the agitated nerves of Mrs. Carlyle, 'dead weary' as she describes herself to have been. 'Infernal serenades of asses, braying as if the devil were in them,' with 'ever so many cocks challenging each other all over the parish,' banished all hope of sleep.

In this first letter from Troston we find the first mention of Lady Harriet Baring, afterwards Lady Ashburton. Mrs. Carlyle ends with : ' God bless you, my dear husband ! I hope you are rested, and going to Lady Harriet, and I hope you will think of me a great deal, and be as good to me on my return as you were when I came away. I do not desire any more of you ! Your own—J. C.'

The Rev. Reginald does not seem to have struck Mrs. Carlyle by the intellect and power which so distinguished Carlyle's old pupil Charles, of whom Lord Houghton speaks in such warm and generous terms in his highly interesting work, 'Monographs.' But she was not in a state of health to appreciate the commonplace, and again, on August 20, bitterly complains to her husband of night-noises, of which a healthy brain and nervous system would have been more or less unconscious : 'Braying, lowing, crowing, cackling, barking, howling, &c., the like of which I have not found in Israel !' In thus expressing herself we must bear in mind that she well knew Carlyle to be equally susceptible to the least disturbance, and could, or at least might, be expected to understand her trouble. She adds : ' In the few moments that I slept, I dreamed that my mother came to me, and said that she knew of a beautiful place where it was so quiet. . . .'

This is, indeed, what Mrs. Carlyle feared would come out of her—' the literature of desperation ; ' and we must bear in mind that, from this time forth, we are speaking of a sick woman, broken permanently in her nervous health and well-being, and seeing all things with the inevitable exaggeration of an overworn brain and saddened hopes. That she was *tragical* and *intense* was absolutely inevitable to one in her physical state, and it would be idle to discuss so sad, so unalterably sad, a condition, in the once bright and dauntless woman.

A 'passing bell' for some old parishioner who had died, rung at an untimely hour, caused acute suffering, sleeplessness and fright to Mrs. Carlyle, who returned to Cheyne Row early in September, and again poured forth her sadness in letters to Mrs. Russell and Mrs. Aitken. It was true of her, as Carlyle had said of himself, that, 'sick children, who long now for this, now for that, are not well off anywhere. The thing they want, I suppose, is to get to sleep well on their mother's bosom.' But that was not to be as yet.

Growing popularity attracted a vast number of visitors to Cheyne Row—to see, if it might be, the author of 'Hero Worship,' 'The French Revolution,' &c., the man who had wrought such a mighty upheaval in thought and literature; and the 'Lion's Wife' had a handsome share of such rich incomings. For among those admirers was one who came to know and to love both these remarkable people, and was Mrs. Carlyle's closest friend through life—Miss Geraldine Jewsbury, a Manchester lady, gifted, brilliant, and herself an authoress, afterwards, also, for many years, reader and reviewer to the 'Athenæum.'

Geraldine was eager, sprightly, original, and warm-hearted—the most congenial nature Mrs. Carlyle could have met with. We, who had the privilege of knowing her in her later years, when she visited her brother, the late Mr. Frank Jewsbury, in Manchester, can never forget the quick, responsive brightness and very marked originality of Geraldine Jewsbury. There were many points of character not dissimilar between her and Mrs. Carlyle; and the friendship was extended to Mr. Carlyle, who received it with less of rapture, perhaps, but never failed to recognize the good points of Geraldine, though her impulsiveness sometimes grated on him momentarily.

Miss Jewsbury was also very intimate with a Mr. and Mrs. Paulet (he, Swiss by birth; she, an English lady), who lived at Seaforth, near Liverpool, and in time Mrs. Carlyle came to know and visit the Paulets. The husband was an estimable man, a merchant in good circumstances, and Mrs. Paulet (*Betsy*, as she soon came to be called in the letters and chats of the ladies) was a charming and gifted woman, attractive in many ways.

Three uncommon women like these found difficulties, no doubt, in a 'three-cornered' friendship, irregularly unreserved and intimate, yet not altogether confidential, equally, amongst the three. From discussing literary subjects they often passed to personal ones, and, as all three were not always present, there arose in time that little 'rift within the lute' which was natural under the circumstances. But peace came out of the agitation, and one of its terms was, that each lady returned to the other every scrap of writing which had passed between them,—so far, at least, as Mrs. Carlyle and Miss Jewsbury were concerned, whose correspondence had been voluminous; and probably in Mrs. Paulet's case also.

All three friends now having passed away, it would be worse than useless to dwell on a storm which never really affected the true heart-friendship between Mrs. Carlyle and Miss Jewsbury, which lasted till the *end*—in 1866. One only letter of this correspondence is in our hands, the sole representative of hundreds—it was lent most kindly by John Stores Smith, Miss Jewsbury's valued friend and literary executor. It was written at the close of Mrs. Carlyle's life, as there is abundant evidence to show, and will be given in its place.

It was in July 1843 that the house in Cheyne Row needed painting and readjustment, and Carlyle had gone to Wales to be out of the annoyance, leaving his wife to look after the workmen, &c., with her maid as companion, in this uncomfortable state of things. And Mrs. Carlyle, suffering as much as her husband did from the smell of paint, ingeniously fitted up 'a sort of gipsy's tent' in the garden, with arm-chair, little table, &c. It was constructed, as she tells her husband, by her own hands, 'out of the clothes' ropes and poles, and the old crumb-cloth out of the library.'

We cannot but remember her gipsy blood, and feel that she unconsciously adopted a plan most congenial to her temperament, and must have thus passed some truly happy hours, for she adds, 'one has no credit in being jolly in such a pretty bower.' Here we have a reference to 'Mark Tapley,' and we may mention that Charles Dickens was now known personally to the Carlyles. Speaking of this 'tent,' Mrs. Carlyle says—'Woman wants but little here below;' we might add the emphatic conclusion of a venerable lady-friend : 'but that little she *must have!*'—and it was not always feasible. Writing to her Uncle John in Liverpool on July 18 Mrs. Carlyle speaks of her home as 'possessed by seven devils— a painter, two carpenters, a paperhanger, two nondescript apprentice lads, and a spy, all playing the devil to the utmost of their powers. . . .' Her tent, too, frail refuge, had an awkward way of falling down on her head at the least puff of wind. In fact, her vivid descriptions of this period of 'earthquaking' are highly characteristic.

Carlyle meantime visited Clifton and Chepstow, and writes to his wife: 'You are very good; write always. Except by your letters, I am, at present, disunited from all the earth.' A visit to Bishop Thirlwall was a memorable incident of this little tour. When Carlyle reflected that his wife was weak, overwrought, and suffering from the heat, he urged her to join him at a seaside lodging at Formby, near Seaforth, where the Paulets lived; but the plan came to nothing. So Mrs. Carlyle remained at Cheyne Row, while her husband again went to Scotland, in what Mr. Froude calls 'a period of eclipse.'

Helen Welsh, her cousin from Liverpool, was now with Mrs. Carlyle, and the house in Cheyne Row began to look clean and pretty. 'Thanks,' she writes to Carlyle, 'for your constant little letters; when you came back, I do not know how I shall learn to do without them. . . . But, my dear, I must stop: you see that my head is bad, and that I am making it worse. Bless you!'

On August 9 Mrs. Carlyle set off, with old Mr. Sterling, to spend a few days at Ryde, where her discomforts seem to have been many and acute. Here occurred the remarkable incident of her enthusiastic meeting with Father Mathew, which shows her keen and impulsive nature at its very height. We give an extract from her letter to her husband, on this subject. The date is August 9, 1843:—

. . . And now let me tell you something which you will perhaps think questionable, a piece of Hero-Worship that I have been after. My youthful enthusiasm, as John Sterling calls it, is not extinct then, as I had supposed; but must certainly be immortal! Only think of its blazing up for Father Mathew! You know I have always had the greatest reverence for that priest ; and when I heard he was in London, attainable to me, I felt that I must see him, shake him by the hand, and tell him I loved him considerably ! I was expressing my wish to see him, to Robertson, the night he brought the Ballad Collector ; and he told me it could be gratified quite easily. Mrs. Hall had offered him a note of introduction to Father Mathew, and she would be pleased to include my name in it. 'Fix my time, then.' 'He was administering the pledge all day long in the Commercial Road.' I fixed next evening.

Robertson, accordingly, called for me at five, and we rumbled off in omnibus, all the way to Mile End, that hitherto for me unimaginable goal ! Then there was still a good way to walk ; the place, the 'new lodging,' was a large piece of waste ground, boarded off from the Commercial Road, for a Catholic cemetery. I found '.my youthful enthusiasm ' rising higher and higher as I got on the ground, and saw the thousands of people all hushed into awful silence, with not a single exception that I saw—the only religious meeting I ever saw in cockneyland which had not plenty of scoffers hanging on its outskirts. The crowd was all in front of a narrow scaffolding, from which an American captain was then haranguing it; and Father Mathew stood beside him, so good and simple-looking! Of course, we could not push our way to the front of the scaffold, where steps led up to it; so we went to one end, where there were no steps or other visible means of access, and handed up our letter of introduction to a policeman; he took it and returned presently, saying that Father Mathew was coming. And he came; and reached down his hand to me, and I grasped it; but the boards were higher than my head, and it seemed our communication must stop there. But I have told you that I was in a moment of enthusiasm; I felt the need of getting closer to that good man. I saw a bit of rope hanging, in the form of a festoon, from the end of the boards; I put my foot on it; held still by Father Mathew's hand; seized the end of the boards with the other; and, in some, to myself (up to this moment), incomprehensible way, flung myself horizontally on to the scaffolding at Father Mathew's feet! He uttered a scream, for he thought (I suppose) I must fall back; but not at all; I jumped to my feet, shook hands with him and said—what? 'God only knows.' He made me sit down on the only chair a moment; then took me by the hand as if I had been a little girl, and led me to the front of the scaffold, to see him administer the pledge. From a hundred to two hundred took it; and all the tragedies and theatrical representations I ever saw, melted into one, could not have given me such emotion as that scene did. There were faces both of men and women that will haunt me while I live; faces exhibiting such concentrated wretchedness, making, you would have said, its last deadly struggle with the powers of darkness. There was one man, in particular, with a baby in his arms; and a young girl that seemed of the 'unfortunate' sort, that gave me an insight into the lot of humanity that I still wanted. And in the face of Father Mathew, when one looked from them to him, the mercy of Heaven seemed to be laid bare. Of course I cried; but I longed to lay my head down on the good man's shoulder and take a hearty cry there before the whole multitude! He said to me one such nice thing. 'I dare not be absent for an hour,' he said; 'I think always if some dreadful drunkard were to come, and me away, he might never muster determination perhaps to come again in all his life; and there would be a man lost!'

I was turning sick, and needed to get out of the thing, but, in the act of leaving him—never to see him again through all time, most probably—feeling him to be the very best man of modern times (you excepted), I had another movement of youthful enthusiasm which you will hold up your hands and eyes at. Did I take the pledge then? No; but I would, though, if I had not feared it would be put in the newspapers ! No, not that ; but I drew him aside, having considered if I had any ring on, any handkerchief, anything that I could leave with him in remembrance of me, and having bethought me of a pretty memorandum-book in my reticule, I drew him aside and put it in his hand, and bade him keep it for my sake; and asked him to give me one of his medals to keep for his? And all this in tears and the utmost agitation ! Had you any idea that your wife was still such a fool! I am sure I had not. The Father got through the thing admirably. He seemed to understand what it all meant quite well, inarticulate though I was. He would not give me a common medal, but took a silver one from the neck of a young man who had just taken the pledge for example's sake, telling him he would get him another presently, and then laid the medal into my hand with a solemn blessing. I could not speak for excitement all the way home. When I went to bed I could not sleep; the pale faces I had seen haunted me, and Father Mathew's smile; and even next morning, I could not anyhow subside into my normal state, until I had sat down and written Father Mathew a long letter—accompanying it with your 'Past and Present !' . . .

It is to be feared that old Mr. Sterling was hardly the companion for Mrs. Carlyle. A noisy hotel had been changed for lodgings, where discomforts of a still more unbearable kind awaited the nervous and sleepless woman. A letter from Miss Jewsbury the next day, in connection with a young servant for whom Mrs. Carlyle was kindly finding a place in Manchester, gave Mrs. Carlyle the excuse for instant return to town. She speaks kindly of old Mr. Sterling, but estimates his conversational powers as low, since, in his decline and suffering, 'he cannot even talk, for every minute needing to roar out " This is torture, by Jove ! My God, this is agony!"' and she ends her letter by subscribing herself 'bug-bitten, bedevilled, and out of my latitude.'

On August 13 she has safely returned to Cheyne Row, and tells her husband, who is still at Scotsbrig, that she was, or ought to be, 'the most thankful woman in Chelsea.' But in the same letter are the words: '*Oh! my mother, my own mother!*' After a good sleep in her own 'red bed,' she awoke to activity, and 'fell immediately to painting and glazing with my own hands, not to ruin you altogether,' and she ends with 'Pray for me!' A German governess, Miss Bölte, whose name often occurs, spent an evening with Mrs. Carlyle, who was trying to place her in a situation—ever anxious, as she was, to help others. Miss Bölte is described as 'a fine, manly little creature.'

Depressing days followed, failing strength, and very unlovely household discomforts, needless to enter on here. Still were the kindly deeds never neglected: the 'five pounds for poor old Mary, before you leave the country;' the gentle reception of Garnier, a revolutionary exile, all out of tune and out of heart, whose troubled soul she smoothed with her tender womanly hand, so that, on parting, he said, 'You have made me pass one evening pleasantly, and I came very miserable.' It was towards the end of this month that Mrs. Carlyle 'realised' the sofa, of which she writes so graphically to her husband, with the eagerness and pleasure of a child describing a new toy.

There was a little disappointment at the fact of Dr. John Carlyle arriving at Cheyne Row on a visit before Carlyle's own arrival. But she bravely says: 'When *you* come, I shall insist on going into some quiet, comfortable room with you, and locking the door till we have had a quiet, comfortable talk. . . .'

These anticipations were not realised. Carlyle returned from his travels 'very bilious,' and, as a consequence, doubtless, irritable, and all the completed labours after order and cleanliness in the house were swallowed up in one wild longing on his part for a quiet place to write in. An 'accursed pianoforte next door' was the deciding aggravation. Something must be done, and that speedily; and many expedients were tried, but without avail, to arrange a quiet room for Carlyle to work in. Mrs. Carlyle writes to Mrs. Aitken in October 1843:

My dear Jane,—Carlyle returned from his travels very bilious and continues very bilious up to this hour. The amount of bile that he does bring home to me, in these cases, is something 'awfully grand !' Even through that deteriorating medium he could not but be struck with a 'certain admiration' at the immensity of needlework I had accomplished in his absence, in the shape of chair-covers, sofa-covers, window curtains, &c., &c., and all the other manifest improvements into which I had put my whole genius and industry, and so little money as was hardly to be conceived ! For three days his satisfaction over the rehabilitated house lasted; on the fourth, the young lady next door took a fit of practising on her accursed pianoforte, which he had quite forgotten seemingly, and he started up disenchanted in his new library, and informed heaven and earth in a peremptory manner that ' there he could neither think nor live,' that the carpenter must be brought back and 'steps taken to make him a quiet place somewhere—perhaps best of all on the roof of the house.' Then followed interminable consultations with the said carpenter, yielding, for some days, only plans (wild ones) and estimates. The roof on the house could be made all that a living author of irritable nerves could desire: silent as a tomb, lighted from above; but it would cost us 120*l*.! Impossible, seeing that we may be turned out of the house any year ! so one had to reduce one's schemes to the altering of rooms that already were. By taking down a partition and instituting a fire-place where no fire-place could have been fancied capable of existing, it is expected that some bearable approximation to that ideal room in the clouds will be realised. But my astonishment and despair on finding myself after three months of what they call here 'regular mess,' just when I had got every trace of the workpeople cleared away, and had said to myself, 'Soul, take thine case, or at all events thy swing, for thou hast carpets nailed down and furniture rubbed for many days!' just when I was beginning to lead the dreaming, reading, dawdling existence which best suits me, and alone suits me in cold weather, to find myself in the thick of a new 'mess:' the carpets, which I had nailed down so well with my own hands, tumbled up again, dirt, lime, whitewash, oil, paint, hard at work as before, and a prospect of new cleanings, new sewings, new arrangements stretching away into eternity for anything I see! 'Well,' as my Helen says (the strangest mixture of philosopher and perfect idiot that I have met with in my life), 'when one's doing this, one's doing nothing else anyhow!' And as one ought to be always doing something, this suggestion of hers has some consolation in it. . . .

Three days of satisfaction were a scanty reward for the continuous and anxious efforts made by Mrs. Carlyle for her husband's comfort. In a letter to Mrs. Sterling she expresses herself vividly on the subject.

Up went all the carpets which my own hands had nailed down, in rushed the troop of incarnate demons, bricklayers, joiners, white-washers, &c. . . . Down went a partition in one room, up went a new chimney in another. Helen, instead of exerting herself to stave the torrent of confusion, seemed to be struck [no wonder] with temporary idiotcy; and my husband himself, at sight of the uproar he had raised, was all but wringing his hands and tearing his hair. . . . Myself could have sat down and cried, so little strength or spirit had I left. . . .

Sad to tell, this re-arrangement of rooms, when completed, proved an entire failure, and the distracted writer, after 'shifting about in the saddest way, like a domestic wandering Jew, returned to his original library.' 'Alas!' adds his wife, 'one can make fun of this on paper, but in practice it is anything but fun, I assure you. There is no help for it, however; a man of genius cannot hold his genius as a sinecure!'

It was in November of this year that Mrs. Carlyle writes of her own suffering to the kind uncle John in Liverpool; piteously bewails her 'solitude' in that bed-chamber, where she has 'transacted so many headaches, so many influenzas,' and says she is 'Oh! so lonely! as in some intermediate stage betwixt the living world and the dead!' For Carlyle was now buried, in his own fashion, namely in the production of his 'Cromwell,' and a notable diminution ensued in the time he could spend with his wife.

It was in June of 1844, that she ventured on a visit to her relatives and friends in Liverpool and that neighbourhood. The winter had again been very depressing. In the March preceding, Carlyle had anxieties about his beloved old mother, and made touching entries in his Journal as to her possible decline. The more slowly advancing decay ever beside him, he failed to see. His 'eyes were holden'! 'Jane,' he says, 'gets better in the bright weather. All is bright here.' But these words were in a letter to cheer his mother. In his Journal he says on May 8: 'My progress in "Cromwell" is frightful. . . . A thousand times have I regretted that this task was ever taken up. . . . I am oftenest very sad.' And so the double sadness went on in these two lives, and other hope was utterly vain.

After a most trying journey Mrs. Carlyle arrived at her uncle's house in Maryland Street, Liverpool, and met the most cordial welcome, but tells her husband that, 'instead of being able to feel glad to see them, something twisted itself about my throat and across my breast, as if I were going to be strangled, and I could get no breath without screaming.' It was at this house that she had met the news of her mother's death. With a not unnatural womanly wilfulness, Mrs. Carlyle wished her husband to miss her presence at Cheyne Row, and rejoiced at the written tokens of this, adding, 'It is curious how much more uncomfortable *I* feel without *you!* I am always wondering, since I came here, how I can, even in my angriest mood talk about leaving you for good and all; for if I were to leave you to-day on that principle I should need absolutely to go back to-morrow to see how you were taking it.'

July 11 found her at Seaforth House, with the Paulets,

whence she wrote lovingly to her husband, over whose birthday gift to her she had 'cried and laughed,' longing to give him 'an emphatic kiss' by way of thanks.

The end of September she was again in her Chelsea home, and Carlyle proceeded on his first visit to the Grange, where Lady Harriet Baring was staying with her father, Lord Ashburton, while Mrs. Carlyle was much occupied with kindly and heroic ministrations to the unfortunate Plattnauer, an anxious guest. Her influence on this man was remarkable, though she herself barely alludes to it, and none can ever know what he owed to her. But it was a dull and joyless time for Mrs. Carlyle, unenlivened, to any appreciable extent, by all the brilliant society that now flocked around her.

The visit to the Grange was soon over, and some fragments from her own note-books, destroyed by herself for the most part, give an idea of her life up to the summer of 1845, when she again visited 'uncle John' and the Paulets. She seems as impatient as ever with the commonplace order of things around her, complains of 'the eternal smell of roast meat' in that hospitable household, and comforts herself in her misery by the reflection that perhaps 'others are more to be pitied that they are *not* miserable.' 'Somehow *I*, "as one solitary individual," would rather remain in hell —the hell I make for myself with my restless *digging*—than accept this drowsy placidity.' This theory, Mrs. Carlyle certainly and most inevitably carried out. We would not 'hear her enemy say so,' but a more thorough and absolute judgment was never made. Her brains 'tormented her' by her own confession. '*But what to do?*' Could Carlyle or any other have helped her materially? We think not. Perhaps a quiet cigarette with Miss Jewsbury, who really loved her, was her greatest solace at this time. A game of chess with Mr. Paulet was also soothing, and she had still spirit enough to sign herself to Carlyle—'Your own *adorable wife.*'

Carlyle was now himself coming north—his wife returning to London. She had written him an angry letter about his changes of plan, and had promptly repented. On August 20 she writes to him, 'husbands are so obtuse. They do not understand one's movements of impatience' want always to be treated with the respect due to genius; exact common-sense of their poor wives, rather than "the finer sensibilities of the heart;" and so the marriage state . . "has come to what ye see "—if not to immortal smash as yet, at least to within a hair's breadth of it.'

By the middle of September the 'Cromwell' was finished, and Carlyle, having spent some few days at Seaforth, went to his own people, while his wife returned to Chelsea, 'to meet again,' as she writes in a letter to a friend, 'when he has had enough of peat-bog, and his platonically beloved silence. . . .' Mrs. Carlyle herself returned for another of those inexplicable 'household earthquakes,' so wearisome even in their mention, and for which she was so eminently unfitted in her weakened state. Her cousin, Helen Welsh, received her, and the visits of Mazzini and others helped her solitude. Her impressions of a grand amateur theatrical representation, got up by Dickens and Foster, with other distinguished co-adjutors, are most amusing, in her letter to Carlyle of September 23, though the evening was fatiguing. But next day a charming call from Alfred Tennyson, 'all to herself,' was one of the pleasant results of her presence on the occasion.

The serious illness of Macready was a pain to Mrs. Carlyle, as he had been present on the said occasion, and in his usual health; and hardly less terrible, in prospect of Carlyle's return, was the re-appearance of a dog which was supposed to have been 'put down' at Christmas. 'The calmness of a great despair' overcame the anxious wife at these unholy barks. 'Oh destiny accursed!' she says, 'what use of scrubbing and sorting? All this availeth nothing so long as the dog sitteth at the washerman's gate.' A skilful note put down the nuisance, and peace reigned once more. 'Thank God,' she writes, 'you still have quietude to return to.' The dog, set at large, 'behaved just like any other rational being.'

On October 7, Mrs. Carlyle writes to her husband—'Ah! my dear; yes, indeed! If I could quench the devil also, you might turn your face homewards with comparative security.' Pecuniary annoyances represent part—only a part—of the diabolic influences here alluded to, but never was more thrifty and conscientious manager than herself, and her extreme over-sensibility alone called forth this outcry.

Early in December the Carlyles paid a long-promised visit to Mr. and Lady Harriet Baring at Bay House, Alverstoke, Hants, and the first impression made on Mrs. Carlyle by her brilliant hostess was evidently a favourable one. In a letter to Mrs. Russell on returning from Bay House, she describes Lady Harriet as 'the very cleverest woman, out of sight, that I ever saw in my life (and I have seen all our " distinguished authoresses "), moreover, she is full of energy and sincerity, and has, I am sure, an excellent heart.' Yet here lay the source of a bitter and terrible alienation between the two who had so faithfully hitherto stepped beside each other in sunshine and storm. But a lull came first, and in the summer of 1846 Mrs. Carlyle again visited her Lancashire friends, being joined by Carlyle in August after his six silent weeks in Annandale. 'Sad as death,' he says, in his retrospective annotation, 'on my own and the world's confusions and perversities, and the tragedies bred there for oneself and others.'

From Seaforth Mrs. Carlyle wrote in much depression to her friend, Mrs. Russell of Thornhill, and on the 14th she writes to Carlyle, who was still at Chelsea, of her 'suffocating misery' at not having received her regular birthday letter from him. She had been to ask for the letter, and the postmistress had said there was none that day. She had walked home 'in a tumult of wretchedness.' She tells him her tormenting thoughts: 'Were you,' she writes, 'so out of patience with me that you had resolved to write to me no more at all? Had you gone to Addiscombe, and found no leisure there to remember my existence? Were you taken ill, so ill that you could not write? . . .' Some explanation is needed here. There had been deep unhappiness in the little household. Carlyle had written to a dear, trusted friend, Erskine of Linlathen, on July 11, 'My wife went off a few days since to Lancashire. She had been in a very weakly way, . . . had much need of quiet and fresh air. . . . I, too, am battered and fretted into great sorrow of heart, that will be difficult to cure in this world.'

CHAPTER XIX

A. D. 1846-1847

The dark cloud—Carlyle's anxiety—Mrs. Carlyle seeks counsel—Mazzini's honourable and noble advice—The flight to Seaforth—Birthday gift and gentle words—Renewed counsels—Renewed bitterness—Lord Houghton's estimate of Lady Harriet Baring—Contrasts—Sad thoughts—Clough's Poem—Visit to W. E. Forster—Again at Addiscombe — Hopeless misunderstanding—The healing of the wound rendered impossible.

ALTHOUGH Carlyle attributed his consuming and constant discontent partly to ' the nature of the beast,' we know that he had much to try him, to try *any* man, at this special time. A thick cloud of wretchedness had followed a visit paid by Mrs. Carlyle to Addiscombe. She had returned, as she said, 'with a mind all churned to froth,' and after most painful scenes, had fled to the Paulets at Seaforth and failed to report her safe arrival. Carlyle wrote in alarm: ' My dear,' he said, ' I hope it is only displeasure, or embarrassed estrangement from me, that robs me of a note this morning. I will not torment myself. Perhaps an unfriendly letter would be worse. Never have we parted so before, and all for *nothing!* Adieu, dearest, for that is always your title, if madness prevail not. Do not doubt of me, do not yield to the Enemy of us all, and may God bless thee always!'

But Mrs. Carlyle had been too deeply stirred, and, before leaving London, had taken the strong step of consulting a justly esteemed friend, Mazzini, at this painful crisis. His replies shew how nobly worthy he was of the critical confidence. 'Awake, arise, dear friend!' he writes. ' Beset by pain we must go on, with a sad smile and a practical encouragement from one another. Your life proves an empty thing, you say! Empty? Have you never done good? Have you never loved? Think of your mother, and do good. Set the eye to Providence. It is not a piece of irony that God has placed you here; can't you trust Him a little longer?'

Again, on July 13, after receiving some gentle words from his wife, Carlyle wrote enclosing his faithfully-remembered birthday present, this time a little card-case with tender messages. 'Accept my little gift,' he writes, 'and kiss it as I have done.' The letter, with its enclosure, had been overlooked, and it was the delay of two hours in its delivery which called forth the painful words we have quoted. When once safely in her hand, she again writes to her husband, ' I wonder what love-letter was ever received with such thankfulness?'

... 'Yes,' she continues, 'I have kissed the dear little card-case; and now I will lie down awhile and try to get some sleep, at least to quiet myself. Oh! why cannot I believe it, once for all, that, with all my faults and follies, I am "dearer to you than any earthly creature"?' (this last phrase, by the way, originally quoted from one of Cromwell's letters to his wife).

Mrs. Carlyle had again written to Mazzini, and again received honourable and gentle counsel. On July 15 he wrote to her: 'Yes! Sad as death; but not basely sad. ... You believe in God; don't you think, after all, that this is nothing but an ephemeral trial, and that He will shelter you to your journey's end under the wide wing of His paternal love?

You had, have, though invisible to the eyes of the body, your mother, your father, too. Can't you commune with them? I know that a single moment of true fervent love for them will do more for you than all my talking! Were they now what you call living, would you not fly to them, hide your head in their bosom and be comforted, and feel that you owe to them to be strong—that they may never feel ashamed of their own Jane? Why, can you think them to be *dead*, gone for ever, their loving immortal souls annihilated? Can you think that this vanishing for a time has made you less responsible to them? *Can you, in a word, love them less because they are far from sight?* I have often thought that the arrangement by which loved and loving beings are to pass through death is nothing but the last experiment appointed by God to human love; and often, as you know from me, I have felt that a moment of true soul-communing with my dead friend was opening a source of strength for me unhoped for, down here. Did we not often agree about these glimpses of the link between ours and the superior life? Shall we now begin to disagree? Be strong then, and true to those you loved, and proud, nobly proud in the eyes of those you love or esteem. Some of them are deeply, silently suffering, but needing strength too, needing it perhaps from you. Get up and work; do not set yourself apart from us. When the Evil One wanted to tempt Jesus, he led Him into a solitude. Believe me, my dear friend, ever yours,

JOSEPH MAZZINI.

This sympathy could not root out the deep pain from her heart, but no words could have been wiser, had she but known.

This time was an eminently dreamy one for Mrs. Carlyle. On hearing of the death of the old minister at Auchtertool, and of her cousin Walter Welsh's succession to the appointment thus suddenly vacated, she writes to Mr. Carlyle—

What a mighty problem we make about our bits of lives, and Death as surely on the way to cut us out of 'all that,' at least, whatever may come after . . . one may go a far way in scepticism; may get to disbelieve in God and the devil, in virtue and in vice, in love, in one's own soul; never to speak of time and space, progress of the species, rights of women, greatest happiness of the greatest number, 'isms,' world without end; everything, in short, that the human mind ever believed in, or 'believed that it believed in'; only not in death. The most outrageous sceptic even I, after two nights without sleep—cannot go ahead against that fact—a rather cheering one on the whole—that, let one's earthly difficulties be what they may, death will make them all smooth sooner or later, and either one shall have a trial at existing again under new conditions, or sleep soundly through all eternity. That last used to be a horrible thought for me, but it is not so any longer. I am weary, weary to such a point of moral exhaustion, that any anchorage were welcome, even the stillest, coldest, where the wicked should cease from troubling, and the weary be at rest, understanding both by the wicked and the weary *myself*.

Carlyle had, as he says, left home, not guessing at all how ill she was. How should he guess? He had no means of guessing; no clue to the desolation of that heart of hers!

From Liverpool Mrs. Carlyle went on to Miss Jewsbury's quiet place in Manchester, and this faithful friend ministered, as she best knew how, to the storm-tossed spirit and exhausted frame. Nor was the task an ungrateful one, for her guest writes on August 23: 'It has brought back something like color into my face and something like calm into my heart. . . .'

From Scotsbrig Carlyle took a short trip to Ireland, Dublin, Belfast &c., while what he calls 'a sordid form of servile chaos' went on in the house at Cheyne Row. After eight years, the valued, though not faultless domestic, 'Kirkcaldy Helen,' had left the Carlyles, and the presence of 'a temporary servant' seems to have driven the little household almost to despair. The return of Helen on probation, ended in 'open and incurable drunkenness,' and once more, in December 1846, Mrs. Carlyle was wretched in her domestic arrangements, was herself three weeks ill in bed with a doctor daily attending her, and quite worn out with what she calls, in a letter to Mrs. Sterling (Susan Hunter), 'the disgusting history.' It was clearly a case wherein 'the patient must minister to herself,' and as the real cause of suffering lay deeper than in the short-comings of servant-girls; it may be well to say something here of the undoubted sorrow caused to Mrs. Carlyle by Carlyle's friendship with Lady Harriet Baring, afterwards Lady Ashburton.

Carlyle was fastidious, and his most attractive opening into literary society was through the Ashburtons. Had he neglected to follow up this opportunity, London society might, in consequence of his own peculiarities, have been in some sense closed to him. As guest in that house, he met on equal terms many distinguished men of rank and letters, and though he may have spoken of them afterwards in ludicrously caustic and severe terms, he was perfectly alive to the advantage of meeting them. Lady Ashburton, on her part, a happy, brilliant, and ambitious woman, prominent in the best society in town, naturally courted the presence at her frequent social gatherings of Thomas Carlyle, one of the 'lions' of the day, one whose crude and startling originality gave to her evenings a flavour unattainable elsewhere. And it was interesting and 'piquant,' no doubt, to outsiders, to hear this hostess, with her own marked individuality, speak in sparkling and unfettered terms, drawing forth yet more unbridled rejoinders from Carlyle.

Lord Houghton's short memorial of Lady Ashburton in 'Monographs' is most interesting to those who care about the Carlyles. Prefaced by an admirable portrait, and written with a sincere admiration and that chivalry with which the writer would be sure to treat of a woman's characteristics—it does not impress us favourably; and very little penetration is needed to convince the thoughtful reader that those two natures were antagonistic, and could by no means amalgamate. Mrs. Carlyle had *her* peculiar characteristics, Lady Harriet Baring had *hers*. If the latter had been repressed in her childhood—as she tells Lord Houghton—the consequences were unfortunate, for as she frankly adds: 'I was constantly punished for my impertinence, and you see the result: *I think I have made up for it since!*' And if Mrs. Carlyle had been an idolised only child, as she had been, she 'made up for it' in another way, and, in her acutely sensitive state, felt pain where no pain was intended, and bitterly resented that 'demeanour of superiority' shown by Lady Harriet Baring to others than to herself, to none, surely, in whom it evoked more irretrievable suffering.

The invitations to Bath House were almost invariably to

the two—Carlyle and his wife—but were often only accepted by the former, who, utterly unconscious of the harm that was being done, paid a penalty out of all proportion to the fancied slight—as any one will admit who reads the letters and journals of Mrs. Carlyle, written during the twelve years of this largely imaginary, or at least avoidable, grievance. That the ' King of the Forest' should amiably show his claws and be put through his paces in the drawing-rooms of Bath House, to a crowd of admiring and sometimes curious guests, was, no doubt, very gratifying to Lady Harriet and her friends. The other side of the question, none the less natural, is, that Mrs. Carlyle, who had clung to her husband through the hard, lonely days of obscurity and non-success, having held him up by her unfailing belief in his powers, and given health and strength lavishly, to make his path smooth for him—now began to feel as if, after all, it were not she who reaped the golden harvest of his rapidly growing success, but this brilliant and fashionable lady, whom she could not feel to be her superior intellectually, and who knew none of the dark, terrible, sunless hours spent in the Chelsea home, when a despair of all things cast at times so real and so tangible a cloud over the married pair. Poverty had been hard, loneliness had been hard, but these she could bear, the other she could *not* bear.

To speak of jealousy in any ordinary sense of the word, would be manifestly absurd; but the burden was heavy, and a long period of cutting sorrow ensued. We can only pity, with a true and tender pity, so much wretchedness. A less womanly woman would have suffered less, but here was one eminently feminine to the heart's core, and persistently craving those little marks of tenderness so dear to woman, so outstripping all that the most splendid genius can do, in the way of rendering a woman's life sweet, harmonious, and altogether acceptable.

We do not blame Carlyle. Even with that mother whom he so dearly loved, the intercourse was mainly composed of a silent sitting by the fireside of an evening, in the old 'house-place,' with a tranquillising pipe of tobacco, or of his returning from his long rambles to a simple meal, partaken of in comparative silence; and now and then, at meeting or parting, some pious and earnest words from the good soul to her son. And how can we expect that it could dawn on him to be different with this eager, passionate-hearted wife! He could not know it; and she could not teach him. At one time, dyspeptic and pre-occupied, he took to dining alone, hoping to avert digestive difficulties, but it followed that Mrs. Carlyle also dined alone—a dreary arrangement for her; for even in handing the salt to a woman, both tenderness and courtesy may be shown, which shall make that trifling action almost a caress.

There is a short poem by the late Arthur Hugh Clough —that fine and gentle spirit—which has always associated itself, to our thinking, with the position of this married pair. We quote the poem in this place as intensely expressive. Its appropriateness will at once strike the reader.

Qua cursum Ventus.

As ships, becalmed at eve, that lay
   With canvas drooping, side by side,
Two towers of sail at dawn of day
   Are scarce, long leagues apart, descried;

When fell the night, upsprung the breeze,
   And all the darkling hours they plied,
Nor dreamt but each the self-same seas
   By each was cleaving, side by side:

E'en so—but why the tale reveal
   Of those whom—year by year unchanged,
Brief absence joined anew to feel,
   Astounded, soul from soul estranged?

At dead of night their sails were filled,
   And onward each rejoicing steered:—
Ah, neither blame, for neither willed,
   Or wist what first with dawn appeared!

> To veer how vain! On, onward strain,
>   Brave barks! In light, in darkness too,
> Through winds and tides, one compass guides,—
>   To that, and your own selves, be true.
>
> But O blithe breeze, and O great seas,
>   Though ne'er, that earliest parting past,
> On your wide plain they join again,
>   Together lead them home at last!
>
> One port, methought, alike they sought,
>   One purpose hold where'er they fare,—
> O bounding breeze, O rushing seas,
>   At last, at last, unite them there!

Carlyle's unconsciousness of the actual cause of his wife's pain makes us very tender in thinking of them both. In August, 1846, writing to her from Scotsbrig, he says: ' Oh, my dearest, how little I *can* make thee know of me! . . . Adieu, my own Jane, whom nothing can divide from *me*!" The silence on his wife's part that was causing Carlyle such pain, arose from a plan he had made to join the Barings, while in Scotland, on a few days' tour, Mrs. Carlyle being cordially invited to join the party. But she was in no mood to do so; and the five days given to the trip were anything but propitious. Carlyle deeply felt the coldness which was unaccountable to him, and when he did receive a letter from his wife, he was full of good resolutions and penitence. ' Home,' he writes, ' is the word, and remember one thing, to write a little oftener to me, and as near the old tone as you can come! . . .' On August 29, he writes: ' But there will come a day when all that will be intelligible again. I should be miserable if I thought there would not!' There was a blindness in the eyes of *both* these noble natures and only Death was to remove it.

It is interesting to note Mrs. Carlyle's sound and original views on ' altruism' as given in an extract of a letter from her to her cousin Helen Welsh of Liverpool, and dated

Chelsea: Jan. 20, 1847.

Dearest Helen,—One hears much fine talk in this hypocritical age about seeking and even finding one's own happiness in 'the happiness of others;' but I frankly confess to you that I, as one solitary individual, have never been able to confound the two things, even in imagination, so as not to be capable of clearly distinguishing the difference; and if every one would endeavor, as I do, to speak without cant, I believe there would be a pretty general admission on the part of sinful humanity that to eat a comfortable beef-steak when one is hungry yields a satisfaction of a much more positive character than seeing one's neighbour eat it? For the fact is, happiness is but a low thing, and there is a confusion of ideas in running after it on stilts. When Sir Philip Sidney took the water from his own parched lips to give it to the dying soldier, I could take my Bible oath that it was not happiness he felt; and that he would never have done that much-admired action if his only compensation had been the pleasure resulting to him from seeing the dying soldier drink the water; he did it because he could not help himself; because the sense of duty, of self-denial, was stronger in him at the moment than low human appetite; because the soul in him said, do it; not because utilitarian philosophy suggested that he would find his advantage in doing it, nor because Socinian dilettanteism required of him a beautiful action! . . . .

Part of January and February of 1847 was spent by the Carlyles with the Barings at Bay House, near Alverstoke, where Mrs. Carlyle was again very ill—though still able, at times, to enjoy the bright society around her. Part of August was spent at Matlock, where W. E. Forster visited the Carlyles and shewed much kindness. Responding to his pressing wish, they spent a fortnight with him at Rawdon Hall, whence Carlyle departed for Scotsbrig.

Lord Houghton remarks, with some *naïveté*: 'It was with no disregard of her sex that Lady Ashburton (as she had then become) preferred the society of *men*.' Possibly, Mrs. Carlyle may have shared this preference, but the visits to the Barings certainly gave no pleasure or profit to *her*, and the long years up to 1857, when Lady Ashburton died, were among the hardest in the life of Mrs. Carlyle—awakening in her a quicker sense of the want in her own life, to which Carlyle was blind, and which she felt all the more while he sought the society of Lady Ashburton, in his own simplicity and absence of all knowledge of the pain he caused. This sorrow as to the intercourse with the Baring family was a constant fret to the lonely wife. It shewed sometimes in a silent bitterness—sometimes in still more bitter utterances. It would have been as nothing had essentials been different.

July 15, 1847, was another of Mrs. Carlyle's now dreaded birthday anniversaries. Gifts and loving tokens, including a brooch from Carlyle, had caused her to ' fall a-crying: ' there were too many sad associations mixed up with the little festival. She describes herself to Helen Welsh as ' unable to sleep or eat, hardly able to sit upright,' and adds that her husband urges her to try a change to Haddington, where the kind Misses Donaldson would receive her with open arms. She speaks of herself as 'already worn out' with the effort of writing the letter. This ended in a week's visit to the Grange, where Mrs. Carlyle's health continued very feeble, and again the year ended in discouragement. Mr. Froude has told the whole story of that unhappy year with truth and admirable delicacy, and it would be idle to do other than refer the reader to his 'Carlyle's Life in London,' vol. i., chapter xiv., where every detail is given. It only remains to say: ' Oh, the pity of it !—the pity of it !'

The painful subject was tacitly left, unhealed, but for the most part held in the background—no open breach of the friendly footing was admitted—but that is often the very worst way of curing an evil, easier at the moment, possibly, but entailing untold complications later on. September, therefore, found Mrs. Carlyle at Cheyne Row again; her husband still at Scotsbrig. Old Mr. Sterling had died, and Mrs. Carlyle describes herself to John Forster as ' a sadder and a wiser woman.' So the year closed sadly enough; though the anxiety of poverty had been some time removed, a deeper care had taken its place! And still the kindly visits of friends failed to cheer the drooping spirit; outside sources of pleasure and interest could not lighten the cloud which weighed on Mrs. Carlyle.

Lady Harriet Baring did not mend matters by well-meant assiduities: her medical emissary, Dr. Fleming, gravely assuring the delicate and suffering Mrs. Carlyle that Lady Harriet considered she had brought all her illness by 'unheard-of imprudence in diet.' But this did not prevent Mrs. Carlyle from again visiting Lady Harriet Baring at Addiscombe, a step surely taken to please Carlyle. She returned to Cheyne Row on October 1, writing to Carlyle 'before starting,' lest she should be too ill to do so immediately on her return, and knowing he would be anxious about his poor 'Goody.' We cannot resist the thought that a continual correspondence *from a distance*, during some of these sad years, would have been no imperfect substitute for personal intercourse between this married pair. Carlyle feeling that Lady Harriet was the most considerate of hostesses, must have been pained by his wife's embittered account of the short visit to that house where *he* felt himself at ease.

The selfish indifference of one of Lady Harriet's housemaids left Mrs. Carlyle, unable to light her bedroom fire. Chilly and feeble as she was, this was a cruel neglect. It cannot be supposed that the hostess knew anything of this discomfort, but the effect was equally painful. Lady Harriet, however, always thought Mrs. Carlyle needed '*bracing*,' instead of the tenderest care at all times. The delicate woman keenly felt that her frequent ailing was treated as 'hypochondria,' and this was certainly an erroneous supposition, and galling to a high spirit. It is painful to find Mrs. Carlyle saying, in a letter to her husband, 'When I look at my white, white face in the glass, I wonder how anyone can believe I am fancying!'

CHAPTER XX

A. D. 1847-1849

Return to Cheyne Row—Renewed illness—Bitter reflections—Disappointment—Confidences to Uncle John Welsh—A winter's visit of Carlyle to the Barings—Mrs. Carlyle remaining at Cheyne Row—Remonstrances of Miss Jewsbury—Long illness of Mrs. Carlyle—Consultations with John Forster—Visit to Addiscombe—Death of Lord Ashburton—Carlyle's tour in Ireland—The forgotten plaid—Mrs. Carlyle visits Lady Harriet Baring (now Lady Ashburton) at Alverstoke—Brilliant society but no sleep—Death of John Sterling—Declining health of Jeffrey—Haddington—Betty Braid, the 'old nurse'—Scenes of childhood revisited—'Matthew Baillie'—Mrs. Carlyle visits her father's grave—Sunny Bank—Sad and loving meetings—'Old Jamie'—Manchester and Miss Jewsbury—Illness of Helen Welsh of Liverpool.

MRS. CARLYLE returned home only to fall ill again, and was too weary at the end of a week's so-called '*rest*,' to be able to bear to listen to the lengthy discussions of Mazzini and Dr. John Carlyle on the subject of 'Dante,' and speaks of 'sending them both away together'; a sign that much was amiss, as the brilliant, versatile woman could certainly have turned the talk into what direction she pleased, had she not been exhausted in mind and body, disheartened, indifferent.

A call from Lady Harriet Baring gave some slight satisfaction. On October 9 Mrs. Carlyle says, speaking of this visit: 'I could not but think from her manner that she had bethought her I had been rather roughly handled on my last visit.' It may have been so, but where the prosperous and the unhappy are brought into any sort of forced intercourse, every touch is a wound.

In November of 1847 Mrs. Carlyle writes an unusually sharp and biting letter to John Forster. The causes of bitterness were various and so potent, as to draw from the writer the half-jesting determination of *suiciding* herself. Inability, from illness, to go to Notting Hill to see a bust of Carlyle, then in progress, makes her say, 'Unfeeling as it looked to let myself be withheld by any weather from going to see my husband's bust, I thought it would really be more unfeeling to risk an inflammation in my husband's wife's chest, which makes my husband's wife such a nuisance, as you, an unmarried man, can hardly figure.' Then, she writes it with tears in her eyes, she cannot go to the theatre on Monday, whither Forster was to take them, and, most serious of all, Carlyle was furious at her looking over 'proofs' of a novel by her friend, Geraldine Jewsbury, declaring that she did not know bad grammar when she saw it any better than Miss Jewsbury did, and that if she had any faculty, she might find better employment for it, etc. This last was hard to bear, for Mrs. Carlyle had a finished and remarkable literary style of her own, and would have made a brilliant use of it, had she not, from the first, been overshadowed by the towering genius and exacting personality of her husband.

The middle of December 1847 finds her pouring out her sad thoughts and her flashing wit to her uncle, John Welsh, in Liverpool, having, as she tells him, 'coughed herself all to fiddle-strings in the course of a week,' and feeling 'the family affections bloom up strong.' She speaks of Miss Martineau and mesmerism in terms more striking than complimentary. Animal magnetism she calls 'a damnable sort of tempting of Providence,' from which she holds herself entirely aloof.

'In January 1848,' says Mr. Froude, 'came an indispensable visit to the Barings. Mrs. Carlyle was to have gone, and they were to have stayed four weeks, but the winter was cold; she was feeble and afraid of a chill.' Pressing invitations from Lady Harriet, and urgent letters from her husband, took no effect on her determination to remain where she was. Writing on January 17 to her husband, then at Bay House, Alverstroke, she says:

I will never, with the health I have, or rather have *not*, engage to leave home for a long fixed period another winter. . . . Besides, is not home—at least, was it not, in more earnest times—' the woman's proper sphere'? Decidedly, if she ' have nothing to keep her at home,'—as the phrase is—she should find something, or die! . . . Amusement, after a certain age, is no go; even when there are no other nullifying conditions: it gets to be merely distraction. . . . To be sure, it is hard on flesh and blood, when one has ' nothing to keep one at home,' to sit down in honest life-weariness and look out into unmitigated zero. . .

And Carlyle is writing to her, ' Why do I complain to poor thee ? . . . Only, if *you* had been strong I would have told you how very weak and wretched *I* was.' Ten days proved enough for Carlyle of the restraints of society, after which he fairly 'fled home,' and soon obtained the consolation of glimpses of future work, his only anodyne.

Mrs. Carlyle again consulted John Forster in her ' delicate embarrassment ' of not wishing Miss Jewsbury's forthcoming novel to be dedicated to herself and Mrs. Paulet, ' not wishing,' as she wrote, ' to give pain to Geraldine, still less to give offence to my husband.'

A long illness of three months closed with a visit to the Barings at Addiscombe, Carlyle being in solitude and his beloved silence at Chelsea.

How strong the link, after all, that bound this strangely assorted couple. Writing on April 13, 1848, to her husband Mrs. Carlyle says: ' I have nothing to complain of here as to diet, or hours, or noise; and I have not had one well moment, day or night, *except that day you came*.'

But all was sadly amiss with Mrs. Carlyle's health, and being left one evening alone, unexpectedly, at Addiscombe, she describes it as ' like a morphia dream '—the first mention of a drug to which, in after days, we know she was forced to resort, occasionally, under medical advice.

The return for a time of the old servant Helen, promised comfort, but all Mrs. Carlyle's charitable efforts could not rescue the girl from bad habits, which ended in 'a final crash.' She was, however, quickly and satisfactorily replaced. Mrs. Carlyle, revived in spirit, was busy making a screen covered with prints. Her fine artistic taste thus found some occupation—though she complains that books 'take no hold' on her, and that, 'being an only child,' she 'never wished to sew!'

A change had taken place at Addiscombe. The kindly old Lord had died in May, and Mr. Baring was now Lord Ashburton.

It was in July of this year, 1849, that Carlyle went for a six weeks' tour in Ireland.* His wife had seen him off on his journey, then went home and cried a little, then found he had left his plaid behind in the bustle of departure. It was a chilly day, and after a frantic desire to plunge into the water and swim after him with the plaid in her mouth, she had dismissed the idea, proceeded to the kitchen, and silently boiled her strawberries, like a practical woman. She then betook herself to Bath House,† to accompany Lady Harriet, now Lady Ashburton, to Addiscombe, driving thither in an open carriage, and arriving, 'shivering with cold, excessively low, and so vexed about the plaid. No sympathy there! thank God! . . . All day I was fancying you shivering like myself.'

A brilliant house-party was now assembled at Addiscombe, none wittier among that company than was Mrs. Carlyle herself, who paid for her bright sallies by insomnia and headache, and complained of the 'tearing spirits' everyone was in! when, her short visit over, she had some of these lively spirits in to afternoon tea. Too tired to keep another engagement of her own, she 'read the new Copperfield,' but had talked too much for sleep.

A visit to W. E. Forster, *en route* for Auchtertool, occurs on July 20, and Mrs. Carlyle's account of her experiences at

---

* Carlyle had sailed from London on June 30, 1849, for Dublin on his Irish tour.

† The town-house of the Ashburtons.

Ben Rhydding will be read in its place. That eager, nerve-tortured frame was a bad subject for 'packing.'

It was on July 17, 1849, that Carlyle, then at Cork, ended a long and interesting letter to his wife: 'Adieu, dear Jeannie. O adieu! My heart and head are very weary; in all dispiritment I turn (as by old want) to *you*! . . . This birthday I was among the Knockmeledown mountains, . . . and could send my dear Goody no gift—only wishes, wishes!' And only three days later his wife ended her letter to him, with the words, 'God bless you! All to be said worth the saying lies in that!' The shadows had begun to fall thickly on this pathway, never a sunny one; the beloved and loyal John Sterling had died in September of 1844, and now the kind Jeffrey was fast fading away.

Carlyle had spent an unsettled and mainly joyless summer, while Mrs. Carlyle had gone on from her cousin's, at Auchtertool Manse, Kirkcaldy, to Haddington, saddest and dearest of places to her, unvisited now by her for twenty-three years; indeed, ever since her marriage. There was for her a solemn gladness in the midst of all the newly-awakened pain; but Carlyle was 'hag-ridden': a miserable few days at Auchtertool, where he stopped to see his wife, was followed by a most uncomfortable visit to the Ashburtons in a Highland shooting-box, Glen Truin,* and he again fled to Scotsbrig. But even the peaceful influences there failed to give him rest, so utterly was he 'out of tune.'

While he was on this visit, his wife wrote to him from the hospitable roof of the Misses Donaldson, at Sunny Bank, Haddington, and wrote of 'headache and heartache,' which attended her even in that charmed circle. The meeting between her and old Betty Braid, as given in the 'Letters and Memorials,' is most touching. It was something for the weary, sad woman to sit on her old nurse's knee and be called her 'dear bairn!' She called also on three of her father's

* Lord Ashburton's deer-hunting station, in Macpherson of Cluny's country.

sisters, Elizabeth, Ann, and Grace Welsh. Mrs. Carlyle tells us that they were 'unlike him.' She would never have admitted the claim of any mortal to be *like* him.

But the real significance of the Haddington visit lay in Mrs. Carlyle's intensely sorrowful revisiting of old scenes of her childhood—as told in the narrative from her leaving Rawdon, when she looked so ill that W. E. Forster insisted on accompanying her to Morpeth, where she had arranged to spend the night, to her actual arrival at Sunny Bank. A new morning 'bright as diamonds,' followed the drizzling day of the journey, and in conversation with W. E. Forster, Mrs. Carlyle, in a quiet walk which rendered her 'unusually communicative,' spoke of the fact that her maternal grandmother was 'descended from a gang of gipsies '—was, in fact, grand-niece to Mathew Baillie, who 'suffered at Lanark,' that is, was hanged there, and this fact, told probably in a spirit of playfulness, was felt by Forster as 'a genealogical fact,' which made Mrs. Carlyle at length intelligible to him: 'a cross between John Knox and a gipsy.' ' By the way,' she adds, ' my uncle has since told me that the wife of that Mathew Baillie, Margaret Euston by name, was the original of Sir Walter Scott's "Meg Merrilies."' Whatever of gipsy ' strain' was attributed to Mrs. Carlyle, and justly, as we think, she was none the less tender-hearted, loving, sensitive, to an uncommon degree.

The emotions of that Haddington visit were overpowering. Arrived at her journey's end, July 25, 1849, she says:—

There I was at the end of it ! Actually in the 'George Inn,' Haddington, alone, amidst the silence of death !

I sat down quite composedly at a window, and looked up the street toward our old house. It was the same street, the same houses; but so silent, dead, petrified ! It looked the old place just as I had seen it at Chelsea in my dreams, only more dreamlike ! Having exhausted that outlook, I rang my bell, and told the silent landlord to bring tea and take order about my bedroom. The tea swallowed down, I notified my wish to view 'the old church there,' and the keeper of the keys was immediately fetched me. In my part of Stranger in search of the Picturesque, I let myself be shown the way which I knew every inch of, shown 'the school-house' where myself had been Dux, 'the playground,' 'the boolin' green,' and so on to the church-gate; which, so soon as my guide had unlocked for me, I told him he might wait, that I needed him no further.

The churchyard had become very full of graves; within the ruin were two new smartly got-up tombs. *His** looked old, old; was surrounded by nettles: the inscription all over moss, except two lines which had been quite recently cleared—by whom? Who had been there before me, still caring for his tomb after twenty-nine years? The old ruin knew, and could not tell me. That place felt the very centre of eternal silence—silence and sadness, world without end! When I returned, the sexton, or whatever he was, asked, 'Would I not walk through the church?' I said 'Yes,' and he led the way, but without playing the cicerone any more; he had become pretty sure there was no need. Our pew looked to have never been new-lined since we occupied it; the green cloth was become all but white from age! I looked at it in the dim twilight till I almost fancied I saw my beautiful mother in her old corner, and myself, a bright-looking girl, in the other! It was time to 'come out of that!' Meaning to return to the churchyard next morning, to clear the moss from the inscription, I asked my conductor where he lived—with his key. 'Next door to the house that was Dr. Welsh's,' he answered, with a sharp glance at my face; then added gently, 'Excuse me, me'm, for mentioning that, but the minute I set eyes on ye at the "George," I jaloosed it was her we all looked after whenever she went up or down.' 'You won't tell of me?' I said, crying, like a child caught stealing apples; and gave him half-a-crown to keep my secret, and open the gate for me at eight next morning. Then, turning up the waterside by myself, I made the circuit of The Haugh, Dodd's Gardens, and Babbie's Butts, the customary evening walk in my teens; and, except that it was perfectly solitary (in the whole round I met just two little children walking hand in hand, like the Babes of the Wood), the whole thing looked exactly as I left it twenty-three years back;

* Her father's.

the very puddles made by the last rain I felt to have stepped over before. But where were all the the living beings one used to meet? What could have come to the place to strike it so dead? I have been since answered—the railway had come to it, and ruined it. At all rates 'it must have taken a great deal to make a place so dull as that!' Leaving the lanes, I now went boldly through the streets, the thick black veil, put on for the occasion, thrown back; I was getting confident that I might have ridden like the Lady Godiva through Haddington, with impunity, so far as recognition went. I looked through the sparred door of our old coach-house, which seemed to be vacant; the house itself I left over till morning, when its occupants should be asleep! Passing a cooper's shop, which I had once had the run of, I stept in and bought two little quaighs; then in the character of travelling Englishwoman, suddenly seized with an unaccountable passion for wooden dishes, I questioned the cooper as to the past and present of his town. He was the very man for me, being ready to talk the tongue small in his head about his town's-folks—men, women, and children of them. He told me, amongst other interesting things, 'Doctor Welsh's death was the sorest loss ever came to the place,' that myself went away into England and—died there!' adding a handsome enough tribute to my memory. 'Yes! Miss Welsh! he remembered her famously, used to think her the tastiest young lady in the whole place; but she was very—not just to call proud—very reserved in her company.' In leaving this man I felt more than ever like my own ghost; if I had been walking after my death and burial, there could not, I think, have been any material difference in my speculations.

My next visit was to the front gate of Sunny Bank, where I stood some minutes, looking up at the beautifully quiet house; not unlike the 'outcast Peri' done into prose. How would my old godmother and the others have looked, I wondered, had they known who was there so near them? I longed to go in and kiss them once more, but positively dared not; I felt that their demonstrations of affection would break me down in a torrent of tears, which there was no time for; so I contented myself with kissing the gate (!), and returned to my inn, it being now near dark. Surely it was the silentest inn on the planet! not a living being, male or female, to be seen in it except when I rang my bell, and then the landlord or waiter (both old men) did my bidding promptly and silently, and vanished again into space. On my re-entrance I rang for candles, and for a glass of sherry and hot water; my feet had been wetted amongst the long grass of the churchyard, and I felt to be taking cold; so I made myself negus as an antidote, and they say I am not a practical woman ! Then it struck me I would write to Mr. Carlyle one more letter from the old place, after so much come and gone. Accordingly I wrote till the town clock (the first familiar voice I had heard) struck eleven, then twelve; and, near one, I wrote the Irish address on my letter, and finally put myself to bed—in the 'George Inn' of Haddington, good God ! I thought it too strange and mournful a position for ever falling asleep in; nevertheless, I slept in the first instance, for I was 'a-weary a-weary,' body and soul of me !

.   .   .   .

In the earliest morning she haunted the place, finding it hard to believe the people were 'only asleep, and not dead'— 'Non omnis moriar '—truly, while such warm emotion flowed and overflowed this tender heart, there was still vital force in the dead past, however lifeless the present had become !

The touching meeting with the old ladies at Sunny Bank came off next day, when, with heart thumping 'like, like anything,' the delicate woman went through the ordeal of a welcome of love and tears, and, finally, an attached old man-servant, once with Dr. Welsh, now ostler at the George, called to see Mrs. Carlyle. 'And I threw my arms around his neck—that did I,' says Mrs. Carlyle, while 'he stood quite passive and pale, with great tears rolling down.' And by and by the omnibus took the traveller to the railway, and she was 'back into the present,' as she says, with the keen and almost disastrous emotions of the last few days left behind, and cousin Jeannie (now Mrs. Chrystal) to welcome her to Edinburgh, 10 Clarence Street, whence to her aunt's for a few days, a brief visit to Scotsbrig, and then home to Chelsea.

The holiday had been unfavourable in many ways, and

from Liverpool, on her way home, Mrs. Carlyle writes to her husband on September 14—he being still at Scotsbrig—in depressed spirits. She was, however, to have the happiness of seeing Miss Jewsbury in Green-heys, Manchester, before her actual return to Chelsea, and there would be much unburdening of the heart in the visit. The Liverpool visit was unusually sad from the fact that Helen Welsh was in hopelessly ill health. 'She protests that she is getting better,' writes Mrs. Carlyle, 'but there is death in her face.'

CHAPTER XXI

A. D. 1849–1851.

Introduction to James Anthony Froude—Arthur Clough—Spedding —Froude's impressions—Mutual loneliness of the Carlyles—Mrs. Carlyle's letter to Mrs. Aitken—Note to John Forster—Visit to The Grange by Carlyle—' Nero ' and ' Shandy '—Nero's letter— Failing ideals—Society felt to be hard work by Mrs. Carlyle— Latter Day Pamphlets concluded—Carlyle in Wales—Renewed household ' earthquakings ' at 5 Cheyne Row—Failing strength of Mrs. Carlyle—Sad thoughts—Fruitless regrets and good resolutions.

THE month of June 1849 had been marked by a very important event, which we cannot pass over here. For it was early in this year—before Carlyle's Irish tour—that Carlyle made the acquaintance of James Anthony Froude, that acquaintance which was so soon to ' enter the region, and take the place, with the things that cannot die.' The first introduction had been made through Arthur Hugh Clough, who, we believe, left Oxford about the same time as Mr. Froude, and whose poems, few as they are, remain to show how brilliant a genius and how noble a nature were comparatively prematurely extinguished.

The ' Sage of Chelsea ' was, at this time, about fifty-four years old (we quote from Mr. Froude), ' tall, upright, beardless, the eyes, which became lighter with age, of a deep violet, with fire burning at the bottom of them, which flashed out at the least excitement.'

Mr. Froude, who was accompanied by his friend Spedding, describes this first visit, on a June evening, when, the talk in the garden ended, Mrs. Carlyle gave them tea indoors. Mr. Froude says, ' Her features were not regular, but I thought I had never seen a more interesting looking woman. Her hair was raven black, her eye dark, soft, sad, with dangerous light in them. Carlyle's talk was rich, full, and scornful; hers delicately mocking. She was fond of Spedding, and kept up a quick, sparkling conversation with him, telling stories at her husband's expense, at which he laughed himself as heartily as we did.' This graphic description gives our readers the best possible account of these remarkable people, as they appeared at this time. *Beneath* lay the depths yet to be sounded by that friend.

Carlyle, writing in his journal of that same year says, 'How lonely am I now grown in the world; how hard, ... all the old tremulous affection lies in me, but it is as if frozen. So mocked, and scourged, and driven mad by contradictions, it has, as it were, lain down in a kind of iron sleep. . . . God help me! God soften me again!' A piercing cry this from a man's heart.

And Mrs. Carlyle, writing about the same time to the good mother-in-law at Scotsbrig, says: 'The settling down at home after all these wanderings has been a serious piece of work for both Mr. C—— and myself; for me, I have only managed it by a large consumption of morphia. . . . My visit to Scotsbrig was the one in which I had the most unmixed satisfaction; for along with my pleasure at Haddington and Edinburgh, there was almost more pain than I could bear!'

A kind letter from Mrs. Aitken, of Dumfries, written in the same month, brought a reply which must be given here:

To Mrs. Aitken, Dumfries.

5 Cheyne Row: October, 1849.

My dear Jane,—Your letter was one of the letters that one feels a desire to answer the instant one is done reading it—an out-of-the-heart letter, that one's own heart (if one happen to have one) jumps to meet. But writing, with Mr. C. waiting for his tea, was, as you will easily admit, a moral impossibility; and after tea there were certain accursed flannel shirts (Oh! the alterations that have been made on them!) to 'piece!' and yesterday, when I made sure of writing you a long letter, I had a headache, and durst not either write or read, for fear of having to go to bed with it. To-day, I write; but with no leisure, though I have no 'small clothes' to make—nor any disturbance in that line (better for me if I had); still I get into as great bustles, occasionally, as if I were the mother of a fine boisterous family.

Did you hear that I found bugs in my red bed on my return? I, who go mad where a bug is! and that bed 'such an harbour for them'—as the upholsterer said! Of course, I had it pulled in pieces at once, and the curtains sent to the dyeing—at immense expense—and ever since I have been lying in the cold nights between four tall, bare posts, feeling like a patient in a London hospital. To-day, at last, two men are here putting up my curtains, and making mistakes whenever I stay many minutes away from them; and as soon as their backs are turned, I have to go off several miles in an omnibus to see Thackeray, who has been all but dead, and is still confined to his room, and who has written a line to ask me to come and see him. And I have a great sympathy always with, and show all the kindness in my power to, sick people—having so much sickness myself, and knowing how much kindness then is gratifying to me.

So, you see, dear, it is not the right moment for writing you the letter that is lying in my heart for you. But I could not, under any circumstances, refrain from telling you that your letter was very, very welcome; that the tears ran down my face over it—though Mr. C. was sitting opposite, and would have scolded me for 'sentimentality,' if he had seen me crying over kind words merely; and that I have read it three times, and carried it in my pocket ever since I got it, though my rule is to burn all letters! Oh, yes! *there is no change in me*, so far as affection goes, depend upon that! But there are other changes, which give me the look of a very cold and hard woman generally!

I durst not let myself talk to you at Scotsbrig, and, now that the opportunity is passed, I almost wish I had! But I think it not likely, if I live, that I will be long of returning to Scotland. All that true, simple, pious kindness that I found stored up for me there, ought to be turned to more account in my life. What have I more precious?

Please burn this letter—I mean, don't hand it to the rest; there is a circulation of letters in families that frightens me from writing often: it is so dificult to write a circular to one!

... For me, I am really better; though I may say, in passing, that Mr. C.'s 'decidedly stronger' is never to be depended on in any account he gives of me, as, so long as I can stand on my legs, he never notices that anything ails me: and I make a point of never complaining to him unless in case of absolute extremity. But I have, for the last week, been sleeping pretty well, and able to walk again, which I had not been up to since my return.

About the bonnet: send it by any opportunity you find, just as it is: I can trim very nicely myself, and, perhaps, might not like Miss Montgomery's colour. But I cannot have it for nothing, dear! If Miss G. won't take money, I must find some other way of paying her.

God bless you, dear Jane, and all yours! Remember me to James: and never doubt my affection for yourself, as I shall never doubt yours for me.

Ever,
J. W. C.*

In this letter Mrs. Carlyle delineated herself truly when she said, 'There is no change in me, so far as affection goes. ... But there are *other* changes.' There were changes unseen by mortal eye, but telling their stern record to the Unseen Listener perhaps! There may have been, at this time, a desperate longing after a fuller life—an impatience of discordant and hopeless realities—the 'Shall I go on, or no?' so simply written, but the fruit of such complicated difficulties in human lives. Unchanged in her old attachments and her lasting powers of tenderness, she certainly was.

Thackeray, who had been dangerously ill, had asked Mrs. Carlyle to come and see him; and she, sick and suffering herself, was promptly setting out on the kind errand.

Mrs. Aitken's letter had brought the tears to Mrs.

---

* See 'Letters and Memorials,' Vol. II. Letter 117.

Carlyle's eyes. She spoke truly as to many outward manifestations; but our own opinion, founded no less upon these letters than on intimate conversation with many who knew and loved her, causes us vehemently to protest against harsh judgment being formed of her. She never complained to her husband—what woman of spirit would have done so? She fought her fight out, in more or less loneliness, 'alongside' of a man who truly *loved* her, but was incapable of showing her the tenderness she needed. He himself was conscious, at times, of a want in himself, dimly and vaguely felt and never put into words. The time for *deeds* was past, while *she*, driven in on herself, was intent on doing her part, making no sign, save by scornful and bitter manifestations, which were unlikely to draw tenderness out of any man, least of all out of Thomas Carlyle!

Very characteristic is a note written by Mrs. Carlyle to John Forster in November 1849, beginning piously, 'God's will be done, dear Mr. Forster,' in regard of an invitation to meet Mr. Dickens, which Mrs. Carlyle was too ill to accept. She goes on: 'If one said otherwise, *it would do itself all the same.*' A book she here mentions as by a young authoress, is, presumably, 'John Halifax,' whose beloved and accomplished writer, afterwards Mrs. Craik, became an intimate friend of Mrs. Carlyle, as time went on. Mrs. Carlyle's comment on Miss Mulock's book, which we suppose to have been 'John Halifax,' is too significant to be passed over. Writing to Forster again in December 1849, after thanking him for the book, she says, 'It quite reminds one of one's own "love's young dream." I like it, and I like the poor girl who can still believe, or even "believe that she believes," *all that.* God help her! . . .'

About this time a much humbler element of happiness entered her saddened life, in the shape of the little dog '*Nero*,' who was an attached pet of Mrs. Carlyle's, and who lies buried in the garden at Cheyne Row, after ten years of companionship, such as dogs sometimes know how to give.

In December, Mrs. Carlyle begins a note to John Forster, 'I died ten days ago, and was buried at Kensal Green—at least, you have no certainty to the contrary. . . .' This was a reminder of an unkept promise to visit her when she needed cheering.

A sad letter to Mrs. Russell, of Thornhill, marks the last day of 1849. Nervous suffering had almost conquered the brave spirit of Jane Welsh Carlyle; she had been detained in Manchester by severe illness, when anticipating a joyful though necessarily short visit to Miss Jewsbury; and she had fallen into a lassitude, inevitable after such prolonged suffering. The little dog 'Nero' is mentioned as a relieving novelty; but the clouds drew close about that bright personality, so ready to shine out with the smallest encouragement, under circumstances that should be congenial; too few, alas! in that life so heavily handicapped.

It was in January 1850 that Carlyle paid a short visit to The Grange,—Robert Lowe, Delane (of the 'Times'), with Monckton Milnes, being the other guests. Lady Ashburton had playfully given Carlyle the designation of 'Boreas' about this time. No letter was received by him from his wife on this occasion, save the graceful and clever one written as from little Nero, which we quote from 'Letters and Memorials:'

To T. Carlyle, The Grange, Alresford, Hants.

5 Cheyne Row, Chelsea: Tuesday, Jan. 29, 1850.

Dear Master,—I take the liberty to write to you myself (my mistress being out of the way of writing to you she says) that you may know Columbine and I are quite well, and play about as usual. There was no dinner yesterday to speak of; I had for my share only a piece of biscuit that might have been round the world; and if Columbine got anything at all, I didn't see it. I made a grab at one of two 'small beings' on my mistress's plate; she called them heralds of the morn; but my mistress said, 'Don't you wish you may get it?' and boxed my ears. I wasn't taken to walk on account of its being wet. And nobody came, but a man for 'burial rate;' and my mistress gave him a rowing, because she wasn't going to be buried here at all. Columbine and I don't mind where we are buried.

This is a fine day for a run; and I hope I may be taken to see Mohe and Dumm. They are both nice well-bred dogs, and always so glad to see me; and the parrot is great fun, when I spring at her; and Mrs. Lindsay has always such a lot of bones, and doesn't mind Mohe and Dumm and me eating them on the carpet. I like Mrs. Lindsay very much.

Tuesday evening.

Dear Master,—My mistress brought my chain, and said 'Come along with me, while it shined, and I could finish after.' But she kept me so long in the London Library, and other places, that I had to miss the post. An old gentleman in the omnibus took such notice of me! He looked at me a long time, and then turned to my mistress, and said 'Sharp, isn't he?' And my mistress was so good as to say, 'Oh yes!' And then the old gentleman said again, 'I knew it! easy to see that!' And he put his hand in his hind-pocket, and took out a whole biscuit, a sweet one, and gave it me in bits. I was quite sorry to part from him, he was such a good judge of dogs. Mr. Greig from Canadagua and his wife left cards while we were out. Columbine said she saw them through the blind, and they seemed nice people.

Wednesday.

I left off, last night, dear master, to be washed. This morning I have seen a note from you, which says you will come tomorrow. Columbine and I are extremely happy to hear it; for then there will be some dinner to come and go on. Being to see you so soon, no more at present from your

Obedient little dog,
NERO.

This same little dog had been lost for a day, and 'floods of tears' shed over his absence. He and the cat, 'Columbine,' were a merry pair of playthings, though Mrs. Carlyle had said that Nero was, of course, neither so pretty nor so clever as 'Shandy,' of whom Carlyle had written to Miss Welsh in 1822 that he was 'a dog of worth, undoubtedly.'

Poor Shandy is not quite forgotten, for Lieutenant-Colonel David Davidson, in his charming ' Memories of a Long Life ' (Douglas, Edinburgh, 1890), gives a portrait of the animal, the work of one of those itinerant artists so often seen in those days. This one, Brooks, had been engaged to paint the boy brothers of Colonel Davidson,* and Shandy had been borrowed of Mrs. Welsh to give effect to the group.

More interesting is Colonel Davidson's vivid recollections of Mrs. Carlyle herself, as he knew her before he went to India, at the age of sixteen, she being some few years older. ' I see her now,' he says, ' her raven locks and dark, liquid eyes, contrasting with her fair complexion; and features which, if not quite regular, yet flashed with bright intelligence, softened in tender sympathy, or sparkled with the choicest fun.'

Times were changed in 1850. 'The mould was smelled above the rose,' the tint was that of long suffering and struggle. Lady Ashburton, gay and full of smartness, had given Mrs. Carlyle the name of 'Agrippina' at this time, since *Nero* was her companion; but the joke must have failed to arouse much real merriment in Mrs. Carlyle, who was craving of Mrs. Russell, of Thornhill, ' a slip of the Templand sweetbriar,' in memory of that mother whose loss was never forgotten.

In March, Mrs. Carlyle spent a few days at Addiscombe, and wrote to ' Master Nero' under cover to T. Carlyle, Esq., words half sweet, half bitter, calling him ' My poor orphan ! my dear good little dog !' but adding, 'The lady for whom I abandoned you—*to whom all family ties yield*—is pretty well again, as far as I can see.'

In a letter to Mrs. Aitken, written in April, she says: ' My "beau-ideal" of existence this long while has been growing further and further from that "getting on," or rather "*got* on," in society which is the aim of so much female aspiration and effort.' Here, again, she speaks of Nero, and

* See Appendix.

says she is ' no longer alone any more.' But surely a closer and dearer companionship was needed by the sensitive and delicate woman, beloved whenever she was truly understood, and open to the least touch of human tenderness.

Mrs. Carlyle found London society rather hard work. She would have taken much delight in the slip of Templand sweetbriar, sent duly by kind Mrs. Russell, but it was ' past hope,' having ' hurried itself to put out leaves when it should have been quietly taking root—a procedure,' she adds, ' not confined to sweetbriars !' Her bitter view of London society tells of sad unhappiness at her own heart, for London society is very excellent and pleasant and desirable, to those who bring the requisite state of mind, and has as often, we suppose, served as a panacea and antidote, as it has caused revilings such as are showered upon it by this suffering lady. ' People dare not let themselves think or feel in this centre of frivolity and folly,' she writes in July 1850; 'they would go mad if they did, and universally commit suicide.'

On the last day of this month, Carlyle, having finished the ' Latter Day Pamphlets,' went off to Wales, ' solitary and silent,' his wife still in weak health. ' Not much of it,' she had written to Mrs. Russell, ' but *I make it do !*' Her letters to her husband at this period were not enlivening, sparkling as they are with native wit and originality. Again the ' beaming spirits' of callers are complained of, the silence and sadness of others found equally hard to bear.

' Took morphine last night,' she writes on August 4 to her husband, ' and slept some. . . .' Towards the end of that month she writes to him:

Yes! yes! I *have* composed myself — am quiet. You shall have no more wail or splutter from me on this occasion. If I had been an able-bodied woman, instead of a thoroughly broken-down one, I should surely have had sense and reticence enough not to fret you, in your seclusion, with details of my household money. . . . I was really no more responsible for what I wrote than a person in a brain fever would have been. . . .

Truly 'the grasshopper had become a burden' to Mrs. Carlyle.

The house needed some ordinary cleaning, but it is not often that ' sweeps, white-washers, and carpet-beaters ' cause such distraction to the lady of the house. Mrs. Carlyle was ill, and unfit for the least annoyance. It was, literally, to her as 'the Sack of Troy,' relieved at times by the reading of new books, and successful games of chess with Anthony Sterling. The early return to town of Erasmus Darwin in September brightened her a little, and a three hours' visit from Elisabeth Pepoli soothed her, but proved a farewell—unsuspected at the time by Mrs. Carlyle, who adds later: 'Alas! what a way to part!'

Carlyle was now at Scotsbrig, and had innocently asked his ever-attentive wife for some '*buttons*' not attainable where he was. He had assured her that if the buttons arrived on *Wednesday* they would be in abundant time. To which her sharp reply is, ' I should think they would, and " don't you wish you may get them?"' Two months of household ' earthquaking ' had left her weak and irritable. The buttons were, no doubt, bought and sent at the earliest possible moment.

Carlyle was about to return from Scotland and Mrs. Carlyle going on a visit to the Grange. That she felt for *his* sensitiveness and what it entailed on him, is touchingly apparent in a letter to him, dated September 23, when he was still at Scotsbrig.

Alas! dear (she writes), I am very sorry for you. You, as well as I, are too vivid; to you as well as to me has a skin been given much too thin for the rough purposes of human life. . . . It does not at all raise my spirits that you are likely to arrive here (at Cheyne Row) in my absence. You may be better without me as far as my *company* goes. I make, myself, no illusion on that head. . . . God knows how gladly I would be sweet-tempered, and cheerful-hearted, and all that sort of thing, for your single sake, if my temper were not soured and my heart saddened beyond my own power to mend them.

And Carlyle, also soured and saddened, was incapable of binding up those wounds; all his love, and he did love her in his own way, was powerless to make her happy.

We think there was a deeper understanding between those two isolated natures than the world could ever know of, and that the long years of faithful holding together tell of it, to those who can enter reverently within the veil, though hardly perhaps to that much larger class who would 'rush in where angels fear to tread.'

The visit to the Grange, another of those small martyrdoms undergone by Mrs. Carlyle to please her husband, began early in October; and the first sensation of the guest on arrival was a disposition to lay her head down on the table and cry; her next impulse, the wild one of taking the next train back to Chelsea and her husband. But the knowledge that either step would be thought 'ridiculous,' quenched the two longings effectually. She had some sweet thoughts in her lonely, sleepless hours. It was only in August that her husband had written to her, 'Thanks to thee—oh! know that I have thanked thee sometimes in my silent hours as no words could ! . . . . the thing that is in my heart is known, or can be known, to the Almighty Maker alone !'

But to take real, daily human comfort from such words as these, unaccompanied by those manifestations so dear to a human heart—the look, the kiss, the touch with love in it—would have been asking too much; and the gap remained, the loneliness, the desolation; and though some of us may smile at some of Carlyle's 'miseries,' no one, we think, certainly no true *woman*, can see just cause for the half-pitying judgment, made by some, on the long-drawn-out mental and bodily suffering of Mrs. Carlyle.

He wrote to her on his arrival at Scotsbrig that he was 'a very unthankful, ill-conditioned, bilious, wayward and heartworn son of Adam.' And we can only respectfully conclude that it was with him *as he said.*

A short visit to friends in Cumberland brought his holiday

to a close; he had promised his wife to be as amiable as he *could* on his return; and in answer to her bitter regret that her company was now become so useless to him, had said, 'Oh, if you could but cease being conscious of *what* your company is to me.' Thoughts of his 'poor Goody' blotted out the fine scenery of the Lake district; Carlyle felt himself most miserable—begging pity and pardon from poor 'Goody, whom God bless!'

CHAPTER XXII

A. D. 1851-1853

Carlyle's visit to the Marshalls—Tennyson and his bride—Disgust at the Exhibition of 1851—Visit to Malvern—Verdict thereon—Miss Gully's letter—Mrs. Carlyle again at the Grange—Repairs at Cheyne Row—Visit to Macready—Carlyle's 'Life of Frederick'— He sails for Rotterdam—A serious undertaking—Mrs. Carlyle visits Lady Ashburton—Carlyle's second German tour—Discomforts — Return to 5 Cheyne Row of Mrs. Carlyle—Further 'earthquakings'—A second visit of Mrs. Carlyle to the Lady Ashburton—Sleeplessness — Depression—The old letter—Carlyle's return—Commencement of 'Frederick'—Mrs. Carlyle with the John Carlyles at Moffat—Return to softer conditions at Chelsea.

IT was at the Marshalls', at Coniston, that Carlyle met Tennyson, then lately married, and approved Mrs. Tennyson's wit, sense, and 'glittering blue eyes;' 'augured,' in fact, 'well of the adventure.' But his own faithful wife was distracted at his return in her absence. She would have rushed back from the Grange to meet him. Carlyle would not hear of this, nor would Lady Ashburton. Prepared for a lonely home, he says, ' I shall know better than ever I did what the comfort is, to me, of being received by you when I arrive worn out, and you welcome me with your old smiles. . . .' As a compromise, Carlyle accepted Lady Ashburton's proposal that he should spend a short time at the Grange with his wife before finally settling down in Chelsea for the winter. It was an unhappy time with Carlyle, the oft-times suspected 'Nadir' of his fortunes was felt to be in full force. He felt 'lonely, shut up,'—silently prayed for *work*, his one solace on earth.

It was the middle of October before the Carlyles were again at Cheyne Row. A quiet winter was marked for Mrs.

Carlyle by rather better health; and Christmas found her busy with kindly gifts to old servants and pensioners in Scotland; Mrs. Russell being her sympathetic almoner in these deeds of love. A painful accident, which caused her to strike her chest against the end of the sofa, caused some little disquietude, but the apprehension was presumably out of proportion to the actual injury.

Early in 1851, the visit of a highly sentimental young lady, whose guardians desired to place her with the Carlyles, disturbed Mrs. Carlyle very much. The young lady seems to have simplified matters by making an early marriage, to the relief of perplexed guardians and friends. Mrs. Carlyle tells her uncle, John Welsh: 'Indeed, you can have no notion how the whole routine of this quiet house was tumbled heels-over-head. It had been, for three days and three nights, not Jonah in the whale's belly, but the whale in Jonah's belly. ...'

In the same letter is an account of a visit to Pentonville Prison, equally inimitable in its caustic satire. The '*solitary system*' might not have been bad for Carlyle, who, in the spring of this same year confides to his Journal that he is 'weak, very irritable too,' and that it would be best for him to be set to work 'maistly in a place by himsel'.' The latter expression is quoted from a 'half-mad friend of James Aitken.' Human help, as Mr. Froude says, there could be none. His disgust at the Exhibition of 1851 drove him and his wife to Malvern, where for a few weeks he was the guest of Dr. Gully—'paid his tax to contemporary stupor, and found by degrees that *water*, taken as medicine, was the most destructive drug he ever tried.'

A letter written many years afterwards by Miss Ellen Gully, daughter of Dr. Gully, gives some interesting personal impressions. The letter was written to the wife of a Unitarian minister in Southport.

I have been wanting to talk to you about the Carlyles (she writes), but have never had time. ... I read the 'Reminiscences,' and I thought it a melancholy production ... it was very interesting, and it was well to let it be known that he regretted his selfishness to his wife, but his groans (in Italian) and endearing expressions concerning her, I think it was a mistake to print. . . . Why should a spendid, bad-tempered man have all his impulsive sayings and doings criticised, while worthless humorous fellows, whose only business is to attend to the 'etiquettes,' and who would make a faultless picture, are allowed to rest in their graves? Many of Carlyle's sayings which I have since seen complained of as vindictive and ungrateful, were, I feel certain, said only in a humorous way to raise a laugh in which he himself would join. . . . I think Carlyle ought never to have married *anybody*—he ought to have lived alone and had a good cook. Mrs. Carlyle was wasted on him entirely, and thrown into a sphere of life and duties for which she was quite unsuited—he, in his richest days, would never have more than one servant (*this was afterwards changed*), and you know how servants-of-all-work *cook*; and he, dyspeptic, tore his hair if the meat was tough. Their hospitality was beautiful . . . they neither of them cared a bit about food, only he could not digest common cookery ! . . . I don't myself see that he had any right to indulge in the delight of a witty wife, and yet indulge in his idiosyncrasy of only having one cheap servant. . . . I must admit that he was, at times, selfish and not kind to his wife, when we knew them. Totally inconsiderate of her health—I remember one or two occasions, on which she, suffering far more than he, was sent journeys by him in order to secure his comforts. . . .

So much for Miss Gully's opinions, which no doubt sprang from a close and sympathetic observation. And in writing of a woman, it is well sometimes to know what another woman thinks !

The month at Malvern over, Carlyle fled to Scotsbrig, and his wife to her kind and loving friends, the Jewsburys, at Manchester; being determined to keep up some little remnant of 'water cure' all the same. She speaks warmly of the Gullys in her first letter to Carlyle, dated September 5, 1851. 'The more I think of these people,' she says, 'the more I admire their politeness and kindness to us.'

December found Mrs. Carlyle again at the Grange, much

depressed by three weeks' bad cold contracted there, much exercised in her mind as to customary gifts to her poor friends at Dumfries, and again turning to Mrs. Russell, of Thornhill, whose ready kindliness never failed her.

It is amusing to read that Mrs. Carlyle, who had been seeing much of Macaulay at this time, admits that, for 'copious talking, he beats Carlyle hollow,'—but not in *quality*, apparently.

The year 1852 opened dismally enough with 'repairs' of the house in Cheyne Row. We are left to wonder why two people 'without incumbrance,' did not straightway walk into some *other* house, 'ready swept and garnished,' sooner than undertake what is called 'thorough repair,' when it entailed so much inevitable suffering! But we conclude that they would rather 'dree their weird,' or that no other idea ever occurred to them. Mrs. Carlyle writes in the summer of 1852, to Mrs. Russell, of Thornhill, as to this new 'earthquaking. She was, as she says, 'needed to keep the workmen from falling into continual mistakes,' but it was a relief to her when Carlyle went off to Mr. Erskine of Linlathen! Mrs. Carlyle was tired out. 'If you saw me,' she writes to Mrs. Russell, ' sitting in the midst of falling bricks and clouds of lime-dust, and a noise as of battering-rams, you wouldn't wonder that I make my letter brief.'

The dying off of the little Templand sweet-briar just now grieved her! 'I am vexed,' she says, 'and can't help feeling the sweet-briar's unwillingness to grow with me; a bad omen, somehow.'

Mrs. Carlyle's letters to her husband at this time have something of despair, almost of desperation, in them. Her visit to the dying Mrs. Macready is told with deep and simple pathos. The omens were not hopeful as to her own health, cheery as are her accounts of herself. The journey was a long one to Sherborne, *viâ* Frome, and Mrs. Carlyle says she rendered herself at Paddington station with a bag on one arm and her 'blessed' (Nero) in a basket on the other.

In August, Mazzini's mother died, and again the office of

consoler fell on her to whom it was, perhaps, one of the few consolations she was susceptible of, in her weak and weary state.

And now Carlyle's mighty and restless spirit had at length conceived another design. He would write the Life of Frederick the Great, and with a view to collecting material, started from the port of Leith, on board the Rotterdam steamer *en route* for Bonn, and other places, on August 30, 1852. 'For Carlyle to write a book on Frederick'—as Mr. Froude justly says—'would involve the reading of a mountain of books, memoirs, journals, state-papers. The work with Cromwell would be child's play to it'—and so it proved! That tremendous book made prolonged and entire devastation of any satisfactory semblance of home-life, or home-happiness.

It was in December of 1851 that Lady Ashburton asked Mrs. Carlyle to spend that month with her, Carlyle being buried in 'Jomini and the Seven Years' War.' It was not easy for Mrs. Carlyle to accept, with due graciousness, this well-meant invitation, and she took counsel with Dr. John Carlyle. 'Heaven knows,' she wrote, 'what is to be said from me individually! If I refuse this time, she will quarrel with me outright! That is her way, and, as quarrelling with *her* would involve also quarrelling with Mr. C., it is not a thing to be done lightly.' Mrs. Carlyle went, however, to the Grange, while her husband remained shut up with his preliminary work. He managed later to join his wife at the Grange, and finished the year there.

Six months of comparative quiet followed before Carlyle sailed again for Rotterdam on a second German tour, in August 1852. A characteristic anecdote occurs prior to this voyage in a letter from Mrs. Carlyle to the mother at Scotsbrig. Carlyle had been suffering from indisposition, it would seem, and said to the servant, 'I should like tea for breakfast this morning, but *you need not hurry*.' The fact was, he wished a little extra time for his ablutions, but the servant was much agitated, and thought it such an unlikely thing for the master to say, that 'it quite made her flesh creep.'

And now Carlyle was grappling with the discomforts of foreign travel, and his wife had paid another visit to Addiscombe, returning, sleepless and fatigued, to temporary lodgings at No. 2 Cheyne Row, her weary feet finding no rest. In September, she was again in her own chaos at No. 5, and straightway took regularly ill, 'in desperate agony, with a noise going on around me like the crack of doom. . . . I have passed a good many bad days in this world, but certainly never one so utterly wretched from mere physical and mental causes as yesterday.' This was her own sad account.

It may be contended that mere inconvenience ought not to produce such dire consequences. In a healthy system the effects would be different, no doubt, but disease had made sad inroads on Mrs. Carlyle's nervous powers, and she simply spoke of things *as she felt them*, the true test of effect, and so far of absolute *fact*, in such matters. That there are people who love the sound of the 'hurdy-gurdy' at night, and of the early cock at dawn, did not prevent poor John Leech dying of London noises.

It was in this year that Dr. John Carlyle was engaged to be married, and Mrs. Carlyle's comment is that, 'having known each other for fifteen years, it is possible they mayn't be marrying on a basis of fiction.' Facts were present to *her*, poor soul, when she lay on her back, 'in an agony,' directing and hounding on the workmen who were to make 5 Cheyne Row a comfortable and desirable residence for Mr. Carlyle on his return.

On September 13, 1852, Mrs. Carlyle had been hearing from her husband, and writes, 'What a pity you can't get any good sleep,' adding, 'It is not German beds only, however, that one cannot get sleep in. Three nights ago, in desperation, I took a great dose of morphia for the same state of things, and was thankful to get four hours of something like forgetfulness by that "questionable" means!' Thomas Erskine of Linlathen had been writing to Mrs. Carlyle that 'he loved her much, and wished he could see what God intended her for!' Her answer, as quoted by herself to Carlyle, is a sad one.

I answered his letter (she says), begging him to tell me 'what God intended me for,' since he knew and I didn't. It would be a satisfaction even to know it. It is surely a kind of impiety to speak of God as if He, too, were 'with the best intentions always unfortunate.' Either I am just what God intended me for, or God cannot 'carry out' His intentions, it would seem. And in that case I, for 'one solitary individual,' can't worship Him the least in the world.

Some lives seem so dedicated to inevitable suffering that we can only bow the head and refrain from explanations— any mere matter-of-fact discussion on the subject is useless.

Long histories of petty domestic worries, crushing enough in their way, and needless to dwell on here, fill many of these letters to Carlyle. Workmen had been dilatory, and Mrs. Carlyle says, on October 5, to her husband: 'I have not a word of comfort to give; I am wearied and sad and cross, and feel as if death had been dissolved into a liquid and I had drunk of it till I was full! Good gracious! that wet paint should have the power of poisoning one's soul as well as one's body!' It is not always thus, surely; but here was a soul and body ill-attuned, sick, sad, lonely.

Turning over some boxfuls of old letters, Mrs. Carlyle came upon Dr. Welsh's 'Day-Book,' removed the cover, and found a large letter lying inside, addressed to her in her mother's handwriting—'with three unbroken seals of her ring.' It was not, alas! the wished-for letter of farewell,' but contained the deed making over Craigenputtock to Mrs. Welsh, executed some time before the marriage to Thomas Carlyle, to whom, on the mother's death, the property had again been legally transferred.

A few words, only, from the mother's hand, were written in the envelope of this unexpectedly found letter. 'When this comes into your possession, my dearest child, do not forget my sister. G. W., Templand: May, 1827.' That gentle sister had long passed away—and Mrs. Carlyle could do nothing all the day after finding the letter but weep, with that saddest grief which attends the past and the irretrievable.

The breaking-in of thieves into the unfinished house was quite a healthy diversion compared with such sadness—and Mrs. Carlyle's account to Dr. John Carlyle of this latter event is truly excellent reading. In December she writes, on the last day of the year:

To Mrs. Russell, Thornhill.

5 Cheyne Row: Friday, Dec. 31, 1852.

My dear Mrs. Russell,—Here is another year; God help us all! I hope it finds you better than when I last heard of you from my friends at Auchtertool. I have often been meaning to write to you without waiting for a New Year's Day; but in all my life I never have been so driven off all letter-writing as since the repairs began in this house. There were four months of that confusion, which ended quite romantically, in my having to sleep with loaded pistols at my bedside! the smell of paint making it as much as my life was worth to sleep with closed windows, and the thieves having become aware of the state of the premises. Once they got in and stole some six pounds' worth of things, before they were frightened away by a candlestick falling and making what my Irish maid called 'a devil of a row,' it was rather to be called 'an angel of a row,' as it saved further depredation. Another time they climbed up to the drawing-room windows, and found them fastened, for a wonder? Another night I was alarmed by a sound as of a pane of glass cut, and leapt out of bed, and struck a light, and listened, and heard the same sound repeated, and then a great bang, like breaking in some panel. I took one of my loaded pistols, and went downstairs, and then another bang which I perceived was at the front door. 'What do you want?' I asked; 'who are you?' 'It's the policeman, if you please; do you know that your parlour windows are both open?' It was true! I had forgotten to close them, and the policeman had first tried the bell, which made the shivering sound, the wire being detached from the bell, and when he found he could not ring it he had beaten on the door with his stick, the knocker also being off while it was getting painted. I could not help laughing at what the man's feelings would have been had he known of the cocked pistol within a few inches of him. All that sort of thing, and much else more disagreeable, and less amusing, quite took away all my spirit for writing; then, when Mr. C—— returned from Germany, we went to the Grange for some weeks; then when I came home, and the workmen were actually out of the house, there was everything to look for, and be put in its place, and really things are hardly in their places up to this hour. Heaven defend me from ever again having any house I live in 'made habitable!'

Carlyle had returned from Germany, in October, 'half dead . . . out of those German horrors of insomnia, indigestion, and continued chaotic wretchedness.' He really reminds us of a definition of the term '*amphibious,*' occurring, we think, in one of Dickens's works—as applied to a creature which 'cannot live in the water, and dies on the land.' Carlyle fled upstairs to his poor 'Heroic Helper,' and found that 'she, too, is fighting, has not conquered, that beast of a task, undertaken voluntarily for one unworthy. . . .'

A short visit to the Grange ended this chaotic state of things, and, once more, 5 Cheyne Row was free of workmen and some peace was possible! And now began the actual work of 'Frederick,' which occupied the early months of 1853, and was only completed in January 1865. In July Mrs. Carlyle had gone off to Moffat, where John Carlyle, now married, had taken a house—and, strange to say, there was still *painting* to be done in Cheyne Row. It was a ghastly time to the over-sensitive Carlyle—the smell of the paint and the crowing of 'quite newly-invented cocks' in the long, light summer mornings!' And above and below all, the want of 'sweet accord' between the married pair! 'Oh Jeannie,' he wrote to her, 'you know nothing about me just now! . . your lynx-eyes do not reach into the inner region of me, and know not what is in my heart—what, on the whole, always was and will always be there. I wish you did ! I wish you did !'

Sitting all alone in his Chelsea garden he meditated on his miseries; in one letter eloquently dilating on them, in the next apologising for his weakness.

'But what could I do?' he said, 'fly for shelter to my mammy, like a poor infant with its finger cut; complain in my distress to the one heart that used to be open to me?'

'Greater than man, less than woman,' as Essex said of Queen Elizabeth. The cocks were locked up next door, and the fireworks at Cremorne were silent, and the rain fell and cooled the July air; and Carlyle slept, and the universe became once more tolerable.*

* From Froude's *History of Carlyle's Life in London*, Vol. ii. p. 131.

CHAPTER XXIII

A. D. 1853-1856

Declining health of old Mrs. Carlyle at Scotsbrig—Mrs. Carlyle hastens to her—Womanly tenderness—The danger staved off—Return to Chelsea—Death of John Welsh of Liverpool—Visit of the Carlyles to the Grange—The 'soundless' room at Chelsea—Return of Mrs. Carlyle—Noises—Death of Helen Welsh—Death of Carlyle's mother—Wifely sympathy—Miss Jewsbury comes to live in London—Miss Fox—Mazzini's farewell—Mrs. Carlyle's Journal—Deep misery—Sympathy—Budget of a ' Femme Incomprise.'

AT this time the good old mother at Scotsbrig shewed signs of fatal decline. The tidings of anxiety reached Mrs. Carlyle at Moffat, where she was still the guest of Dr. and Mrs. John Carlyle. Only a few days before she had been humorously complaining of being kept awake on the night of her arrival by '*a hyæna,*' escaped from some travelling menagerie, then she had had a narrow escape of accident on the steep slope of a hill, but the greater trouble was to come.

It was in a letter to Mrs. Braid (the much-loved old servant 'Betty,') dated July 13th 1853, that Mrs. Carlyle speaks of this anxiety. 'He (Carlyle),' she writes, 'is very melancholy and helpless, left alone, at the best of times; and now, I am afraid, he is going to have a great sorrow in the death of his old mother.'

Mrs. Carlyle, with true womanly tenderness, hurried away from Moffat to assist in nursing, and wrote beautiful and comforting letters to her husband, which were thoroughly appreciated by him. The immediate alarm passed, and Mrs. Carlyle was able to return safely to Chelsea, breaking her journey at Liverpool, weeping much on her way thither, partly, no doubt, from over-strain and fatigue, and partly at the wrench it always gave her to leave her beloved Scotland. Carlyle in his annotation upon this letter says—'feet bleeding by the way, over the thorns of this bewildered earth.'

In the letter to her husband, just quoted from, Mrs. Carlyle says, '*Thanks for never neglecting*——'

It was in October that John Welsh of Maryland Street died, to the grief of all who knew him. Mrs. Carlyle, writing to his daughter Helen, says: 'It was well he should die thus, gently and beautifully, with all his loving kindness fresh as a young man's; his enjoyment of life not wearied out; all our love for him as warm as ever. . . .'

And now came the anything but soundless building of a supposed '*soundless*' room for Carlyle to write in, he having reached, on August 1853, another 'nadir' of suffering! The Carlyles both then betook themselves to the Grange for Christmas, after occupying Addiscombe alone for some weeks previously at the kind request of the Ashburtons. The first 'silent apartment had turned out the noisiest in the house, with infernal additions of cocks and macaws.'

Two days rest here, at the Grange (for Mrs. Carlyle), were cut short by an awkward accident in the shape of a blow on the head, which shocked the nerves and took away sleep, and ended, somewhat unexpectedly, in her retiring to look after the difficulties in Chelsea. The clever woman had the keepers of nuisances legally bound down to silence by means of a timely five-pound note, and a written agreement with penalty attached. But news of Helen Welsh's death arrived almost at the same time, she having survived her father but a few weeks.

It was within a week of Christmas that Carlyle, still at the Grange, had distinctly worse news of his mother, and hurried away to Scotsbrig. In his Journal of January 8th, 1854, he writes: 'The stroke has fallen, my dear old mother is gone from me!' There was yet time for a brief farewell.

The womanly sweetness with which Mrs. Carlyle writes to her husband on this bereavement tells its own sure tale.

Oh, my dear (she writes), never does one feel oneself so utterly helpless as in trying to speak comfort for great bereavements. I will not try it. . . . And yet all griefs, when there is no bitterness in them, are soothed down by Time. And your grief for your mother must be altogether sweet and soft. You must feel that you have always been a good son to her; that you have always appreciated her as she deserved, and that she knew this, and loved you to the last moment . . . made doubly sure to you by her last look and words. Oh! what would I have given for last words, to keep in my innermost heart all the rest of my life. . . .

But the infinite distance lay between them.

Carlyle, probably, felt anything but the calming assurance suggested by his wife. It is not natural or possible in the first days of piercing pain! but the tie between him and his mother had been no ordinary one, and there was a deep loneliness in his heart.

The year 1854 was spent almost entirely in London. The book on 'Frederick' loomed, as a huge thundercloud, over that little horizon. The offer of quarters at the Grange was not favourably received, and the July heats found the Carlyles still in London.

We cannot feel that Mrs. Carlyle ever took kindly to the 'purple and fine linen' of those in more opulent circumstances than was she herself. Muddy boots and a soaked mackintosh met a more cordial welcome from her, as a rule, than did the daintily dressed occupant of a cosy brougham, with its pair of high-stepping greys. It was not snobbishness, not envy; but it was an indubitable fact, and had its root in pride, in conscious superiority, in the sense of being the second and not the *first* person in some of her guests' minds. So we think. Again, there were the deep, unquenchable attachments to old home associations, which she could share with Mrs. Russell or 'Old Betty,' but not with any of the fine, fashionable folk who now surrounded her. So she was sensitive at the inhabiting of the Grange during the absence of its owners—dreaded 'the five housemaids,' and it was, after all, not very surprising that it should be so.

A bright prospect was now held out in the intention of Miss Jewsbury to come and live in London, 'a real gain' as Mrs. Carlyle puts it. And it was always a refreshment, even to outsiders like ourselves, to come in contact with that bright and unique personality.

The Crimean War haunted Mrs. Carlyle day and night. Near relative she had none, in danger, but there was Colonel Sterling to be thought of, and she says in November 1854 to Mrs. Russell: 'I read the list of killed and wounded always with a sick dread of finding his name.'

So Carlyle struggled through the dark, gloomy days with his 'unexecutable book'; and Mrs. Carlyle, after vainly looking for a suitable seaside cottage, finally decided to remain at Chelsea, and did so, over-worn, fatigued, and sleepless!

We are forced to remember that Mrs. Carlyle could not be what is called *happy* anywhere, whatever may have been the impression of those who only saw this gifted pair at times and briefly. The late Miss Caroline Fox formed, at first, an impression hardly borne out by facts. 'They are a very happy pair,' she says. 'She plays all manner of tricks on her husband, telling wonderful stories of him in his presence, founded almost solely on her bright imagination . . . .' and as early as 1847 Caroline Fox quotes Mrs. Carlyle as saying, 'I often wonder what right I have to live at all.' Now, too, she spoke of the world's hollowness, and of every year deepening her sense of this; of half a dozen real friends as far too magnificent an allowance for anyone to calculate on—she would suggest *half a one:* 'those you really care about *die.*' Of Thomas Erskine, whom they both loved, Mrs. Carlyle said, 'He always soothes me, for he looks so serene, as if he had found peace.'

She, poor woman, certainly had *not* done so!

In June 1849 Miss Fox 'steamed to Chelsea, and paid Mrs. Carlyle a humane little visit.' 'I don't think,' says Miss Fox, ' she roasted a single soul or even body. She talked in rather a melancholy way of herself and of things in general, professing that it was only the Faith that all things are well put together—which all sensible people *must* believe —that prevents our sending to the nearest chemist's shop for six-pennyworth of arsenic. . . .' 'We said a few modest words,' adds the gentle Quakeress, 'in honour of existence, to which she answered, "*But I can't enjoy Joy*," as Henry Taylor says.'

Miss Fox also records Mazzini's farewell words to Mrs. Carlyle on his departure at the time of the Milan insurrection. 'Mrs. Carlyle had said he took leave of her as one who never expected to see her again: he kissed her and said, " Be strong and good until I return."' In Mazzini Mrs. Carlyle lost a true friend, strong and brave enough to see her faults, and to say a timely word. Miss Fox, too, would have been a great comforter, had circumstances cast the lot of the two women together more closely. Little real help was possible, however, at the present time, when the deep dissatisfaction of Mrs. Carlyle at her husband's repeated visits to the Ashburtons at Bath House was accentuated by all the stress of a sick body and a sick mind—past help ! We cannot but think that had it been possible for Mr. Carlyle to see clearly one fraction of the pain he was causing, he might easily have given up this friendship, all blameless as it was in itself, and let the *greater* supersede the *less*. For the peace of her, whom he had vowed to cherish, *was*, after all, the main thing, and were the wish ever so unreasonable, most men would have seen it and acted out the wife's desire. But he was *not* like other men, and he did not see. Had he once *seen*, we do not doubt the result !

As it was, the sadness became very heavy. Some extracts from a journal kept by Mrs. Carlyle shew the depth of her pain. We quote a few sentences.

Oct. 22, 1855.—' Cut short last night by Mr. C.'s return

from Bath House! That eternal Bath House! I wonder how many thousand miles Mr. C. has walked between here and there, putting it all together, setting up always another milestone and another betwixt himself and me!'

Oct. 25.—'... My heart is very sore to-night, but I have promised myself not to make this journal a "miserere," so I will take a dose of morphia and do the impossible to sleep.'

Nov. 1.—'Fine weather outside, but indoors, blowing a devil of a gale. Off into space then, to get the green mould that has been gathering upon me of late days brushed off by human contact.'

Nov. 6.—'... They must be comfortable people who have leisure to think about going to Heaven! My most constant and pressing desire is to keep out of Bedlam.'

Nov. 7.—'... What a sick day this has been with me! Oh! my mother. Nobody sees when I am suffering now.'

Dec. 4.—'Oh! to cure anyone of a terror of annihilation, just put him on my allowance of sleep, and see if he don't get to long for sleep, sleep, unfathomable and everlasting sleep, as the only conceivable heaven!'

March 24, 1856.—'... Looking back was not intended by nature, evidently, from the fact that our eyes are in our faces, and not in our hind heads. Look straight before you then, Jane Carlyle. ... Look, above all, at the duty nearest hand, and, what's more, *do it!*'

March 26.—'To-day it has blown knives and files; a cold, rasping, savage day: excruciating for sick nerves. Dear Geraldine, as if she would contend with the very elements on my behalf, brought me a bunch of violets and a bouquet of the loveliest, most fragrant flowers. Talking with her all I have done, or could do. "Have mercy upon me, O Lord! for I am weak. ... O Lord, heal me, for my bones are vexed. My soul also is sore vexed—but Thou, O Lord! how long?"'

If the Journal was not a 'Miserere,' it was truly a 'De Profundis.'

August 1855 had witnessed a painful experiment. The Ashburtons, knowing how Carlyle needed rest, had again offered Addiscombe to him and Mrs. Carlyle, and thither they repaired. But it proved a failure, and Mrs. Carlyle went back to Chelsea with some suddenness, causing much pain to her husband, who wrote at once to her in the tenderest terms, only wishing her to find rest if she could.

Christmas of 1855 found the Carlyle's again at the Grange —but the visit was a very unhappy one for Mrs. Carlyle— sick and sad, she struggled on! It was in the autumn of 1855 that the Journal was begun from which such sad extracts have been given; the Journal from which, after her death, Carlyle first came to know how unhappy she had been, and that *he* had been partly the cause.

Few women could have composed the sparkling and able 'Budget of a Femme Incomprise,' dated February 12, 1855 —unique amongst feminine productions. Carlyle received it with roars of laughter and promptly complied with the modest demands made on him. 'Excellent,' he says, 'my dear, clever Goody; thriftiest, wittiest and cleverest of women.' He did not feel the hidden bitterness of the whole thing. We give the ' Budget ' * in full.

Budget of a Femme Incomprise.

I don't choose to *speak* again on the *money question!* The 'replies' from the Noble Lord are unfair and unkind, and little to the purpose. When you tell me 'I pester your life out about money,' that 'your soul is sick with hearing about it,' that 'I had better make the money I have serve,' 'at all rates, hang it, let you alone of it'—all that I call perfectly unfair, the reverse of kind, and tending to nothing but disagreement. If I were greedy, or extravagant, or a bad manager, you would be justified in 'staving me off' with loud words; but you cannot say *that* of me (whatever else)—cannot *think* it of me. At least, I am sure that I never 'asked for more' from you or anyone, not even

* From Froude's *History of Carlyle's Life in London*, Vol. ii. p. 162.

from my own mother, in all my life, and that through six-and-twenty years I have kept house for you at more or less cost according to given circumstances, but always on less than it costs the generality of people living in the same style. What I should have expected you to say rather would have been: 'My dear, you *must* be dreadfully hampered in your finances, and dreadfully anxious and unhappy about it, and quite desperate of *making it do*, since *you* are "asking for more." Make me understand the case, then. I can and will help you out of that *sordid* suffering at least, either by giving you more, if that be found prudent to do, or by reducing our wants to within the present means.' That is the sort of thing you would have said had you been a perfect man; so I suppose you are not a perfect man. Then, instead of crying in my bed half the night after, I would have explained my budget to you in peace and confidence. But now I am driven to explain it on paper 'in a state of mind'; *driven*, for I cannot, it is not in my nature to live 'entangled in the details,' and I *will not*. I would sooner hang myself, though 'pestering you about money' is also more repugnant to me than you dream of.

You don't understand why the allowance which sufficed in former years no longer suffices. That is what I would explain to the Noble Lord if he would but—what shall I say?—*keep his temper*.

The beginning of my embarrassments, it will not surprise the Noble Lord to learn, since it has also been 'the beginning of' almost every human ill to himself, was *the repairing of the house*. There was a destruction, an *irregularity*, an *incessant recurrence of small incidental expenses*, during all that period, or *two* periods, through which I found myself in September gone a year, *ten* pounds behind, instead of having some pounds saved up towards the winter's coals. I could have worked round 'out of that,' however, in course of time, if habits of *unpinched* housekeeping had not been long taken to by *you* as well as myself, and if new unavoidable, or not-to-be avoided, *current* expenses had not followed close on those incidental ones. I will show the Noble Lord, with his permission, what the new current expenses *are*, and to what they amount per annum. (Hear, hear! and cries of 'Be brief!')

1. We have a servant of 'higher grade' than we ever ven-

tured on before; more expensive in money. Anne's wages are 16 pounds a year; Fanny's were 13. Most of the others had 12; and Anne never dreams of being other than *well fed*. The others *scrambled* for their living out of ours. Her regular meat dinner at one o'clock, regular allowance of butter, &c., adds at least three pounds a year to the *year's* bills. But she plagues us with no fits of illness nor of *drunkenness*, no *warnings* nor complainings. She does perfectly what she is *paid* and *fed* to do. I see houses not so well kept with 'cook,' 'housemaid,' and 'manservant' (Question !). Anne is the last item I should vote for retrenching in. I may set her down, however, at six additional pounds.

2. We have now gas and water 'laid on,' both producing admirable results. But betwixt 'water laid on' at one pound, sixteen shillings per annum, with *shilling* to turncock, and water carried at fourpence a week, there is a yearly difference of 19 shillings and four pence; and betwixt *gas* all the year round and a few sixpenny boxes of lights in the winter the difference may be computed at *fifteen shillings*. These two excellent innovations, then, increase the yearly expenditure by one pound fourteen shillings and four pence—a trifle to speak of; but you, my Lord, born and bred in thrifty Scotland, must know well the proverb, 'Every little mak's a mickle.'

3. We are higher *taxed*. Within the last eighteen months there has been added to the Lighting, Pavement, and Improvement Rate ten shillings yearly, to the Poor Rate one pound, to the sewer rate ten shillings; and now the doubled Income Tax makes a difference of 5*l*. 16*s*. 8*d*. yearly, which sums, added together, amount to a difference of 7*l*. 16*s*. 8*d*. yearly, on taxes which already amounted to 17*l*. 12*s*. 8*d*. There need be no reflections for want of taxes.

4. Provisions of all sorts are higher priced than in former years. Four shillings a week for bread, instead of two shillings and sixpence, makes at the year's end a difference of 3*l*. 18*s*. Butter has kept all the year round 2*d*. a pound dearer than I ever knew it. On the quantity we use—two pounds and a half per week 'quite reg'lar'—there is a difference of 21*s*. 8*d*. by the year. Butcher's meat is a penny a pound dearer. At the rate of a pound and a half a day, *bones* included—no exorbitant allowance for three people—the difference on that at the year's end would

be 2*l.* 5*s.* 6*d.* Coals, which had been for some years at 21*s.* per ton, cost this year 26*s.*, last year 29*s.*, bought judiciously, too. If I had had to pay 50*s.* a ton for them, as some housewives had to, God knows what would have become of me. (Passionate cries of 'Question! Question!') We burn, or used to burn—I am afraid they are going faster this winter—twelve tons, one year with another. Candles are *riz*: composites a shilling a pound, instead of 10*d.*; dips 8 pence, instead of 5*d.* or 6*d.* Of the former we burn three pounds in nine days—the greater part of the year you sit so late—and of dips two pounds a fortnight on the average of the whole year. Bacon is 2*d.* a pound dearer; soap ditto; potatoes, at the cheapest, a penny a pound, instead of three pounds for 2*d.* We use three pounds of potatoes in two days' meals. Who could imagine that at the year's end that makes a difference of 15*s.* 2*d.* on one's mere potatoes? Compute all this, and you will find that the difference on *provisions* cannot be under twelve pounds in the year.

5. What I should blush to state if I were not *at bay*, so to speak: ever since we have been in London *you* have, in the handsomest manner, paid the winter's butter with *your own money*, though it was not in the bond. And this gentlemanlike proceeding on your part, till the butter became uneatable, was a good two pounds saved me.

Add up these differences:—

	£	s.	d.
1. Rise on servant	6	0	0
2. Rise on light and water	1	14	0
3. On taxes	7	16	8
4. On provisions	12	0	0
5. Cessation of butter	2	0	0

You will find a total of £29 10 8

My calculation will be found quite correct, though I am not strong in arithmetic. I have *thochtered* all this well in my head, and *indignation* makes a sort of arithmetic, as well as verses. Do you finally understand why the allowance which sufficed formerly no longer suffices, and pity my difficulties instead of being angry at them?

The only thing you *can* reproach me with, *if you like*, is that fifteen months ago, when I found myself already in debt, and everything *rising* on me, I did not fall at once to *pinching* and *muddling*, as when we didn't know where the next money was to come from, instead of 'lashing down' at the accustomed rate: nay, expanding into a 'regular servant.' But you are to recollect that when I first complained to you of the *prices*, you said, quite good-naturedly, 'Then you are coming to bankruptcy, are you? Not going to be able *to go on*, you think? Well, then, we must come to your assistance, poor *crittur*. You mustn't be made a bankrupt of.' So I kept my mind easy, and retrenched in nothing, relying on the promised 'assistance.' But when 'Oh! it was lang o' coming, lang o' coming,' my arrears taking every quarter a more alarming cypher, what could I do but put you in mind? Once, twice, at the third speaking, what you were pleasantly calling 'a great heap of money'—15*l*.—was— what shall I say?—flung to me. Far from *leaving anything* to meet the increased demand of another nine months, this sum did not clear me of debt, not by five pounds. But from time to time encouraging *words* fell from the Noble Lord. 'No, you cannot pay the double Income Tax; clearly, I must pay that for you.' And again: 'I will burn as many coals as I like; if you can't pay for them somebody must!' All resulting, however, thus far in '*Don't you wish you may get it?*' Decidedly I should have needed to be more than mortal, or else 'a born daughter of Chaos,' to have gone on without attempt made at ascertaining what *coming to my assistance* meant: whether it meant 15*l*. without a blessing once for all; and if so, what retrenchments were to be permitted.

You asked me at last money row, with withering sarcasm, 'had I the slightest idea what amount of money would *satisfy me*. Was I wanting 50*l*. more; or forty, or thirty? Was there any conceivable sum of money that could put an end to my eternal botheration?' I will answer the question as if it had been asked practically and kindly.

Yes. I have the strongest idea what amount of money would '*satisfy*' me. I have computed it often enough as I lay awake at nights. Indeed, when I can't sleep now it is my 'difficulties' I think about more than my sins, till they become 'a real mental awgony in my own inside.' The above-named sum, 29*l*., divided into quarterly payments, would *satisfy* me (with a certain parsimony about little things, somewhat less might do), I engaging my word of a gentlewoman to *give back* at the year's end whatever portion thereof any diminution of the demand on me might enable me to save.

I am not so unpractical, however, as to ask for the whole 29*l.* without thought or care where it is to come from. I have settled all that (Derisive laughter, and Hear, hear !), so that nine pounds only will have to be disbursed by you over and above your long-accustomed disbursements (Hear, hear !). You anticipate, perhaps, some draft on your waste-paper basket. No, my Lord, it has never been my habit to interfere with your ways of making money, or the rate which you make it at; and if I never did it in early years, most unlikely I should do it *now*. My bill of ways and means has nothing to do with making money, only with disposing of the money made. (Bravo ! hear !)

1. Ever since my mother's death you have allowed me for old Mary Mills 3*l.* yearly. She needs them no more. *Continue these three pounds for the house.*

2. Through the same long term of years you have made *me* the handsomest Christmas and birthday presents; and when I had purposely disgusted you from *buying me things*, you gave me at the New Year 5*l.* Oh I know the meaning of that 5*l.* quite well. *Give me nothing;* neither money nor money's worth. I would have it so anyhow, and continue the 5*l.* for the house.

3. Ever since we came to London you have paid some 2*l.*, I guess, for *butter*, now become uneatable. Continue that 2*l.* for the house; and we have already *ten* pounds which you can't miss, not having been used to them.

4. My allowance of 25*l.* is a very liberal one; has enabled me to spend freely for myself; and I don't deny there is a pleasure in that when there is no household crisis; but with an appalling deficit in the house exchequer, it is not only no pleasure but an impossibility. I can keep up my dignity and my wardrobe on a less sum—on 15*l.* a year. A silk dress, 'a splendid dressing-gown,' 'a milliner's bonnet' the less; what signifies that at my age ? Nothing. Besides, I have had so many 'gowns' given me that they may serve for two or three years. By then, God knows if I shall be needing *gowns* at all. So deduct 10*l.* from my personal allowance; and continue that for the house.

But why not transfer it *privately* from my own purse to the house one, and ask only for 19*l*.? It would have sounded more modest—*figured* better. Just because 'that sort of thing' don't please me. I have tried it and found it a bad *go*: a virtue *not* its own reward! I am for every herring to hang by its own head, every purse to stand on its own bottom. It would worry me to be thought rolling in the wealth of 25*l*., when I was cleverly making 15*l*. do, and investing 10*l*. in coals and taxes. Mrs. —— is up to that sort of self-sacrifice thing, and to finding compensation in the sympathy of many friends, and in smouldering discontent. I am up to neither the magnanimity nor the compensation, but I am quite up to laying down 10*l*. of my allowance in a straightforward, recognised way, without standing on my toes to it either. And what is more, I am determined upon it, *will not* accept more than 15*l*. in the present state of affairs.

There only remains to disclose the actual state of the exchequer. It is empty as a drum. (Sensation.) If I consider twenty-nine more pounds indispensable—things remaining as they are—for the coming year, beginning the 22nd of March, it is just because I have found it so in the year that is gone; and I commenced that, as I have already stated, with 10*l*. of arrears. You assisted me with 15*l*., and I have assisted myself with 10*l*., five last August, which I took from the Savings Bank, and the five you gave me at New Year, which I threw into the coal account. Don't suppose—'if thou's i' the habit of supposing'— that I tell you this in the *un*devout imagination of being *repaid*. By all that's sacred for me—*the memory of my father and mother* —what else can an irreligious creature like me swear by? I would not take back that money if you *offered* it with the best grace, and had picked it up in the street. I tell it you simply that you may see I am not so dreadfully greedy as you have appeared to think me latterly. Setting *my* 10*l*. then against the original arrears, with 15*l*. in assistance from *you*, it would follow, from my own computation, that I should need 14*l*. more to clear off arrears on the weekly bills and carry me on, paying my way until 22nd of March, next quarter-day. (Cries of Shame! and Turn her out!) I say only '*should need*.' Your money is of course yours, to do as you will with, and I *would like* to again 'walk the causeway' carrying my head as high—as—Mr. A., the upholsterer, owing no man anything. and *dearly I would like* to 'at all rates let YOU alone of it,' if I knew who else had any business with my housekeeping, or to whom else I could properly address myself for the moment; as what with that expensive, most ill-timed dressing-gown, and *my* cheap ill-timed chiffonnier, and my half-year's bills to Rhind and Catchpole, I have only what will serve me till June comes round.

If I was a man, I might fling the gauntlet to Society, join with a few brave fellows, and 'rob a diligence.' But my sex 'kind o' debars from that.' Mercy! to think there are women —your friend Lady A., for example ('*Rumeurs!*' Sensation)— I say for *example*; who spend not merely the additamental pounds I must make such pother about, but *four times my whole income* in the *ball* of one night, and none the worse for it, nor anyone the better. It is—what shall I say?—'curious,' upon my honour. But just in the same manner Mrs. Freeman might say: 'To think there are women—Mrs. Carlyle, for example— who spend 3*l*. 24*s*. 6*d*. on one dressing-gown, and I with just *two loaves* and eighteen pence from the parish, to live on by the week.' There is no bottom to such reflections. The only thing one is perfectly sure of is 'it will come all to the same ultimately,' and I can't say I'll regret the loss of myself, for one— I add no more, but remain, dear Sir, your obedient humble servant,   JANE WELSH CARLYLE.

And yet we fear that, as Mr. Froude says, 'his was the soft heart, and hers the stern one.' A sternness *born of repressed tenderness* is very stern indeed, and, in this sense perhaps, it *was* so—to all appearance. That fiery heart, in its unseen fetters, could not always be amiable—but like 'poor Brutus—with himself at war, forgot the shews of love to other men.'

CHAPTER XXIV

A. D. 1856–1858

Position between Mrs. Carlyle and Lady Ashburton—The Scotch journey—Carlyle at 'The Gill'—Mrs. Carlyle at Auchtertool—'Seeking and finding'—Sunny Bank—Tender Remembrances—The return to London—Death of Lady Ashburton—Tribute to her—Bitter reflections—Scotland again—First readings of a portion of 'Frederick'—Wifely pride—Mrs. Carlyle's return to Cheyne Row—Discouragement—The kindness of Mr. Henry Larkin—Another visit to Germany—Mrs. Carlyle at Lann Hall—Holm Hill—Letters to Mr. Larkin—Cheyne Row once more—Second marriage of Lord Ashburton—Mrs. Carlyle's thoughts of her mother—The visit to 'Humbie' and Auchtertool—Carlyle again in Annandale with his own people.

We cannot overlook the 'strained relations' between Mrs. Carlyle and Lady Ashburton. *Intention* to wound, there cannot have been, but 'evil is wrought by want of thought, as well as want of heart'—and with all her gifts, we cannot see that Lady Ashburton possessed that blessed one of being able to put herself into other peoples places, mentally, and from the heart—that gift upon which so much of the deepest harmony of life depends. I quote an incident from Mr. Froude's book, referring to this incident, slight in itself, and only important as an illustration of the position in which Mrs. Carlyle was placed on many occasions.

A small incident in the summer of 1856, though a mere trifle in itself, may serve as an illustration of what she had to undergo. The Carlyles were going for a holiday to Scotland. Lady Ashburton was going also. She had engaged a palatial carriage which had been made for the Queen and her suite, and she proposed to take the Carlyles down with her. The carriage consisted of a spacious saloon, to which, communicating with it, an ordinary compartment with the usual six seats in it was attached. Lady Ashburton occupied the saloon alone. Mrs. Carlyle, though in bad health and needing rest as much as Lady A., was placed in the compartment with her husband, the family doctor, and Lady A.'s maid; a position perfectly proper for her if she was a dependent, but in which no lady could have been placed whom Lady Ashburton regarded as her own equal in rank. It may be that Mrs. Carlyle chose to have it so herself. But Lady A. ought not to have allowed it, and Carlyle ought not to have allowed it; for it was a thing wrong in itself. One is not surprised to find that when Lady A. offered to take her home in the same way she refused to go. 'If there were any companionship in the matter,' she said bitterly, when Carlyle communicated Lady A.'s proposal, 'it would be different; or if you go back with the Ashburtons it will be different, as then I should be going as part of your luggage without self-responsibility.' Carlyle regarded the Ashburtons as great people, to whom he was under obligations, who had been very good to him, and of whose train he, in a sense, formed a part. Mrs. Carlyle, with her proud, independent, Scotch republican spirit, imperfectly recognised these social distinctions. This, it may be said, was a trifle, and ought not to have been made much of. But there is no sign that Mrs. Carlyle did make much of what was but a small instance of her general lot. It happens to stand out by being mentioned incidentally—that is all. But enough has been said of this sad matter, which was now drawing near its end.

It is hard to say where things *end* or *begin*, with the subtle combinations presented by human hearts.

Something remains, always, of what has entered deeply into deep natures.

Arrived in Scotland, the party soon separated—Carlyle leaving his wife with her cousins at Auchtertool, and proceeding to his sister Mary's, at The Gill, Annan—'seeking and finding perfect solitude, kindness, and silence.' Mrs. Carlyle wrote him from Auchtertool Manse, of the comfort she felt with her good cousins there, but said she was 'sad as death.'

A short visit to her aunt's at 'Craigenvilla,' Edinburgh, did not help to lift the weight of bodily and mental depression—and by August 9, 1856, Mrs. Carlyle was once more at Sunny Bank, Haddington, the home of her godmother, Miss Donaldson. One of that kind group had died (Miss Kate), so the welcome was mixed with tears. 'Everybody is so kind to me—Oh! so kind, that I often burst out crying with pure thankfulness to them all.' So wrote Mrs. Carlyle to her husband, who was still at his sister's house, The Gill. The parting from Haddington was again a wrench. Mrs. Carlyle returned to her aunt's at 'Craigenvilla.' Many tender recollections of the Haddington visit appear in the letters to Carlyle. 'The people at Haddington,' she writes, 'seem all to grow so good and kind as they grow old!' Among the loving gifts showered on Mrs. Carlyle by the kind ladies at Sunny Bank were two canaries—'born in our own house, the darlings!' she says; a good substitute for the disreputable 'Chico!'

On August 26, a letter from Mr. Carlyle, arriving at the same time with one from Aunt Ann,* who was on a visit in Dumfriesshire—just at the moment of breakfast, caused quite a flutter, sufficient to make these excellent ladies forget to 'ask the blessing.' Mrs. Carlyle was amused, and regretted to old 'Betty' that her aunts should live 'in such a fuss of religion.' But the aunts were dear to their niece, who was glad she had made this return visit to them.

An invitation to some castle in Scotland had come to Mrs. Carlyle, and was felt to be very unacceptable. 'The honour of the thing'—she writes to Carlyle on August 23—'looks too mean, and scraggy, and icy a motive to make me go a foot length—or trouble myself the least in the world, with all

---

* One of the surviving daughters of John Welsh of Penfillan (Grace, Elisabeth and Ann—aunts, therefore, of Mrs. Carlyle).

those tears and kisses I brought from Haddington, still moist and warm on my heart. . . .'

Returned to Auchtertool, an unwise exertion made to hear Dr. Guthrie on the Sunday she passed in Edinburgh, left Mrs. Carlyle again very suffering. The eloquence of that great preacher did not make 'the game worth the candle' in this case.

In September Mrs. Carlyle visited Scotsbrig, while her husband was with the Ashburtons at Kinloch, Luichart, Dingwall. An unusual degree of irritation is shown in the two letters Mrs. Carlyle wrote him during this visit, the fret of the proposal that she should travel back to London with the Ashburtons seemed to cut her to the quick.

Lady Ashburton is very kind to offer to take me back (she had said). Pray make her my thanks for the offer. But, though a very little herring, I have a born liking to 'hang by my own head.' . . .

The concentrated bitterness of the words must have struck home.

And now comes a letter written after the Carlyles had both returned to 5 Cheyne Row, and dated October 10, 1856. Again Mrs. Carlyle unburdens some of her heart-sadness to Mrs. Russell of Thornhill. 'Oh! my dear, my dear, my dear!' she begins. 'To keep myself from going stark mad I must give myself something pleasant to do for this one hour. . . .' And then comes a lengthy narrative of ill-health and grievances small and great, none small to *her*, poor, overwrought woman! Home troubles—and servant troubles— 'a house full of bugs and evil passions'—as she herself graphically states it! Even the kind Geraldine Jewsbury could not stem this torrent of discomfort! Mrs. Carlyle ends by begging the Russells, in a body, to think of her and love her!

Carlyle had deeply felt his wife's expressions as to the proposed journey from Scotland to London, under Lady Ashburton's convoy. He said her feeling was 'wholly grounded on misknowledge, or in deep ignorance of the circumstances . . .' and there was reason in his so saying, *with the light he had.*

The year 1857 was to be a memorable one for these two strangely-mated beings. January found them dining at different hours—little cheer at either meal, we must suppose. Mrs. Carlyle was trying exercise in an omnibus—' some fourteen miles of shaking, at the modest cost of one shilling.' Mr. Carlyle's horse was giving him the highest satisfaction. 'The canaries,' writes Mrs. Carlyle in her letter to Mrs. Austin at The Gill, 'are the happiest creatures in the house— the dog next.' This account was indicative of scanty joy in the home—among the '*humans*,' as the Americans say.

But a great cause of suffering was about to be removed, and very unexpectedly. We quote from Carlyle.* He says: 'Monday, May 4, 1857.—At Paris, on her way home from Nice, Lady Ashburton (born Lady Harriet Montague) suddenly died: suddenly to the doctors and those who believed them; in which number, fondly hoping against hope, was I.' In his Journal at the time, May 6, 1857, he thus chronicles the event: 'A great and irreparable sorrow to me, yet with some beautiful consolations in it too. . . . To her I believe it is a great gain; and the exit has in it much of noble beauty, as well as pure sadness worthy of such a woman. Adieu! Adieu! Her work—call it grand and noble endurance of *want* of work—is all done!' Many years later, Mr. Froude tells us of Carlyle's expressions regarding her. 'She was the greatest lady of rank I ever saw, with the soul of a princess and a *captainess*, had there been any career possible to her but that fashionable one.'

Lord Houghton, in his 'Monograph' on Lady Ashburton says: 'The imperfect health against which Lady Ashburton had long struggled with so much magnanimity, resulted in a serious illness at Nice in 1857, and she died with resignation and composure at Paris on her way to England. She was

* *Letters and Memorials of Jane Welsh Carlyle.*

buried in the quiet churchyard, near to the home her presence had gladdened and elevated.'

Carlyle was present at the funeral, at Lord Ashburton's particular entreaty, and was now more at leisure to consider the other woman, whose martyrdom of suffering had never, perhaps, seemed quite so noble and attractive, and to whom 'want of work' was *not* added as an extra call for sympathy. It would seem that a short visit to Addiscombe was paid by the Carlyles some time after the event of Lady Ashburton's death, for Carlyle says: 'I rode much about with Lord Ashburton in intimate talk, and well recollect this visit of perhaps a week or ten days. . . . My Jane's miserable illness now over, a visit to Haddington was steadily in view all summer.' So of these two women the 'one had been taken and the other left'—the 'mill to grind' being quite overpoweringly hard for the one that was *left*. We marvel that the frail physique stood it out nearly another ten years, but *her* hour was not yet come!

On July 8, 1857, we find Mrs. Carlyle writing to her husband, who was at Chelsea, from her old quarters, Sunny Bank, Haddington. 'They are the same heavenly kind creatures,' she says, speaking of her entertainers, the Misses Donaldson —and again, 'I cannot write, I am so wearied; oh, so dreadfully wearied! . . . If you could fancy me in some part of the house out of sight, my absence would make little difference to you, considering how little I see of you, and how preoccupied you are when I do see you.' This savors not of indifference, but of an unsubdued, unabated, craving for love and notice from her husband.

Lord Ashburton had sent gifts to Mrs. Carlyle, personal reminiscences of his late wife, the receipt of which had overcome her very much, making her 'like to cry!' There was pain on all hands for her just now.

It was while on this visit to Haddington, that she visited her own old home, little altered, and full of associations. It was young Dr. Howden who lived there now, with his wife—that 'young girl-wife, who was so lovely and wrote poetry—God help her!' Having left Haddington Mrs. Carlyle writes on August 3 from Auchtertool, whither she had gone on a short visit, in language decidedly hyperbolical. She speaks of having to 'assume the muzzle of politeness' in other people's houses; but evidently found it hard to *keep hers on*. She refused other invitations, but hoped for a few days more at Sunny Bank before returning to London.

Her own ill-health caused much of the discomfort that steadily attended her. At sight of Carlyle's own letters to her she would now turn quite sick, and have to catch at a chair, and sit down trembling, before opening one. We must bear in mind the very forcible language habitually used by Mrs. Carlyle, both as to her 'domestic earthquakings' and other matters! At this very time she writes to Carlyle of a cousin, Jeannie, who, 'with her suite, did not arrive till yesterday. The baby,' she says, 'is about three fingerlengths long; the two nurses nearly six feet each.' The reader must smile, Carlyle himself must have been meant to smile, at the lively exaggeration, and this test might be applied to much that Mrs. Carlyle said, in her years of suffering especially; but it is impossible altogether to discount what she says of her own physical pains, which were, indeed, beyond words to describe.

A short visit to Craigenvilla was marked by a most appreciative and loving tribute to the portion of 'Frederick' now submitted to her. 'Oh! my dear!' she says, 'what a magnificent book this is going to be! *The best of all your books!*' This letter Carlyle calls 'the one bit of pure sunshine that visited my dark and lonesome, and in the end, quite dismal and inexpressible enterprise of 'Frederick'!

And now August 28 found Mrs. Carlyle again at Sunny Bank, with the old ladies who loved her so. She read to them, with wifely pride, the 'sheets' of 'Frederick,' but was wishing to be at home, and dreading the fatigue of the journey. The remembrance of her unfortunate journey northwards in July haunted her yet. It had been very bad, owing to an over-crowded railway carriage and unusual discomforts. Carlyle had lamented it tenderly at the time, and had written: 'You shall go into no more wretched saving of that kind—never more!' alluding to the second-class carriage.

Carlyle had been kind to the canaries and to little 'Nero' in his wife's absence; he wished to be kind and to make things easy for her. Her approval of the opening of 'Frederick' had delighted him. 'It would be worth while to write books,' he says, 'if mankind would read them as you do.' So the prospect was more cheery, and early in September Mrs. Carlyle returned, 'and there was joy in Nero, and in the canaries, and in creatures more important.' But the 'Friedrich affair' was a terrible trial, of thirteen years in all, and its shadow soon fell again over the passing gleam of joy.

It was in the July of 1858 that Mrs. Carlyle had written to her husband, then at Scotsbrig, of the difficulty of always writing and reporting her bad health. She wished it—in legal phrase—'taken as read' that she had sleepless nights, and nervous suffering. She had no other tale to tell, though Carlyle in his love, and his indomitable and blind hopefulness, always expected better things.

Suppose (she writes), instead of putting myself in the omnibus the other day, and letting myself be carried in unbroken silence to Richmond and back again, I had sat at home, writing to you all the thoughts that were in my head. . . . Not a hundredth part of the thoughts in my head have been, or ever will be, spoken or written—as long as I keep my senses, at least. Only don't *you*, the apostle of silence, find fault with me for putting your doctrine in practice. There are days when I must speak things all from the lips outwards, or things that, being of the nature of self-lamentation, had better never be spoken. . . .

It was in this month, namely, on July 19, 1858, that mention is made of Mr. Henry Larkin, who for the last three years had been rendering the most valuable and devoted help to Carlyle in his 'Frederick' and in many other literary matters, Carlyle appreciated the love-given services of this able young man. In a note in the 'Letters and Memorials' he calls him 'a helper sent me by the favour of Heaven, as I often said and felt in the years to come. . . . Never had I loyaller or more effective help. . . . A man to thank Heaven for, as I still gratefully acknowledge.'

After much personal conversation with Mr. Larkin, we feel we owe him much. Himself of a refined and sympathetic nature, he was able to understand both Mr. and Mrs. Carlyle. And it was to the latter that he was enabled to show a brother's kindness, and from whom he received a grateful and tender friendship. It was not till 1862 that Mr. Larkin actually *became* the 'neighbour' he had long proved himself, to the Carlyles—by taking up his abode, after his marriage, at No. 6 Cheyne Row—mainly at Mrs. Carlyle's wish. The article, 'A Ten Years' Reminiscence,' written by Mr. Larkin, to which reference has been made as having appeared in the 'British Quarterly,' July 1881, is vivid and deeply interesting, as throwing much light on the sad closing years of Mrs. Carlyle's life.

Early in August she was at Bay House, with the Ashburtons, and improved in health. 'I am quite comfortable, morally,' she writes on August 7; it was but a few weeks since Carlyle had written to her:

My poor little Jeannie, my poor, ever-true life-partner, hold up thy heart! We have had a sore life-pilgrimage together, much bad road . . . little like what I could have wished or dreamt for thee ! . . . Oh, forgive me ! forgive me for the much I have thoughtlessly done and omitted; far, far at all times from the poor purpose of my mind. And, God help us, *thee*, poor suffering soul, and also *me!*

These piercing expressions of sadness were written while Carlyle was in the fulness of his mental powers, and must be set against the judgment of those who regard the des-

Dr! the one living Doctor I know, or know of, in w[hom] I have retained confidence. His previous treatment, an unceasing cares at the leg and his wife's devoted ni[ght?] prevented the malady gaining ground, and I am up now after only two days and a half in bed — about as w[ell] as I was before — only a little uncertain on my leg, a little confused with th[e] effects of Morphia, a little less "conceited about my im-provement", and a great deal less impatient to set out for London! Set out I must however, as early as is consistent with ordinary prudence — for h[ave] idea of M.r Carlyle going

not at home, seeking
ings like a madman
& never finding them!" and
his depending on the
der mercies of Charlotte
r his diet — leaves me no
t — partly on Charlotte's
count, I confess, as well
on his own." —
So far as I can make
t from his programme
ten in the style of
"Lamentations of Jeremiah"
— will arrive at Chelsea
ne time of Thursday —
will sail from Antwerp
— Wednesday he says "y 21st
v d — and twenty four hours
re and then — ." " Then
will be at Chelsea," I fancy
to mean —

I write to tell you, th[at]
you may go and see a
him on Friday — And
a Mother to him poo
Babe of genius till I.
which will be in th[e]
beginning of next we[ek]
I expect — if all conti[nues]
to go well with my hou[se]
affairs — You need
not give Charlotte a[ny]
more board-wages — s[he]
will live with her Ma
on tick as usual, till
come and resume the ch[arge]
of that unhappy househol[d]
I calculate on leaving th[is]
on Friday — but shall b[e]
a few days amongst m[y]
L? relations — Love to you
Mother — it has several ti[mes]

which would probably have saved myself and 'others' all further trouble with me, had it not befallen in the house of a Dr.!—the one living Doctor I know, or know of, in whom I have retained confidence. His judicious treatment and unceasing cares at the beginning, and his wife's devoted nursing, prevented the malady gaining ground, and I am up now—after only two days and a half in bed—about as well as I was before, only a little uncertain on my legs, a little confused with the effects of morphia, a little less conceited about my 'improvement,' and a great deal less impatient to set out for London ! Set out I must, however, as early as is consistent with ordinary prudence—for the idea of Mr. Carlyle going about at home, *seeking things* like a madman, and never finding them ! 'and of his depending on the tender mercies of Charlotte for his diet, leaves me no rest—partly on Charlotte's account, I confess, as well as on his own !'

So far as I can make out from his programme, written in the style of *The Lamentations of Jeremiah*, he will arrive at Chelsea some time of Thursday. He will sail from Antwerp on Wednesday, he says, 'if not sooner'—and 'twenty-four hours more and then—'; 'then he will be at Chelsea,' I fancy this to mean.

I write to tell you, that you may go and see after him on Friday—and be a mother to him, poor Babe of Genius, till I come, which will be in the beginning of next week, I expect—if all continue to go well with my bodily affairs. You need not give Charlotte any more board-wages—she will live with her master on *tick* as usual, till I come and resume the charge of that unhappy household. I calculate on leaving this on Friday—but shall be a few days amongst Mr. C's relations. Love to your mother—it has several times crossed my mind with pleasure what a beautiful *pincushion* I have to go home to ! !

Yours affectionately,
JANE CARLYLE.

An amusing incident is given by Mr. Larkin as to this home-coming of Mrs. Carlyle. She had written to him from Thornhill a most urgent note to meet her, on her arrival at Euston, and given all particulars. But Mr. Larkin met the train and saw no trace of her, waited and carefully kept a sharp look out—no Mrs. Carlyle appeared! So, in some anxiety, he returned home, and called next day at 5 Cheyne Row to find her innocently wondering *why he had not met her!* 'That it was a well-meant trick,' Mr. Larkin never doubted;' nor, on consideration, do we.

Carlyle had returned from Germany 'broken and degraded'—but the already finished volumes of his 'Frederick' were out of the printer's hands and were extremely successful. '*Much babbled of in newspapers*,' he says, characteristically, in his Journal of December 8, 1858.

At this time a memorable event took place, Lord Ashburton married again—a Miss Stuart Mackenzie—and this lady was a true and kind friend of Mr. and Mrs. Carlyle, and afterwards of *him* in his loneliness. No misunderstanding now clouded the intercourse with the Ashburton family. The Dowager Lady Sandwich, mother of Lady Harriet Baring, continued to be a much-loved friend of Mr. and Mrs. Carlyle—as, indeed, she had been throughout. Lord Ashburton and his new wife had, however, gone at once to Egypt, so that acquaintance had not begun (with the successor to Lady Harriet) at the time of which we write. The clean house, a little maid, radiant with 'virtue its own reward,' and a jet black kitten, failed to keep up any cheer in Mrs. Carlyle's heart. The London atmosphere, she said, weighed on her like a hundredweight of lead.

Writing to Mr. J. G. Cooke on or about December 22, 1858, she says, in condolence on the death of this gentleman's mother: 'Yes; the longer one lives in this hard world motherless, the more a mother's loss makes itself felt and understood. . . . It is sixteen years since my mother died, *as unexpectedly*, and not a day, not an hour, has passed since that I have not missed her, have not felt the world colder and blanker for want of her. . . .'

Besides the want of the mother's sympathy, there were other blanks and irretrievable causes of pain in Mrs. Carlyle's life—many lying exclusively *in herself*, in a temperament pitiably unsuited to 'human nature's daily food,' and finding poison therein.

A dreary winter, that of 1858-59, leaves little to record. It was in June 1859 that, writing to Miss Barnes, the daughter of her kind doctor, she, Mrs. Carlyle, says: 'And if you will bring with you to-morrow evening whatever stock you may have of 'faith, hope, and charity,' I have no doubt but we shall become good friends.'

It had been resolved that the Carlyles should escape the heat of the London summer by a few months spent in Scotland. Rooms had been found in the farm-house of Humbie, near Aberdour, and thither Carlyle went by steamer, with the servant, Charlotte, his horse, and 'the blessed' (Nero). Mrs. Carlyle, in very frail health, went first to Haddington and joined her husband at Humbie after a few days' rest.

The visit to Humbie was not a success. Mrs. Carlyle was too weak to walk in the woods with her husband, too nervous to sit the willing horse 'Fritz,' the gift of the first Lady Ashburton, and October found the two restless natures once more in Chelsea; not, however, before a visit had been paid at Auchtertool, whence Mrs. Carlyle had written a highly original letter of congratulation to Miss Barnes, on the announcement of her approaching marriage. The letter is given here.

To Miss Barnes, King's Road, Chelsea.

Auchtertool House, Kirkcaldy: Aug. 24, 1859.

My dear Miss Barnes,—How nice of you to have written me a letter, 'all out of your own head' (as the children say), and how very nice of you to have remarked the forget-me-not, and read a meaning in it! It was certainly with intention I tied up some forget-me-nots along with my farewell roses; but I was far from sure of your recognising the intention, and at the same time not young enough to make it plainer. Sentiment, you see, is not well looked on by the present generation of women; there is a growing taste for fastness, or, still worse, for strong-mindedness! so a discreet woman (like me) will beware always of putting her sentiment (when she has any) in evidence—will rather leave it—as in the forget-me-not case—to be divined through sympathy; and failing the sympathy, to escape notice.

And you are actually going to get married! you! already! And you expect me to congratulate you! or 'perhaps not.' I admire the judiciousness of that 'perhaps not.' Frankly, my dear, I wish you all happiness in the new life that is opening to you; and you are marrying under good auspices, since your father approves of the marriage. But congratulation on such occasions seems to me a tempting of Providence. The triumphal-procession-air which, in our manners and customs, is given to marriage at the outset—that singing of *Te Deum* before the battle has begun—has, ever since I could reflect, struck me as somewhat senseless and somewhat impious. If ever one is to pray—if ever one is to feel grave and anxious—if ever one is to shrink from vain show and vain babble—surely it is just on the occasion of two human beings binding themselves to one another, for better and for worse, till death part them; just on that occasion which it is customary to celebrate only with rejoicings, and congratulations, and *trousseaux*, and white ribbon! Good God!

Will you think me mad if I tell you that when I read your words, 'I am going to be married,' I all but screamed? Positively, it took away my breath, as if I saw you in the act of taking a flying leap into infinite space. You had looked to me such a happy, happy little girl! your father's only daughter; and he so fond of you, as he evidently was. After you had walked out of our house together that night, and I had gone up to my own room, I sat down there in the dark, and took 'a good cry.' You had reminded me so vividly of my own youth, when I, also an only daughter—an only child—had a father as fond of me, as proud of me. I wondered if you knew your own happiness. Well! knowing it or not, it has not been enough for you, it would seem. Naturally, youth is so insatiable of happiness, and has such sublimely insane faith in its own power to make happy and be happy.

But of your father? Who is to cheer his toilsome life, and make home bright for him? His companion through half a lifetime gone! his dear 'bit of rubbish' gone too, though in a different sense. Oh, little girl! little girl! do you know the blank you will make to him?

Now, upon my honour, I seem to be writing just such a letter as a raven might write if it had been taught. Perhaps the henbane I took in despair last night has something to do with my mood to-day. Anyhow, when one can only ray out darkness, one had best clap an extinguisher on oneself. And so God bless you !

Sincerely yours,
JANE W. CARLYLE.

It was not at the Manse that the Carlyles were now staying, but at a large comfortable house lent by a Mr. Liddell, 'where,' as Mrs. Carlyle writes to her friend Mr. George Cooke, 'we should have done very well had not Mr. C. walked and rode and bathed himself into a bilious crisis, just before leaving Humbie.' She describes her position during a portion of this time, and we fear the instance was not a solitary one, as being 'more like being keeper in a mad-house, than being in the country for quiet and change'; and yet, at the very outset of this ill-fated holiday, Carlyle, writing to his brother John, who was to meet the weary traveller, had said: 'Be soft and good with her: you have no notion what ill any fuss or flurry does her.' The discomforts of Humbie had been too much for both husband and wife—they went afterwards to Auchtertool, as we have said, and Carlyle subsequently into Annandale, to his own people.

CHAPTER XXV

A. D. 1859-1860

Life in Cheyne Row—Mrs. Carlyle's return—George Rennie's death—Letters of Mrs. Carlyle on the subject to Mrs. Dinning of Belford, Northumberland—Carlyle at Thurso Castle—Mrs. Carlyle, with Lady Stanley of Alderley, *en route* for Scotland—Holm Hill—Misunderstanding as to date of Carlyle's return—Mrs. Carlyle returns to Cheyne Row unnecessarily—Carlyle's remorse—Two servants kept.

THESE were dreary days for the subject of this Memoir. To quote from Mr. Froude a peculiarly powerful passage in his 'Life in London,' Vol. II. p. 234:

Mrs. Carlyle grew continually more feeble, continual nervous anxiety allowing her no chance to rally; but her indomitable spirit held her up. She went out little in the evenings, but she had her own small tea-parties, and the talk was as brilliant as ever. If any of us were to spend the evening there, we generally found her alone; then he would come in, take possession of the conversation, and deliver himself in a stream of splendid monologue, wise, tender, scornful, humorous, as the inclination took him—but never bitter, never malignant—always genial, the fiercest denunciations ending in a burst of laughter at his own exaggerations. Though I knew things were not altogether well, and her drawn, suffering face haunted me afterwards like a sort of ghost, I felt, for myself, that in him there could be nothing really wrong, and that he was as good as he was great.

This description is of high value, and gives a vivid picture of part of the home-life at 5 Cheyne Row.

And now Mrs. Carlyle purposed to return all alone to Chelsea, breaking her journey at York. She writes on

September 22, 1859, from Scawin's Hotel, York, to Carlyle at The Gill: 'With the recollection of the agonies of tiredness I suffered on the journey down, and for many days after, still tingling through my nerves . . . . I kept determined not to expose myself to that again'; so she went home without hurry, and Carlyle was to spend a day or two with the Stanleys of Alderley on *his* homeward journey; which gave Mrs. Carlyle a little respite—not un-needed—for she was fatigued and sleepless.

On September 29, she was nailing down drugget—with dismay at seams which had 'given' in the washing—and she was neglecting her dinner and dinner-hour, and not keeping up what little strength she had brought home. By October 3, Carlyle himself had arrived, but a small though deeply felt trouble came first, which concerned the little dog 'Nero.' Just before Carlyle's arrival, 'the night before,' writes Mrs. Carlyle to Mrs. Russell, 'Charlotte went to some shops, taking the dog with her, and brought him home in her arms, all crumpled together like a crushed spider.' A butcher's cart had passed over the little Nero's throat and nearly killed him. The accident distressed Mrs. Carlyle much, and, as we shall see, ended in the dog's death a few months later.

It was about this time that Dr. Russell retired from active medical practice in Thornhill village, and took up his residence in his pretty new home. Of this change, to the new Holm Hill, Mrs. Carlyle says to her friend: 'It will be . . . . more agreeable when you have once *got over the pain of change*.' This, in her own case, we think Mrs. Carlyle never did.

There was a short visit to the Grange in January 1860. It was much enjoyed by Mrs. Carlyle, but about a fortnight after the return to Cheyne Row 'Nero' died, after much suffering. Mrs. Carlyle wrote on Feb 1, to Mr. Barnes, who had evidently ministered to the poor little beast's painless removal from life: 'My gratitude to you will be as long as my life, for shall I not, as long as I live, remember that poor little dog? Oh, don't think me absurd, you, for caring so much about a dog. Nobody but myself can have any idea what that little creature has been in my life. My inseparable companion during eleven years; ever doing his little best to keep me from feeling sad and lonely!'

The weary year wore on. Events there were, but some very sad ones. George Rennie, her old friend and lover, lay dying in his house at 32 York Terrace, Regent's Park. His wife had written to Mrs. Carlyle that he was at the point of death, and that *she*, as his oldest friend, should know it. The summons was promptly responded to, and it was the companion of his childhood, the love of his early manhood, who received his last breath and closed his eyes. It was another link with Haddington taken from Mrs. Carlyle, and it was keenly felt. She it was who broke the news of George Rennie's death to his aunt, Mrs. Dinning, the 'Grace Rennie' of the dear old days. The letter, and one written a few days later, have been kindly placed in our hands, and are given here—touching in their evidence of deep feeling. It is with reverence that they have been transcribed.

No. I.

Copy of letter from Mrs. Carlyle to Mrs. Dinning, The Terrace, Belford, Northumberland.

(*Postmark*.—March 24, 1860.)

32 York Terrace, Regent's Park: Friday 23rd (March, 1860).

My dear '*Grace Rennie*' of long ago,—It must be something like forty years since I saw your sweet face, or had any exchange of words with you! Still, I recollect you well and kindly. I wonder if *you* have any recollection of *me*—of the little Jeannie Welsh you were so kind to, and your nephew George so much in love with? At least you will recollect my name, and the fact of my existence, when recalled to you by this letter; and you will recollect my beautiful mother, who was fond of you, well—after all this life time, I am writing to you, not to recall *myself* to your mind, but to tell you what you ought to be told, not merely officially, but with some words of sympathy and detail.

George—*your* George Rennie and *my* George Rennie, is dead —died yesterday morning at six o'clock—having been insensible from the previous Sunday. By a strange fatality, it was I who watched by him thro' his last night on earth. I, his first love, who received his last breath and closed his eyes! Was it not a strange, sad thing; after so many separations—so many tossings up and down this weary earth! His wife wrote to me on Tuesday that he was at the point of death, and I, 'as his oldest friend, should know it.' God bless her for that thought— death abolishes all forms and ceremonies; so I went to her at once, and begged to be let stay. She granted my petition, indeed she was quite worn out with sleeplessness and anxiety, and was needing the help of one (who) could give it with such fellow-feeling as I could. After that, I never left him till all was over. He never was conscious for an instant—but still it was a satisfaction to have *been with him* at the last. Mrs. Rennie begged me to stay with *her*, she was so desolate; tho' she bears up bravely, and I was willing, for his sake, to be of any earthly use to her, so long as my husband will spare me from my own house.

If I saw you, I could tell you much about George that you would like to hear; but just now I am so sorrowful and tired, that I must content myself with saying, tho' he kept up no intercourse with his relations, it was not from a cold or changed heart. A few weeks before his death I spoke to him about that part of his conduct which displeased me, and found that *pride, reserve*,—his soured temper about the world—was at the bottom of it all; he spoke affectionately of his aunt Grace, and said he would take the first opportunity of going to see her —' would do many things too long neglected, could he only get rid of those depressing headaches that made his life miserable.'

I think you will like to know this was his intention, tho' never to be fulfilled; and I offered to Richard to write the letter he would else have written himself to tell you of his father's death—that along with the news you might receive the comfort to your good heart (it cannot be changed from the heart I knew it), which the assurance of his kind feeling towards you is calculated to give, and which *I* only, perhaps, had heard from him.

Never was there a man—as I told him then—who did himself

more injustice. I believe he had the warmest, truest heart, but it was encased in pride and distrust of others' affection for him, making it of no use to them or himself.

God bless you !   Yours affectionately,
JANE WELSH CARLYLE.

If you would write me a line one day, wouldn't I like to hear of you from yourself. I never passed thro' Darlington, in coming or going to Scotland, without thinking, 'Wasn't it in this neighbourhood that Grace Rennie went to live?'

I daresay you will hardly be able to read this scrawl, I am so tired.

No. II.

Letter from Mrs. Carlyle to Mrs. Dinning, The Terrace, Belford, Northumberland.

(*Dated on envelope.*—March 31, 1860.)

5, Cheyne Row, Chelsea.

Oh, you dear, nice woman ! I should like to put my arms round your neck and give you a hearty kiss ! It is such a pleasure to meet with anyone in this changeful world whom one can recognise for *the same*, after forty years, and *you* look out of that letter on me, the same 'Grace Rennie' that was such a favourite in my old home. Not that if we should see one another face to face, we should not, I daresay, be mutually struck with a certain sorrowful wonder at the alteration in our appearance; for, 'Eh, sir' (*sic*), as the old Ayrshire lady said on meeting, after a lifetime, the companion of her youth, 'Eh, sir (*sic*), forty years makes a great odds on *a girl*.' In outward appearance, yes. None of us can carry off an additional forty years without 'a great odds' being perceptible to 'the naked eye.' But, thank God, there *are* people—not many, but a few—who do continue to keep their inner selves the same—who *won't* let years get *into* their hearts and minds to carry on any hardening, deteriorating process there ! And you are such a one, dear Grace, I could swear from your letter to me, and also from my recollection of your eyes; it wasn't what is called 'the Devil's beauty' (youth) that your eyes were so beautiful with, but the beauty that comes of a loving, honest heart.

I have not seen your 'Henry,' nor heard of him. Please to give him my address yourself (it is written at the top of this sheet). . . . Tell him, moreover, that *after four* is the surest time for finding me, and that a *Chelsea* omnibus will bring him to within a few yards of my door.

I shall like so much to see him. . . .

Dear Grace, the things that are in my heart and memory about poor George, would find more response from *you*, I am sure, than from *her*; and some day we shall surely meet, to have a long talk about him. I don't know whether I shall be going to Scotland this year; I was not minded to go, having spent all last summer there; and my husband being too busy with his book for taking any holyday (*sic*) at all this coming summer. But a new motive for going has arisen, which *may*, perhaps, overcome the motives for staying at home.

You remember Sunny Bank and the Miss Donaldsons?—my mother's ever kind, most trusted friends. They and I have never lost sight of one another; their love for me has been like the love of a mother. Of late years, since they were reduced to *two* (the two eldest), and very suffering and sad, I have gone to visit them every two years or oftener, besides writing to them once a week. They cared so much for seeing me, and hearing from me, and it was such a pleasure to me to be of any comfort to them in their dreary, lonely, suffering times. Now, Miss Donaldson (the eldest), who has been blind, deaf, and *dying* for the last two years, but with as warm a heart and as clear a mind as she had in her prime, is dead; and none of us can be other than thankful at *her* release. But poor Miss Jess—the last of them all—and, since ever I remember, the most ailing of them all—to think of *her*, *alone*, at Sunny Bank, to struggle with ever-increasing infirmities; *that* makes me very sorrowful, and if she would like me to come to her, when the London neice, and other relatives who have gathered about her, but will soon 'tire of the dullness,' leave her to her solitary fate, why, I should just have to provision my husband for two or three weeks, give my servant as minute instructions about him as if he were a three-years-old baby—(*Baby just old enough to get into the fire*), and take the 'North British.' Then, as sure as you live, I would get out at Belford and have a few hours' talk with you, 'face to face, and soul to soul'—(as one's poetry book had it long ago.

Why should one cease to be poetical because one is getting near to sixty? I see no reason).

But if I go at all, it will not be for two or three months yet; and very likely I may not go north this year. Let us hope in that case that we may meet another year. Meanwhile, after having been kindly remembered by you for forty years, I need not fear being forgotten by you in one. And so, good-by dear, with best wishes for all your belongings,

JANE WELSH CARLYLE.

Little record marks the months of a spring and summer evidently felt to be most depressing. In August of this year, 1860, Carlyle went to Thurso Castle, as the guest of Sir George Sinclair, and took his work with him. The 'Frederick' still weighed horribly upon the biographer. In one of his annotations on a letter of his wife to Mrs. Russell, earlier in the year, he said: 'My darling must have suffered much in all this—how much! . . . Never once by word or sign, in all her deep misery, did she hint what she, too, was suffering. . . . *Me* only did she seem to pity in it!' Thurso proved a congenial resting and working place for Carlyle, and his wife writes one of her sparkling letters to the kind host, Sir George Sinclair, saying: 'Pray do keep him as long as you like.'

It was strange that 5 Cheyne Row was again the scene of a domestic 'earthquaking.' 'Upholsterers and painters plashing away for their lives; and a couple of bricklayers tearing up flags in the kitchen.'

To Carlyle himself, his wife complained that a letter just received from him would read charmingly in his biography, and might be quoted in Murray's Guide Book, but said that she, 'as one solitary individual, had not been charmed with it at all.' But she was too ill and weak to be 'charmed' at this time. She was to have some Scotch air, too, and was on her way to the Stanleys of Alderley, Congleton, Cheshire, to break the long journey by the rest, and Lady Stanley's great kindness. Miss Jewsbury and Mr. Larkin, kind and sympathising friends, 'saw her off', at Euston on August 23, 1860. From Alderley Park, she meant to go to the attached relations at The Gill for a few days, and then on to the ever-dear Mrs. Russell of Holm Hill, where she was always happy and soothed. 'To have a doctor for one's host was a consideration of some weight with me,' she writes to Carlyle.

But, two days later, her visions of rest had all turned to ashes. Carlyle had just discovered that he could do no more at Thurso and must get home again. He had really intended prolonging his absence in Annandale before his actual return, but had omitted to make it clear, and Mrs. Carlyle had imagined his absence would have been a much longer one, so the blow to her was a very heavy one. To give up the visit to Mrs. Russell was a hard task—and the poor lady, writing, tells her friend: 'I could sit down and take a hearty cry!'

The length of time needed for posts to and from Thurso aggravated matters, and added an unnecessary bitterness to the change of plan. For, after giving up all her own wishes and hurrying home to Chelsea, a letter was forwarded to Mrs. Carlyle,—a letter which had gone round by Alderley and missed her there,—with the news that, after all, Carlyle had been persuaded to stay on longer at Thurso, and thence to visit friends in Scotland before returning. He wished Mrs. Carlyle could now be persuaded to start again on her travels, but that could not be. She could not, as he had proposed, 'rectify her huge error.' She was not strong enough, and she was too deeply annoyed at the needless disappointment. Her doctor, too, told her that 'no change could do her good that involved fatigue or fret of mind.' So at Chelsea she remained.

A household improvement in the shape of *two* servants, which had been Carlyle's own arrangement, was some help to the wearied mistress of 5 Cheyne Row, and it was in a most humble and dejected state of mind that he arrived late in September. He sincerely wished to be considerate, but failed of it, as some of the best and noblest fail, where a smaller and more ordinary nature will calmly succeed without effort. His sleeping-room being above that of his wife was a cause of suffering to her in her highly nervous condition.

My own wakings up (she writes to Mrs. Austin of The Gill, in October 1860) some twenty or thirty times every night of my life, for years and years back, are as nothing compared with hearing him jump out of bed overhead, once or sometimes twice during a night. . . . Now that my nerves have had a rest, and that I am more 'used to it,' I get to sleep again when all is quiet, but God knows how long I may be up to that. And when he has broken sleep, and I no sleep at all, it is sad work here, I assure you.

CHAPTER XXVI

A. D. 1861-1863

Mrs. Carlyle's craving for her 'one little maid-servant'—Death of Arthur Hugh Clough—Mrs. Carlyle's visit to Ramsgate with Miss Jewsbury—Sleeplessness—Longings to visit Mrs. Russell—Estimate of men—Miss Barnes' marriage—Deaths of dear friends—Folkestone—Mrs. Carlyle accomplishes her visit to Holm Hill and Craigenvilla—'Old Betty'—Visit to Auchtertool—Home again—Illness of Lord Ashburton in Paris—Mrs. Carlyle's wish to go and be useful—Sad letter to 'Old Betty'—The Carlyles at the Grange—Neuralgia or Rheumatism causing Mrs. Carlyle increasing pain—The accident soon after return to Cheyne Row—Carlyle's account—Mr. Froude's account—Mr. Larkin's account.

THE increase in the domestic staff gave no comfort to Mrs. Carlyle. She was constantly being seized, in the dead of night, with a wild desire to clear the house of these newcomers, and take back her 'one little Charlotte,' which she eventually did, retaining the most promising of the two *existing* 'helps,' a young and cheerful girl. The two maid-servants, respectively 19 and 17, kept up, says Mrs. Carlyle, 'an incessant chirping and chattering and laughing . . . pleasant to hear.' So there came a little imported brightness into the sad home.

In this year Arthur Hugh Clough—the pure-minded, conscientious, gifted, loving, and lovable friend—died at Florence. He was much valued by all who knew him, and Mr. Froude was specially anxious that Carlyle should write some few words to his honoured and dear remembrance. But Carlyle could not do it; every moment was claimed by 'Frederick.'

The year 1860 had closed in extreme cold. Gifts of seal furs and soft Indian shawls failed to keep up Mrs. Carlyle's vitality. There is another sort of chill even harder to minister to. 'If one's skin were a trifle thicker, all these worries would seem light,' she says.

Renewed domestic earthquakings rendered the summer of 1861 as trying as ever, and again, a projected visit to Mrs. Russell of Thornhill must be given up—a heavy disappointment! A short visit to Ramsgate with Miss Jewsbury was substituted, but it was not favourable to Mrs. Carlyle's health. The accounts of this 'quiet lodging' are very amusing.

From early morning till late night cries of prawns, shrimps, lollipops—things one never wanted, and will never want . . . . and if that were all. But a brass band plays all through our breakfast, and repeats the performance often during the day, and the brass band is succeeded by a band of Ethiopians, and that again by a band of female fiddlers, and interspersed with these are individual barrel organs, individual Scotch bagpipes, individual French horns.

And even there the trouble did not stop, for to that overwrought brain there were

Hundreds of cocks getting waked up, say, at one in the morning, and never going to sleep again—these cocks—but for minutes, and there are three steeple clocks that strike in succession, and there are doors and gates that slam, dogs that bark occasionally, and a saw-mill, and a mews, and, in short, everything you could wish *not* to hear.

Later on she says: 'Indeed, noise seems to be the grand joy of life at Ramsgate!'

This bitter complaint contrasts strangely with the pathetic letter to Mrs. Russell, written on August 30, soon after Mrs. Carlyle's return to Cheyne Row.

I had set my heart (she writes) on streaming off by myself to Holm Hill, and taking a life-bath, as it were, in my quasi-natural air, in the scene of old affections, not all past and gone, but some still there as alive and warm, thank God, as ever. . . Ah! my dear, your kindness goes to my heart, and makes me like to cry, because I cannot do as you bid me. . . I tried him

(Mr. C.) alone for a few days, when I was afraid of falling seriously ill, unless I had change of air. . . But the letter that came from him every morning was like the letter of a Babe in the Wood, who would be found buried with dead leaves by the robins if I did not look to it.

'This few days' was the visit to Ramsgate; a little later the Carlyles accepted the cordial invitation of the dowager Lady Sandwich, mother of the first Lady Ashburton, to visit her at Harewood Lodge, Berks, but an attack of lumbago, which Carlyle suffered from during that time, took all benefit from the visit.

New Year's Day 1862, opened pleasantly with a dainty little gift of an 'egg-cup,' sent to Mrs. Carlyle by her friend Mr. Cooke, but she was quite unable to face the thought of being present at the marriage of Miss Barnes, and calls the bride-elect, ' Oh you agonising little girl,' for proposing her presence at the ceremony.

An accident to Dr. Russell from the falling of the lid of a safe on his fingers, calls forth a burst of sympathy, followed by some sharp remarks on the conduct of *men generally*. 'Whether,' she writes, 'it be their pride, or their impatience, or their obstinacy, or their ingrained spirit of contradiction, that stupefies and misleads them, the result is always a certain amount of idiotcy, or distraction, in their dealings with their whole bodies.' This was plainly 'badinage,' real *fun*, to be met with a cheery laugh, not real conviction wrapped in bitter words. And this distinction should often be made, by those who can see it, in judging the utterances of Mr. and Mrs. Carlyle.

The dreaded wedding ceremonial of Miss Barnes, in February 1862, *was* graced by the presence of Mrs. Carlyle, after much preliminary warning, at St. Luke's Church.

Warm summer weather brought its freight of sorrows. The deaths of Elisabeth Pepoli, Lady Sandwich, and the bright young American lady, Mrs. Twisleton, pained her sadly. The loss of Lady Sandwich, who was eighty years of age, was the hardest to bear—'the most charming companion, and the warmest, loyallest friend,' writes Mrs. Carlyle to Mrs. Russell on June 5, 1862. So Mrs. Carlyle longed, with an eager, feverish longing, to get away from London, 'to think over all this in quiet'; but she was 'on duty,' her husband still struggling with the two remaining volumes of 'Frederick.' Fortunately Mrs. Carlyle went, ere the month was out, to the Ashburtons at Folkestone, where her husband joined her for a short time, after her first week there. The second Lady Ashburton was a most cordial friend to the Carlyles.

Back again at Chelsea by July 20; things were not cheerful, and when Carlyle accepted an invitation to visit the Marquis of Lothian at Blickling Park, Norfolk, Mrs. Carlyle, declining her part in the visit, resolved to go to her beloved Mrs. Russell at Holm Hill, and wrote to tell her so. There was, as usual, a hindrance. 'This related to a bruised, sprained, or otherwise bedevilled foot,' caused by a fall in stepping back on the pavement and striking her foot violently against the kerbstone, when returning late at night from a call to ask after a sick lady at Islington. The journey was taken, however, and she reported herself better in every way, even 'the foot.'

The departure from Holm Hill, on her return, was, Mrs. Carlyle tells her husband, 'like the partings of dear, old long ago. . . . And then the journey through the hills to that lonely little churchyard' (Crawford, where Mrs. Welsh's grave was), 'all that caused me so many tears, that to-day my eyes are out of my head, and I am sick and sore!' She writes these words from Craigenvilla, where she was visiting her aunts. The date is September 2. On the same day she writes, with desperate sadness, to Mrs. Russell, her late hostess, and speaks of 'going in an omnibus for a dose of morphia to Duncan and Flockhart's.' She, no doubt, had a physician's prescription which could be made up if needful. 'It will calm down my mind,' she says, 'for once—generally my mind needs no calming, being sunk in apathy.' In closing the letter Mrs. Carlyle says: 'Oh, my dear, my dear! Shall I ever forget those green hills, and that lovely churchyard, and your dear, gentle face?'

Seeing 'Betty,' the old Haddington nurse, was another pull at her tired heart. It was this kind ' Betty ' (Mrs. Braid), upon whom Colonel Davidson called and whose graphic account of Dr. Welsh's death is quoted in the appendix.

Mrs. Carlyle felt bound to spend a few days at Auchtertool Manse, with her cousins, the Rev. Walter Welsh and his wife, and she did so, though ' missing that congeniality which comes of having mutually suffered and taken one's suffering to heart. I feel here, as if I were "playing" with nice, pretty, well-behaved children ! I almost envy them their lighthearted capacity for being engrossed with trifles ! And yet *not that*. . . .'

September 30 found her on the eve of departure from Cheyne Row, whither she had not long returned, to stay at Dover with Miss Davenport Bromley, the kindly lady whose bright disposition had procured her, from the Carlyles, the name of 'the flight of skylarks.' Here she felt herself 'less ghastly sick,' found 'Miss B. kind and charming, and the place delicious. . . .'

But it was too late to stave off the suffering of sick nerves by these kind attentions, and October 20, 1862, found her again under the worry of 'servants,' and more or less saddened. Lord Ashburton was ill in Paris, under anxious circumstances. Lady Ashburton was alone to nurse him, and with news of her own mother's death arriving during her husband's illness. A sister of Lady A., who had hurried to her help, had been recalled to London by the serious illness of *her* husband. Mrs. Carlyle, always prompt to help, wrote, offering to go over immediately. But the offer was declined in touching words, 'It would do her no good,' wrote Lady A., 'and would knock me up . . . She was past all human help, and past all sympathy,' she said. 'The poor, dear soul,' writes Mrs. Carlyle, 'had drawn her pen through the last words!—so like her—that she might not seem unkind. . . .'

It was on Christmas Day that she wrote to her old nurse, Mrs. Braid, as 'Dearest Betty,' and says, '. . . I don't wish you a "mirth" and a "happiness" which I know to have passed out of Christmas and New Year for such as us for evermore; passed out of them, along with so much else; our gay spirits, our bright hopes, living hearts that loved us, and the fresh, trusting life of our own hearts. It is a thing too sad for tears. . . .'

On March 2, 1863, she writes to Grace Welsh of having spent a day and night at Ealing, with Mrs. Oliphant, which ' greatly revived her.' But the east winds did their deadly work on her weakened frame; her letters tell of much suffering.

In May 1863 she wrote again to her old nurse, Mrs. Braid, with great tenderness. A tiny green plant that she had brought from her father's grave, had, ' after twelve months in the garden at Chelsea, declared itself a gooseberry bush, and had borne three veritable gooseberries, which, however, dwined and drooped and fell,' whether through mere delicacy ' in the poor, wild thing,' she could not tell.

A week at St. Leonards in June, in the most favourable circumstances, with 'a carriage to drive out in thrice a day; a clever physician for host, who dieted me on champagne and the most nourishing delicacies; and for hostess a gentle, graceful, loving woman,' did good while it lasted, but the old symptoms returned, and August found the Carlyles at the Grange, where Lord Ashburton's continued delicacy of health forbade a large house-party, admitting only the Carlyles and the late Mr. Venables. Mr. Froude says: ' The visit was a happy one, a gleam of pure sunshine before the terrible calamity which was now impending.'

Mrs. Carlyle, in speaking of this visit to Mrs. Russell of Holm Hill, on September 16, says:

In spite of the fine air and beauty of the Grange, and Lady Ashburton's super-human kindness, I had no enjoyment of anything during the three weeks we stayed; being in constant pain, day and night. . . . I think I told you I had pain, more or less, in my left arm for two months before I left London . . . it became worse and worse, and I was driven at last to consult Dr. Quain, when he came down to see Lord A. He told me . . . that it wasn't rheumatism I had got, but neuralgia !—If any good Christian would explain to me the difference between these two things, I should feel edified and grateful.

The pain, whichever it was, proved intractable to treatment and was the forerunner of fatal trouble.

Soon after the return from the Grange, Mrs. Carlyle had ventured on a drive as far as St. Martin's Lane, to call on a cousin of hers, Mrs. Godby. She was later in returning than Carlyle expected. The fact was that on leaving Mrs. Godby, a maidservant accompanied the guest to catch the omnibus which was to take her home. Some excavation in the road prevented the omnibus from coming close to the pavement. Mrs. Carlyle set off quickly to step into it, and was thrown by a passing cab on the kerbstone. Her lamed right arm was powerless to break her fall, and she was helped into a cab and taken home in helpless pain, the sinews of one thigh sprained and lacerated, and the whole system shocked and shaken. Carlyle's own words in the 'Reminiscences' are:

The visit to Mrs. Godby had been pleasant, and gone all well; but now, dusk falling, it had to end. Again by omnibus, as ill-luck would have it. Mrs. G. sent one of her maids as escort. At the corner of Cheapside the omnibus was hailed for (some excavations going on near by, as for many years passed they seldom ceased to do); Chelsea omnibus came; my darling was in the act of stepping in (maid stupid and of no assistance), when a cab came rapidly from behind, and, forced by the near excavation, seemed as if it would drive over her, such her frailty and want of speed. She desperately determined to get on the flag pavement again; desperately leaped and did get upon the kerbstone; but found she was falling over upon the flags, and that she would alight on her right or neuralgic arm, which would be ruin; spasmodically struggled against this for an instant or two (maid nor nobody assisting), and had to fall on the neuralgic arm—ruined otherwise far worse, for, as afterwards appeared, the muscles of the thigh-bone or sinews attaching them had been torn in that spasmodic instant or two; and for three days coming the torment was excessive, while in the right arm there was no neuralgia perceptible during that time, nor any very manifest new injury afterwards either.

The calamity had happened, however, and in that condition, my poor darling, 'put into a cab' by the humane people, as her one request to them, arrived at this door, 'later' than I expected; and after such a 'drive from Cheapside' as may be imagined! I remember well my joy at the sound of her wheels ending in a knock; then my surprise at the delay in her coming up, at the singular silence of the maids when questioned as to that. Thereupon my rushing down, finding her in the hands of Larkin and them, in the greatest agony of pain and helplessness I had ever seen her in. The noble little soul, she had determined I was not to be shocked by it. Larkin then lived next door, assiduous to serve us in all things (did maps, indexes, even joinerings, etc., etc.); him she had resolved to charge with it. Alas, alas! as if you could have saved me, noble heroine and martyr? Poor Larkin was standing helpless; he and I carried her upstairs in an armchair to the side of her bed, into which she crept by aid of her hands. In a few minutes, Barnes (her wise old doctor) was here, assured me there were no bones broken, no joint out, applied his bandagings and remedies, and seemed to think the matter was slighter than it proved to be—the spasmodic tearing of sinews being still a secret to him. For fifty hours the pain was excruciating; after that it rapidly abated and soon altogether ceased, except when the wounded limb was meddled with never so little. The poor patient was heroic, and had throughout been. Within a week, she had begun contriving rope machineries, leverages, and could not only pull her bell, but lift and shift herself about, by means of her arms, into any coveted posture, and was, as it were, mistress of the mischance. She had her poor little room arranged under her eye, to a perfection of beauty and convenience.

It is interesting, also, to add Mr. Froude's account of this disaster.

One evening (he says), after their return, Mrs. Carlyle had gone to call on a cousin at the post-office in St. Martin's Lane. She had come away, and was trying to reach an omnibus, when she was thrown by a cab on the kerbstone. Her right arm being disabled by neuralgia, she was unable to break her fall. The sinews of one thigh were sprained and lacerated, and she was brought home in a fly in dreadful pain. She knew that Carlyle would be expecting her. Her chief anxiety, she told me, was to get into the house without his knowledge, to spare him agitation. For herself, she could not move. She stopped at the door of Mr. Larkin, who lived in the adjoining house in Cheyne Row, and asked him to help her. The sound of the wheels and the noise of voices reached Carlyle in the drawing-room. He rushed down, and he and Mr. Larkin together bore her up the stairs, and laid her on her bed. There she remained, in an agony which, experienced in pain as she was, exceeded the worst that she had known.

Carlyle was not allowed to know how seriously she had been injured. The doctor and she both agreed to conceal it from him, and during those first days a small incident happened, which she herself described to me, showing the distracting want of perception, which sometimes characterized him—a want of perception, not a want of feeling, for no one could have felt more tenderly. The nerves and muscles were completely disabled on the side on which she had fallen, and one effect was that the under jaw had dropped, and that she could not close it. Carlyle always disliked an open mouth; he thought it a sign of foolishness. One morning, when the pain was at its worst, he came into her room, and stood looking at her, leaning on the mantel-piece. 'Jane,' he said presently, 'ye had better shut your mouth.' She tried to tell him that she could not. 'Jane,' he began again, 'ye'll find yourself in a more compact and pious frame of mind if ye shut your mouth.' In old-fashioned and, in him, perfectly sincere phraseology, he told her that she ought to be thankful that the accident was no worse. Mrs. Carlyle hated cant as heartily as he, and to her, in her sore state of mind and body, such words had a flavor of cant in them. True herself as steel, she would not bear it. 'Thankful!' she said to him; 'thankful for what? for having been thrown down in the street when I had gone on an errand of charity? for being disabled, crushed, made to suffer in this way? I am not thankful, and I will not say that I am.' He left her, saying he was sorry to see her so rebellious.

We can hardly wonder after this that he had to report sadly to his brother: 'She speaks little to me, and does not accept me as a sick nurse, which, truly, I had never any talent to be.' Of course, he did not know at first her real condition. She had such indomitable courage that she persuaded him that she was actually better off since she had become helpless than 'when she had been struggling to get out daily and returned done up, with her joints like to fall in pieces.'

For a month she could not move—at the end of it she was able to struggle to her feet and crawl occasionally into the adjoining room. Carlyle was blind. Seven weeks after the accident he could write: 'She actually sleeps better, eats better, and is cheerfuller than formerly. For perhaps three weeks past she has been hitching about with a stick. She can walk too, but slowly without a stick. In short, she is doing well enough—as indeed am I, and have need to be.'*

We now give Mr. Henry Larkin's account of Mrs. Carlyle's accident.†

Carlyle has told us of the serious accident which happened to his wife on her returning home one evening in 1863. I recollect that evening, perfectly, and also the scene of helpless misery which in a few words he so distinctly photographs. But the eye only sees what it brings the means of seeing; and he little thought it was his own presence which had suddenly produced the collapse which struck him so painfully. To make the picture which thus fixed itself on his memory intelligible, it will be necessary to explain, or, perhaps, as he would say, 'to reiterate,' that few men have been constitutionally less able to cope with unexpected difficulties than he was. In any case of confusion or embarrassment, it was sheer misery to have him even standing by and looking on; his own irritable impatience was at once so contagious and so depressing. It was a constant struggle on Mrs. Carlyle's part either to keep him out of the way, or to take the

---

* From Vol. II. of Froude's ' Life in London,' p. 271-3.
† From ' A Ten Years' Reminiscence,' ' British Quarterly.'

oppurtunity of his being away from home, to effect any changes which might have become necessary; and this as much for his own sake as for hers.

On the evening in question, I was sitting quietly at home, when I heard a gentle rap at the door; and was informed that Mrs. Carlyle's servant wished to speak to me. She told me that Mrs. Carlyle had just been brought home in a cab, seriously hurt by a fall, and begged I would come in at once. I went instantly, and found her on a chair in the back room of the ground floor, evidently in great pain. As soon as she saw me, she said, 'Oh, Mr. Larkin, do get me up into my own room before Mr. Carlyle knows anything about it. He'll drive me mad if he comes in now!' We at once consulted as to how we could best carry her up; when, just as we were about to do it, he entered, as he tells us, looking terribly shocked and even angry. I saw he was annoyed at my being there, instead of him; so I said as little as possible, helped him to carry her upstairs, and then left.

On the following morning, I called to inquire how she was, and found she had given word that I was to be asked to go up and see her. She was full of thanks, and told me it would be a great comfort to her if I would come up every morning for five minutes, as she knew she should often be wanting some little thing done; and pleasantly added, 'It will effect many little arrangements for her comfort, which she had thought over during the previous day.'

'For fifty hours,' Carlyle writes in the 'Reminiscences,' 'the pain was excruciating! . . . The poor patient was heroic. . . . In fact her sick-room looked pleasanter than many a drawing-room, all the weakness and suffering of it nobly veiled away. . . . the bright side of the cloud always turned out for me, in my dreary labours.' Very touching is the passage following, on the next page of the 'Reminiscences.' 'Blind and deaf that we are! Oh, think if thou yet love anybody living, wait not till death sweeps down the paltry little dust-clouds and idle dissonances of the moment, and all be at last so mournfully clear and beautiful, when it is too late!'

CHAPTER XXVII

A. D. 1863-1864

Consequences—The first re-appearance of the invalid—Mr. and Mrs. Froude spend a bright evening with the Carlyles—Mr. Simmonds—Ominous signs—Death of Grace Welsh—Decreasing strength of Mrs. Carlyle—Passage from the 'Reminiscences'—Unaidable pain—Maggie Welsh—The strange nurse—Invitation to St. Leonards.

NOT even yet had the dauntless spirit of Jane Welsh Carlyle given in to despair. Carlyle tells how, in a few days after the accident, 'she seemed to be almost happy!' and of her radiant apparition, risen from her bed of sickness after weeks of torture, and come to visit him, as he sate lonely at his work. 'That bright evening,' as Carlyle calls it, was shortly followed by one again bright and memorable, when Mr. and Mrs. Froude had spent the evening at Cheyne Row. Carlyle speaks of them as

the pleasantest; indeed, almost the only pleasant company we now used to have—intelligent, cheerful, kindly, courteous, sincere (they had come to live near us, and we hoped for a larger share of such evenings, of which this probably was the first. Alas! to me, too surely, it was in effect the last!). Cheerful enough this evening was; my darling sat on the sofa talking with Mrs. F. (Froude). They gone, she silently at once withdrew to her bed —saying nothing to me of the state she was in, which I found next morning to have been alarmingly miserable, the prophecy of one of the worst of nights, wholly without sleep and full of strange and horrible pain. And the nights and days that followed continued steadily to *worsen*, day after day, and month after month —no end visible. It was some ten months now before I saw her sit with me again in this drawing room—in body, weak as a child, but again composed into quiet. . . .

Still, Mrs. Carlyle was writing cheerfully to her friends not long after this terrible accident. The letters to Mrs. Simmonds (late Miss Barnes) upon the christening of her baby, are too amusing and characteristic to pass over, written as they were from a thick cloud of pain and discouragement.

*To Mrs. Simmonds.**

My darling,—I am so thankful that you are all right. And to think of your writing on the third day after your confinement the most legible, indeed, the only legible note I ever had from you in my life!

Now, about this compliment offered me, which you are pleased to call a 'favour' (to you). I don't know what to say. I wish I could go and talk it over; but, even if I could go in a cab one of these next dry days, I couldn't drive up your stairs in a cab! I should be greatly pleased that your baby bore a name of mine. But the Godmotherhood? There seems to me one objection to that, which is a fatal one. I don't belong to the English Church; and the Scotch Church, which I do belong to, recognises no Godfathers and Godmothers. The father takes all the obligations on himself (serves him right!). I was present at a Church of England christening for the first time when the Blunts took me to see their baby christened, and it looked to me a very solemn piece of work; and that Mr. Maurice and Julia Blunt (the Godfather and Godmother) had to take upon themselves, before God and man, very solemn engagements, which it was to be hoped they meant to fulfil! I should not have liked to vow and murmur, and undertake all they did, without meaning to fulfil it according to my best ability.

Now, my darling, how could I dream of binding myself to look after the spiritual welfare of any earthly baby? I, who have no confidence in my own spiritual welfare! I am not wanted to, it may, perhaps, be answered—you mean to look after that yourself without interference. What are these spoken engagements, then? A mere form; that is, a piece of humbug.

* 'Letters and Memorials,' Letter 277.

How could I, in cold blood, go through with a ceremony in a church, to which neither the others nor myself attach a grain of veracity? If you can say anything to the purpose, I am very willing to be proved mistaken; and in that case very willing to stand Godmother to a baby that, on the third day, is not at all red!

Yours affectionately,
JANE CARLYLE.

*Letter to Mrs. Simmonds.**

Dear Pet,—I am not the least well and should just about as soon walk overhead into the Thames as into a roomful of people. At the same time, I wish to pay my respects to the baby on this her next grand performance after getting herself born, and to place in her small hands a talisman worthy of the occasion and suitable to a baby born on 'All Saints' Day' (whatever sort of day that may be). As I shouldn't at all recommend running a long pin into the creature, I advise you to wear the brooch in its present form till the baby is sufficiently hardened from its present pulpy condition, to bear something tied round its throat, without fear of strangulation; and then you may remove the pin, and attach the talisman to a string in form of a locket.

But what is it? What does it do? (as a servant of mine once asked me in respect of a 'lord'). What it is, my dear, is an emblematic mosaic made from bits of some tomb of the early Christians, and representing an early Christian device: the Greek cross, the palm leaves, and all the rest of it. Worn by the like of me, I daresay it would have no virtue to speak of; but worn by a baby born on All Saints' Day! it must be a potent charm against the devil and all his works, one would think, for it is a perfectly authentic memorial of the early Christians. I hope you didn't go and drop the 'Jane' after all. Bless you and it.

Affectionately yours,
JANE BAILLIE WELSH CARLYLE.

In the lucid interval, when all was over, Carlyle saw, in looking back, what a terribly sad time this had been for his wife.

* 'Letters and Memorials,' Letter 278.

Silent though she may have been to him, to Mrs. Russell she opened her heart a little; wrote of her constant pain—of the news of the death of her cousin Grace Welsh, one of her Uncle Robert's daughters. The letter, she says, 'quite crushed down the heart' in her for some days. She was easily crushed now! Her sufferings deepened.

Carlyle was still fighting with his 'Frederick'—the final ending of which was his main object in life. He dimly perceived that this book had been a trial to her; began to feel at times that she would die, and he would be truly alone. But the impression was always succeeded by the invincible hope that all might yet be well with her. Carlyle's 'eyes were holden'—he could not see.

Mr. Froude gives some painful details which need not be repeated here. He tells how 'with splendid heroism she had prematurely forced herself to her feet again.' He tells of that memorable evening of which we have spoken, when he and Mrs. Froude once more spent an evening with the Carlyles, and how, that same night, the torturing neuralgic pain had set in—not explainable by doctors.

Carlyle, strangely hopeful, believed all would yet go well with his wife's health. Others saw things differently. Mr. Larkin, who saw her daily, says: 'She was decreasing in strength from day to day and from week to week—sinking into the saddest despondency and gloom of horror. I suppose no one who really watched her, ever expected to see her leave that bed alive. She herself had long given up all real hope!' 'Even then,' Carlyle says, 'she had always something cheerful to tell me. . . . All that was gloomy she was silent upon, and had strictly hidden away.' In the two or three years before the accident he had often talked all his 'half-hours' on subjects connected with his book. As was natural, she showed interest, but answered little; her principal thought being, 'Alas! I shall never see this come to print. I am hastening towards death instead.' And that was *before* the disastrous fall she had now suffered from.

We give a passage from the 'Reminiscences,' referring to this time.

We thought all was now come, or fast coming, right again, and that, in spite of that fearful mischance, we should have a good winter, and get our dismal 'misery of a book' done, or almost done. My own hope and prayer was, and had long been continually that; hers, too, I could not doubt, though hint never came from her to that effect; no hint or look, much less the smallest word at any time, by any accident. But I felt well enough how it was crushing down her existence, as it was crushing down my own, and the thought—that she had not been at the choosing of it, and yet must suffer so for it, was occasionally bitter to me. But the practical conclusion always was, 'Get done with it, get done with it, for the saving of us both that is the outlook.' And sure enough I did stand by that dismal task with all my means; day and night—wrestling with it, as with the ugliest dragon, which blotted out the daylight and the rest of the world to me, till I should get it slain. There was, perhaps, some merit in this: but also, I fear, a demerit. Well, well, I could do no better; sitting smoking upstairs on nights when sleep was impossible, I had thoughts enough; not permitted to rustle amid my rugs and wrappages lest I awoke her and started all chance of sleep away from her. Weak little darling, thy sleep is now unbroken; still and serene in the eternities (as the Most High God has ordered for us), and nobody more in this world will wake for my wakefulness.

My poor woman was what we called 'getting well' for several weeks still. She could walk very little; indeed, she never more walked much in this world; but it seems she was out driving and again out, hopefully for some time. Towards the end of November (perhaps it was in December), she caught some whiff of cold, which, for a day or two, we hoped would pass, as many such had done; but, on the contrary, it begun to get worse, soon rapidly worse, and developed itself into that frightful universal 'neuralgia' under which it seemed as if no force of human vitality would be able long to stand. 'Disease of the nerves' (poisoning of the very channels of sensation), such was the name the doctors gave it, and for the rest could do nothing farther with it, well had they only attempted nothing. I used to compute that they, poor souls, had at least reinforced the disease to trace its natural amount, such the pernicious effect of all their 'remedies' and appliances, opiates, etc., etc., which every one of them (and there came many) applied anew, and always with the like result.

Oh, what a sea of agony my darling was immersed in, month after month—sleep had fled. A hideous pain, of which she used to say that 'common, honest pain, were it cutting off one's flesh or sawing of one's bones, would be a luxury in comparison,' seemed to have begirdled her at all moments and on every side. Her intellect was clear as starlight, and continued so; the clearest intellect among us all; but she dreaded that this, too, must give way. 'Dear,' said she to me on two occasions, with such a look and tone as I shall never forget, 'promise that you will not put me in a mad house, however this go. Do you promise me now?' I solemnly did. 'Not if I do not quite lose my wits?' 'Never, my darling. Oh, compose thy poor, terrified heart.' Another time, she punctually directed me about her burial; how her poor bits of possessions were to be distributed, this to one friend, that to another, in help of their necessities (for it was the poor sort she had chosen—old, indigent, Haddington figures). What employment in the solitary night watches, on her bed of pain! Ah me! ah me!

Many months of this hideous pain supervened on the accident. 'Such a deluge of intolerable pain, indescribable, unaidable pain as I had never seen or dreamt of, and which drowned six or eight months of my poor darling's life as in the blackness of very death. . . . Here, for the first time, I saw her vanquished, driven hopeless, as it were, looking into a wild, chaotic universe of boundless woe,—only death or worse.'

The physicians, generous and skilful, could do little for this tormented, worn-out human body! Tonics failed to strengthen—narcotics failed to soothe. Maggie Welsh, the kind cousin from Liverpool, came in December, and stayed till April. Her well-known face and tones probably gave more comfort to the agonised patient than did the 'varying miscellany' of sick nurses. One in particular caused the invalid much agitation. It was an elderly French nursing sister, whose repeating of her regular devotions annoyed Mrs. Carlyle beyond endurance, knowing Latin as she did, and entirely disagreeing with the said devotions; and the end of it was a rousing up of the household at 3 A. M., when the invalid insisted on the nurse being removed from her room, then and there. It appeared that some spiritual admonitions had been offered to Mrs. Carlyle by this well-meaning nun, so distasteful to the poor racked brain of the invalid as to rouse her to instant action. Silence, apologies, and departure were the result of this adventure.

The kind friends Dr. and Mrs. Blakiston of St. Leonards greatly urged Mrs. Carlyle to visit them at this time, and see what the fine air and their loving attention would do for her. It seemed almost a last resource, so weak had she become, but the idea was not to be hastily abandoned. Hope might come with the change !

CHAPTER XXVIII

A. D. 1864

Mrs. Carlyle's resolution—Mr. Larkin—The terrible journey—Maggie Welsh—Carlyle at Chelsea—Regrets—Despair—The furnished house—Maggie Welsh recalled to Liverpool—Mary Craik—Sad bulletins—Carlyle's visits—Calls of friends—The sufferer too weak to see them—Mrs. Carlyle writes to her aunts—Insomnia—Heavy Days—Futile plans of change—Mrs. Carlyle's horror of returning to Chelsea—Miss Bromley's kindness—Mrs. Carlyle starts for Scotland with Dr. John Carlyle—Spending a night in London on her way—Mrs. Austin—Removal of Mrs. Carlyle to Holm Hill—Her dread of travelling home—The return—The worst over.

MRS. CARLYLE, for her own part, was resolved to make this last effort, even if she died upon the road. All was arranged, and, relying on Mr. Larkin's never-failing kindness, she decided that he was to carry her downstairs and lay her upon a couch from which the attendants would lift her into the invalid carriage, which was to convey her from door to door. ' I don't think you'll find me very heavy,' she said pathetically to Mr. Larkin, who was, indeed, appalled at her loss of weight. ' I carried her down as easily as if she had been a child of twelve years old !' he says. Yet Mrs. Carlyle's height was five foot four inches, and she must have become a mere shadow.

'It was early in March,' says Carlyle in the 'Reminiscences' (perhaps March 2, 1864)—'a cold-blowing, damp, and occasionally raining day, that the flitting thither took effect. . . . Well do I recollect her look as they bore her downstairs: full of nameless sorrow, yet of clearness, practical management, steady resolution. . . . The invalid carriage was hideous to look upon; black, low, base-looking, and you entered it by a window, as if it were a hearse. I knew well what she was thinking.' Mr. Larkin describes this carriage as one

into which the living corpse was to be slid, feet foremost, through a small door behind. I saw at a glance (he says) the whole horror of the thing as it would strike her . . . she was already being carried from the house. I shall never forget the agony of the stifled shriek which she could not suppress, as they lifted and pushed her in. . . . I bade her goodbye, deeply feeling that it was the last poor service I should ever render her. But the end was not yet. . . .

Carlyle, who had attended his wife on this journey, visiting her at every stage, and leaving her meantime in the kind care of Maggie Welsh, returned to London by the late train that same night. He warmly extols the considerate and generous care of Dr. and Mrs. Blakiston, as shown in their reception of their invalid guest—'fine, airy, quiet rooms in the big house, with the loving and skilful hosts.' And he went home cheered and more hopeful. Yet his own settled mood was 'of deep misery frozen torpid.' He had just ended Vol. V. of his 'Frederick' and despaired on finding there must be yet a sixth volume.

It was in June that Mr. Larkin had 'a letter from Mrs. Carlyle, but not in her own handwriting, only dictated, and feebly signed by her—evidently dictated in great depression of heart, in which she said: 'I think you must curse the day you wrote that first letter to Carlyle, which brought you into never-ending trouble with us! . . . . Every emotion, even one of gladness, brings on my torture. . . .'

Carlyle had visited his suffering wife twice or thrice at Dr. Blakiston's house in Warrior Square, St. Leonards, but with little hopeful omen to bring away with him. Maggie Welsh wrote daily bulletins, always striving to be hopeful. There was, indeed, little food for hope. 'Her mood of fixed sorrow,' says Carlyle, 'with no hope in it but of enduring well, was painfully visible.'

It was thought best that the Carlyles should now take a small furnished house at St. Leonards, where Carlyle could join his wife, and where Dr. John Carlyle could also take up his quarters. This plan was carried out early in May, and the anxious family group was assembled at 117 Marina, St. Leonards. Maggie Welsh was called back to Liverpool, by illness in her own family, and Miss Mary Craik, from Belfast, took her place. But this change of abode was preceded by most terrible sufferings on Mrs. Carlyle's part. 'In these seven or eight months of martyrdom,' writes Carlyle (October 1863—May 1864), 'there is naturally no record of the dear martyr's own discoverable; nothing but these small, most mournful notes, written with the left hand, as if from the core of a broken heart.' We quote a few sentences.

To her Husband.

St. Leonards: Friday, April 8, 1864.

Oh! my own darling! God have pity on us. Ever since the day after you left . . . the truth is I have been wretched, perfectly wretched, day and night. . . .

Your loving and sore-suffering
JANE W. CARLYLE.

On April 19 she writes:

How be in good spirits or have any hope but to *die?* When I spoke of going home, it was to *die* there. . . . Oh, have pity on me! . . .

And again, on April 25:

. . . Oh, I would like you beside me. I am terribly alone. But I don't want to interrupt your work, I will wait till we are in our own hired house, and then, if I am no better, you must come for a day.

Your own wretched
J. W. C.

To the aunts at Edinburgh she wrote in great despair in a letter about the end of April, ending with, ' Ah, my aunts, I shall die: that is my belief!'

On an early day in May, Carlyle arrived at ' Marina,' was

pleased to find one good bed-room looking over the sea appropriated to his wife's use, and delighted to meet the resolute, suffering woman dressed, waiting his arrival, though he says: 'She could hardly sit out dinner, and never could attempt it again. With intellect clear and even inventive, her whole being was evidently plunged in continual woe—pain as if unbearable, and no hope left. . . .'

Kind friends came now and then: 'Forster, Twisleton, Woolner, and none of these could she see, not even Miss Bromley, who came twice for a day or more, except the last time—just one hurried glimpse. Nothing could so indicate to what a depth of despair had sunk this once brightest and openest of human souls.'

The Blakistons' unwearied kindness, and the daily drives in the open air—for short times, but often repeated—could no longer help Mrs. Carlyle. Sleep had departed, and the cup of suffering was full to overflowing. The roaring of the sea—at first a lullaby, now, in her weakened state, too loud—kept her awake. The house at Marina had, unfortunately, been taken on for an extra month, till the end of July; but before the middle of July things became intolerable. At first there had been sometimes 'an hour or two of sleep. . . . But this didn't last. . . . And the days were always heavy,' says Carlyle in the 'Reminiscences.' 'What a time, even in my reflex of it! Dante's Purgatory I could now liken it to . . . not his Hell, for there was a sacred blessedness in it withal. . . .'

A change of quarters was inevitable. Bexhill was looked at with this view, then Battle, but always fears of 'noises' made the plans drop into silent abandonment. The home at Chelsea seemed, in its quiet cleanliness, the most attractive change, but Mrs. Carlyle had 'an absolute horror of her old home, bedroom, and drawing-room, where she had endured such torments latterly. 'We will new-paper them, re-arrange them,' said Miss Bromley. And this was actually done in August following. 'That new-papering,' adds Carlyle, 'was somehow to me the saddest of speculations. Alas, darling, is that all we can do for thee? . . .'

After nine nights, or more, totally without sleep, Mrs. Carlyle absolutely determined to go to London, on the way to Scotland, breaking her journey, not at her own house, but at Mrs. Forster's (Palace Gate House, Kensington), and did indeed start by the train from St. Leonards at noon on June 30, escorted by Dr. John Carlyle. At Palace Gate House she found 'much kindness and much state,' did sleep 'some human sleep in my luxurious bedroom, all crashing with wheels.'

But she was absolutely fixed in her purpose to go on at once to Scotland; summoned Dr. John Carlyle to make ready for the evening train to Dumfries, and took a journey of 330 miles, her 'horrible ailment keeping off as by enchantment.' She had left Mary Craik at Chelsea to take care of Carlyle, and was able to report herself from Mrs. Austin's—The Gill —on July 15 in decidedly better case. 'I am very shaky, you will see,' she says, 'but, oh, so thankful for my sleep and ease—would it but last!'

A note of Mr. Froude's in the 'Letters and Memorials' gives a sad account of the failure of these hopes:—

The remainder of that summer has a sad record of perpetually recurring suffering. The carriage broke down in her second drive with her sister-in-law, and she was violently shaken. Mrs. Austin gave her all the care that love had to bestow; but in a farmhouse there was not the accommodation which her condition required, and her friend, Mrs. Russell, carried her off to Holm Hill, where she would be under Dr. Russell's immediate charge.

Dr. John Carlyle had not been altogether sympathetic with his delicate patient, it appears; and she felt it deeply, in her present feebleness.

Her letters to Carlyle at this time are saddening. 'The most touching feature in them,' Mr. Froude writes, 'is the affection with which she now clung to her husband. Carlyle's anxiety, at last awake, had convinced her that his strange humours had not arisen from real indifference. . . .' Indifference between married people leads, we think, to very different results and to much less suffering than is manifest in the relations of these two.

From Holm Hill, Mrs. Carlyle writes on July 23: 'Oh, my dear, I think how near my mother I am, how still I should be, laid beside her. But I wish to live for you—if only I could live out of torment.'

And she thought of her husband in all her pain. On July 25 she writes: ' Mary Craik will go to-day, and you will be alone with town maids, and if I were there I could but add to your troubles.'

Again, on July 27: '. . . I am terribly weak. . . . I seem already to belong to the passed-away as much as to the present—nay, more.'

And on August 5: '. . . It is almost sinfully ungrateful, when God has borne me through such prolonged agonies with my senses intact, to have so little confidence in the future; but courage and hope have been ground out of me. . . . Oh, my dear, I am very weary—my agony has lasted long!'

On August 29: '. . . The thought of how I am ever to make that long journey back, which I made here in the strength of desperation, troubles me night and day. . . . Oh, I am frightened—frightened! A perfect coward am I become—I, who was surely once brave!'

August 30: ' No sleep at all last night: had no chance of sleep for the neuralgic pains piercing me. . . . I am profoundly disheartened. . . .'

September 6: '. . . Oh, if God would only lift my trouble off me so far that I could bear it all in silence, and not add to the trouble of others!'

September 7: 'I cannot write. I have passed a terrible night. . . . Am I going to have another winter like the last? . . .'

September 9: 'I am very stupid and low. God can raise me up again; but will He?'

September 26: '. . . I thank God I got some little sleep last night, for I had been going from bad to worse. . . . Oh, this relapse is a severe disappointment to me—and, God knows, not altogether a selfish disappointment ! I had looked forward to going back to you so much improved, as to be, if not of any use and comfort to you, at least no trouble to you and no burden on your spirits. And now, God knows how it will be. . . Oh, dear, you cannot help me, though you would. Nobody can help me, only God; and can I wonder if God takes so little heed of me, when all my life I have taken so little heed of Him ? . . .'

It was on a mild, clear day (October 1, 1864), that Mrs. Carlyle returned to her home at 5 Cheyne Row, escorted by Dr. John Carlyle. Her worst struggles were now over—no more ' flying from the tormentor, panting like the hunted doe, with all the hounds of the pit in full chase !' All was to be made easy for her now, her room had been beautified and re-modelled with the kind help of Miss Bromley.

She had not been forgotten by her lonely husband during her late absence in Scotland. He had written much to her. On July 29 he had said in his letter to her: ' Oh, darling, when will you come back and protect me ? . . . My thoughts are a prayer for my poor little life-partner who has fallen lame beside me, after travelling so many steep and thorny ways !' And again on August 2: '. . . My poor little friend of friends, she has fallen wounded to the ground, and I am alone—alone !' To Mr. Froude, who was absent from town, and wrote under the impression that Mrs. Carlyle was recovering, he answered, that no such hope was warranted, at present. 'Wish me well, and return, the sooner the better,' he continues.

To Mrs. Carlyle, her husband's letters were frequent and tender, and, now the separation was over, 'she re-appeared in her old circle, weak, shattered, her body worn to a shadow, but with her spirit as bright as ever—brighter, perhaps,' says Mr. Froude. 'A faint, kind, timid smile was on her face,' says Carlyle, speaking of her arrival, 'as if afraid to believe fully; but the despair had vanished from her looks altogether, and she was brought back to me, my own again, as before.'

Her own account of her arrival, as given in a letter to Mrs. Russell, is very spirited and touching at the same time. Mr. Carlyle's rushing out in his dressing-gown, kissing her and weeping over her just as she was in the act of getting out of the cab, and the kisses and embraces of the maids, made this home-coming quite a unique one to her. All were astonished at the improvement in her appearance. She had indeed been snatched back from Death, as it were, and had 'a heavenly sleep' on the first night after her return. 'Oh! my darling,' she writes to Mrs. Russell, 'if I might continue just as well as I am now! But that is not to be hoped. Anyhow, I shall always feel as if I owed my life chiefly to your husband and you, who procured me such rest as I could have nowhere else in this world.' And on October 6 she says to this dear friend: '. . . I feel as if I needed God's help to make me humanly capable of the sort of sacred thankfulness I ought to feel for such a friend as yourself.' The kind Rector's wife had made it easy for Mrs. Carlyle to have the warm, new milk, which had done her good at Holm Hill; she had also plenty of cream, quite good, and went a daily drive in a nice brougham from 1 to 3 P. M.

On October 10, she assures Mrs. Russell that she was 'not the same woman who trembled from head to foot . . . whenever a human face showed itself from without, or anything worried from within.' It was true, the darkest hour was passed, the deepest note of human suffering had been sounded—dawn was at hand. To use Carlyle's own words:

Here ended the most tragic part of our tragedy. Act the 5th, though there lay Death in it, was nothing like so unhappy. The last epoch of my darling's life is to be defined as almost happy in comparison ! It was still loaded with infirmities, bodily weakness, sleeplessness, continual, or almost continual, pain, and weary misery, so far as the body was concerned; but her noble spirit seemed as if it now had its wings free. . . . The battle was over, and we were sore wounded; but the battle was over, and well!

These touching words were written after all was over, indeed, not while Carlyle was more or less blind to the shadow of death which lay on his wife's face, so visible to outsiders.

The emotion of his friend, George Cooke, on his visit to Mrs. Carlyle at Chelsea, after her return from Holm Hill, tells its own tale; for, seeing the wreck before him, he took his friend in his arms and burst into tears. And Lord Houghton, too, who called the same day, was much moved at the change in her.

She speaks in a letter to Mrs. Russell of going to 'Elise' about a bonnet, which was to be 'stripped of its finery.' 'White lace and red roses,' she says, 'don't become a woman who has been looking both Death and Insanity in the face for a year.'

The kindness she received on all hands was almost overpowering to her! All must have seen that her time on earth was not likely to be a long one. Writing to Mrs. Austin on October 18 she says: 'Indeed, it is impossible to tell who is kindest to me; my fear is always that I shall be stifled with roses. They make so much of me, and I am so weak.' And in the same letter she says:

I have always a terrible consciousness at the bottom of my mind that, at any moment, if God will, I may be thrown back into the old agonies. I can never feel confident of life, and of care in life again; and it is best so!

I cannot tell you how gentle and good Mr. Carlyle is. He is busy as ever, but he studies my comfort and peace as he never did before. . . .

How well we can understand Carlyle's words in the 'Reminiscences:' 'The poor bodily department, too, I hoped was recovering; and that there would remain to us a "sweet farewell" of sunshine, after such a day of rains and storms, that would still last a blessed while. . . .'

CHAPTER XXIX

A. D. 1864-1865

The brougham—Mrs. Carlyle's joy at her husband's gift—Illness again—Visit of the Carlyles to Lady Ashburton at Seaton, Devon—Soothing impressions—Discomfort again at Cheyne Row—The 'hereditary housemaid'—At Holm Hill once more—Suffering health—Erskine of Linlathen—Home duties at Cheyne Row—Depression—Letter to Miss Jewsbury.

MRS. CARLYLE'S delicate health had long made it desirable that the means of carriage exercise should be constantly at her command; for years it had been talked of, the plan of her having a brougham of her own, and now the thing was actually done. She had always discouraged the idea; but now Carlyle took the matter into his own hands, and purchased a pretty carriage with a steady mare, ' Bellona,' all her own. And a steady coachman was engaged, Silvester by name; so that long-cherished wish was carried out, not all too late, though delayed. It was hidden from all, that she would breathe her last in that very carriage, bought to preserve and lengthen her fading life.

Talking over this incident of the brougham lately with Mr. Larkin, he told us he never saw Mrs. Carlyle so pleased and radiant as she was at this gift from her husband. ' What gives me the most joy,' she said to Mr. Larkin, ' is, that he did it *entirely himself;* I never suggested it, on the contrary, I had always discouraged the idea.' She felt, no doubt, that this voluntary concession to her increasing weakness, showed a consciousness of her ill-health on her husband's part, and that soothed her. She writes on October 31, 1864, to Mrs. Russell: ' I have now set up a nice little Brougham, or

Clarence (as you call it), all to myself, with a smart grey horse and an elderly driver. . . .'

Carlyle, in an annotation to the letter in which these words occur, says: 'God be for ever thanked that I did not loiter longer. She had infinite satisfaction in this poor gift; was boundlessly proud of it, as her husband's testimony to her. . . .' He then had that *after-knowledge* which opens so wide a gate to our understandings.

All November and December she took her daily drives, saw friends, when able, and was stronger and happier, though the 'servant' trouble still existed.

On January 5, 1865, Carlyle posted his 'last leaf' of the 'Frederick' MS. 'On her face,' he says afterwards, 'there was a silent, faint, and pathetic smile. . . .' The thirteen years of 'Frederick' were over indeed, but not without results.

A letter written by Mrs. Carlyle on February 14 to her old nurse, whose helpless, long-invalided son had died, is very tender. 'Oh, Betty, darling,' she writes, 'I wish I were near you! If I had my arm about your neck and your hand in mine, I think I might say things that would comfort you a little, and make you feel that, so long as I am in life, you are not without a child to love you. . . .'

But such meeting was now impossible. She had again had some sharp suffering—'terrible agony for a few days'—and it was not till March 8 that she and her husband were able to go on a month's visit to Lady Ashburton, at the Dowager Lady Ashburton's pretty cottage—Seaforth Lodge, Seaton, Devonshire.

From this quiet and kindly shelter Mrs. Carlyle writes to Mrs. Russell, reporting but poorly of her own health; but she was cheered by 'the new country, very beautiful. And the sheep, bless them! were not only as white as milk, but had dear, wee lambs skipping beside them. And the river that falls into the sea near here . . . clear as crystal and bright blue . . . and such a lovely and lovable hostess. . . . The insane horror I had conceived of the sea, all in one night, at St. Leonards, has quite passed away.'

She greatly wished Mrs. Russell to visit her in London in the early summer, when Mr. Carlyle would be away, and she left lonely again; but ere that time came, Mrs. Carlyle's health again gave ominous signs of failing. On May 4 she writes to Mrs. Russell: 'I am not worse—indeed, as to the sickness and the sleeplessness, I am rather better in both respects; but I am weak and languid, have little appetite, and am getting thinner. . . . My right arm has gone the way that my left went two years ago, so that I cannot lie upon it, or make any effort with it. . . .'

About May 22 Carlyle was at Dumfries, and thence went to his sister at The Gill, and there was another small 'earth-quaking' of workmen at 5 Cheyne Row, a-papering of the dining-room, and fitting it with book-cases from the top of the house—from the 'Frederick' sanctum. The next fortnight was a distressful one. Mrs. Carlyle came and went between her own disturbed home and her kind friends the Macmillans at Streatham Lane, but remained under much pain. She had 'cried a very little at being left;' but turned at once to practical occupation and what help remained to her.

The mention, in a letter dated Cheyne Row, May 24, 1865, of a servant whom she was then about to engage—Jessie Hiddlestone, daughter of an old servant of Mrs. Welsh's—must be noted, as this servant was eventually engaged, and is alluded to in the letter kindly placed in our hands by Mr. John Stores Smith. We give the letter later on. There is also, in the same letter, the name of Mrs. Warren, who was housekeeper to Mrs. Carlyle during the last few months of her life. These two names, in fact, with the casual mention of a remarkable two days of terrible weather—in which the omnibuses could not run, and Mrs. Carlyle was deprived of her regular carriage exercise—fix the date of that highly interesting letter, otherwise *undated*, as within three months of Mrs. Carlyle's death.

But to go back to June 1865. After severe and continuous pain in the arm, so bad that, to use her own words, it was 'as if a dog were gnawing and tearing at it,' with growing sleeplessness to weaken her still further, Mrs. Carlyle almost gave up hope, and on June 17 was at the Railway Hotel, Carlisle, on her way to Mrs. Russell at Holm Hill. Dr. Quain had advised her to go as soon as possible to Scotland. The right arm was now hopelessly disabled, and she was learning to write with the left one. The charm of Holm Hill was now more or less powerless to revive Mrs. Carlyle. Her vitality was too far spent. By the end of July she was to return home. Carlyle waited at Dumfries for the train that was to take her to London, and travelled as far as Annan with her. Her new servant, Jessie Hiddlestone, was in the same train.

On July 27, she again addressed her husband from Cheyne Row. Her sleep became better, her pain less; but she had made her last railway journey, save and except the one to Folkestone, where she was once again the guest of kind Miss Bromley in August, at Langhome Gardens, Folkestone, and all the good care of her considerate friend did her some good, but the time for restoration was now over and gone. Writing to her husband from Folkestone on August 19, she says: 'But I don't feel the stronger for all this sleep, nor more able to eat or to walk.' To Mrs. Russell she writes, of Miss Bromley: 'She is adorably kind to me, . . . and in such an unconscious way.'

It was disturbing that Mr. Carlyle wished to return to London at this very time, curtailing his wife's reposeful stay at Folkestone. 'But,' she says, 'a demon of impatience seems to have taken possession of Mr. C., and he has been rushing through his promised visits as if the furies were chasing him.' We think it very likely his impatience was to see his sick wife, but that could not be known. In any case, he returned.

There is a beautiful letter, dated August 18, from Mr.

Erskine of Linlathen to Mrs. Carlyle, whom he had hoped to have seen this summer with her husband. We quote a few words:—

'Beloved Mrs. Carlyle,—I suppose you *could not* have come here, and yet it is with some sorrow that I accept this arrangement, as I scarcely expect to have another sight of your dear face on earth. . . .'

Writing to Mrs. Austin in October, Mrs. Carlyle reports her neuralgia better, 'in abeyance,' at least, and Mr. Froude speaks of having met her with her husband about this time at the Dean of Westminster's. The Carlyles also dined with Mr. Froude to meet Mr. Spedding of Mirehouse, Ruskin, and Dean Milman. It was a brilliant occasion in every way.

December 1865 found her again much depressed. 'Bellona,' the mare, had fallen temporarily lame from an injury, and she (Mrs. C.) had unwisely consented to take the air in an omnibus—the nervousness of seeing her husband run after them to stop them, while she waited, was too much for her, so low had her strength fallen! 'I was like to cry with nervousness,' she says, 'to find myself left alone in an open street—and couldn't run after him as he kept calling to me to do—couldn't run at all. . . .'

This was an unfortunate moment for the introduction of nine large hens and one very large cock, who appeared next morning in the garden of the house adjoining. But the indomitable woman *took means* which banished the nuisance, and 'Mr. C.,' she tells her friend, 'clasped me in his arms and called me his " guardian angel "!' It is right to add that Mrs. Carlyle promised, as some recompense for the shutting up of the 'magnificent cock' from 3 P. M. till 10 A. M. to give reading lessons to the small boy of the owner of that bird!

The household went on quietly enough. Mrs. Warren and Jessie did not like each other. This latter, whom Mrs. Carlyle called ' her hereditary housemaid,' was 'more attentive,' says her mistress, 'since I showed myself quite indifferent to her attentions, and particular only as to the performance of her work.'

In January 1866, she writes feelingly on the ill-health of young Robert Welsh, who eventually died of consumption—the letter is to Miss Grace Welsh, Edinburgh. 'It is hard, hard,' she says, 'to tell by what death, slow or swift, one would prefer to lose one's dearest ones, when lose them one must.'

The going down of the steamship 'London' depressed Mrs. Carlyle, among more personal losses. 'I have felt,' she says, 'in a maze of sadness—have had no affinity for any but sorrowful things. . . . But I continue to take my three hours' drive daily. Since I returned from Folkestone in September, I have only missed two days, the days of the snow-storm a fortnight ago, when it was so dangerous for horses to travel that the very omnibuses struck work. . . .'* This circumstance makes the snow-storm to be dated about January 8 or 9, 1866, and we here give the hitherto unpublished letter to Miss Jewsbury, containing the allusion to it, and placed in our hands by Mr. John Stores Smith.

5 Cheyne Row, Friday night.

Oh my dear young woman!—For goodness gracious' sake don't be outstaying your time by ever so long. You are '*wanted*' —not by the police, but by *me!* I want you every day and all, for I have no resource in myself at present, am indeed an unmitigated nuisance to myself, and for any comfort that lies in '*others*'—such others as are get-at-able. Ach!

Since we parted I cannot boast of one moment of *wellness*, day or night! There is nothing serious the matter with me, so far as I know. It is just that 'the weather is cold,' and ' I'm growing old,' and ' my (moral) doublet is not very new. Well-a-day.'

All the same, I am *terribly* in need of having my feet stroked, and being read to, and being told stories to, and being cheered up generally. I come down every morning with a headache, and as

* The letter quoted from here is dated January 23, 1866, and is addressed to Miss Grace Welsh. In this letter the 'snow-storm' alluded to as having happened within a fortnight of the day of writing must have occurred on January 8 or 9.

sick as a dog. The drive out has not the usual enlivening effect in this weather. Indeed, the two last days Silvester declared the attempt 'too dangerous—the many omnibuses having ceased to run;' so I have moped at home, hearing nothing but Mr. C.'s Jeremiads over the 'utter ruin' brought on him by 'that dinner at Forster's and the other at Dr. Quain's.' The '*old*' and '*cold*' are at the bottom of *his* miseries too, I believe; but it would need a bolder woman than *me* to suggest that to him!

When Jessie was mending the fire yesterday, she suddenly addressed me: 'D'ye ken, mem, I *miss* Miss Jewsbury?' 'Impossible!' I answered, for I *had* thought she had said, 'D'ye ken, mem, I *met* Miss Jewsbury!' She stared and said, 'But it is the truth.' 'Perfectly impossible,' I repeated. 'Miss Jewsbury is not in London, she is in Manchester!' 'I ken that fu' weel,' said she snappishly, 'and *that's* just the reason I *miss* her.' Then I saw my mistake. It was the only good sentiment I had heard out of the young woman's head for some time.

I am so disappointed in that 'hereditary housemaid!' Being human, of course she would have faults, and I should find them out in time. But when found out they prove her in all the most important things the very *opposite* of what I took her for; and that *is* humiliating for me, as well as vexatious. She lies like an Irishwoman, is secretive and deceitful as a Welsh woman, is heartless and ungrateful as well as *extremely* bad-tempered—and all the while such a sweet, open countenance; and, when she likes, *fascinating* manners. Mrs. Frank (my kind regards to her) may console herself under *her* household troubles, with the same consolation which alone makes it possible for one to bear up against old age and death!—that it is the *universal doom*.

Mrs. Warren has had a sort of influenza which kept her in a cloud of blue devils for a fortnight. But now she is all right again.

Pray write and fix the time of your return—and *keep it!* I have hundreds of things to tell you.

Affectionately yours,
JANE CARLYLE.

CHAPTER XXX

A. D. 1865-1866

Carlyle offered the Lord Rectorship of Edinburgh University—His wife's wish that he should accept it—His election—His journey northwards with Professor Tyndall—The last parting—Professor Huxley—Mr. Erskine of Linlathen and Carlyle's brothers gathered in Edinburgh—The great day—Immense success—The telegram—The dinner at Forster's—Interview with Professor Tyndall—Excitement—The projected tea-party—The afternoon drive—Sudden death of Mrs. Carlyle—Carlyle receives the news at Dumfries—The unopened letter—Funeral at the Abbey Kirk of Haddington—Epitaph—Reflections.

AND now the 'great outward event of Carlyle's own life, Scotland's public recognition of him, was at hand. This his wife was to live to witness as her final happiness in this world,' so writes Mr. Froude. It was in October of 1865 that the Rectorship of Edinburgh University was formally offered to Carlyle. To this Mrs. Carlyle 'gently urged him.' Early in November he was duly elected. And when March 1866 came, there was much talk of journey and arrangements. It was an exciting and interesting time to Mrs. Carlyle, who was reluctantly compelled to relinquish any idea of accompanying her husband. She would remain quietly at home, and have all the reflected joy and triumph of it. She had her fears of the 'extempore' speech Carlyle would have to make, of its possibly causing him physical discomfort. On Thursday, March 29, all was ready, and Carlyle started on his journey, accompanied by Professor Tyndall; two days were to be spent first at Fryston Hall (Lord Houghton's), and then they were to proceed to Edinburgh.

The anxious thought of Mrs. Carlyle suggested a last measure to ensure her husband's comfort, which *might*, if given in her own case, have prolonged her waning life. She had given him a little flask of fine brandy, to take with him in case of sudden illness. Some of this he actually mixed with water and took ' in that wild scene of the address.'

She had parted from him looking very pale and ill. 'The last I saw of her,' he says in the 'Reminiscences,' 'was as she stood with her back to the parlour door, to bid me her good-bye. She kissed me twice (she me once, I her a second time); and—oh blind mortals! my one wish and hope was to get back to her again and be in peace, under her bright welcome, for the rest of my days, as it were.' But the husband and wife met no more on earth.

Professor Tyndall wrote daily cheering reports to Mrs. Carlyle, and Professor Huxley had joined the party at Fryston. Mr. Erskine of Linlathen had come to Edinburgh to make one of the brilliant assemblage, and Carlyle's two brothers, full of honest pride, were also in Edinburgh to welcome him.

Monday, April 2, was the day of the installation of the new Lord Rector. The record of the magnificent oration given by Carlyle to the students, and of the brilliant success of the whole ceremony, need not be dwelt upon here.

Meantime she, to whom it was the nearest and most urgent thought, was suffering and sleepless at Chelsea, counting the hours in an agony of nervous suspense, till she could hear the result and know that the exertion had not been too much for her husband's strength. She was to dine at Forster's that evening to meet Dickens and Wilkie Collins, and was dressing for the occasion (a birthday dinner) when Professor Tyndall's telegram arrived, which she tore open and read. It ran thus: 'A perfect triumph!' 'Oh,' she says, in her letter to Carlyle of April 3, 'God bless John Tyndall in this world and the next!'

Perhaps this was the most intense moment of joy and

pride that suffering, half-broken heart had known for many a year. For the thread of life was worn very thin, and though, after a restorative, Mrs. Carlyle did dine with John Forster, whose drawing-room she entered 'exultant,' as Professor Tyndall says, 'waving the telegram in the air,' we cannot but think that this flood of excitement helped to hasten the end. For had she not herself recently deplored the fact that joyful and painful emotion were alike hurtful to her? 'She went out,' Carlyle tells us, 'for two days to Mrs. Oliphant, recovered her sleep to the old poor average, or nearly so . . . and was not for many years, if ever, seen in such fine spirits and so hopeful and joyfully serene and victorious frame of mind, till the last moment.' It was the tender glow of sunset. 'Noble little heart,' continues Carlyle. 'Her painful, much-enduring, much-endeavouring little history now at last crowned with plain victory, in sight of her own people and of all the world. . . .' It was, indeed, a sweet 'Indian summer' for her, but all too short.

She had the joy of a personal interview with Professor Tyndall in his room at the Royal Institution on April 16, and heard the minutest details of the great event. She was, in fact, full of joy. 'I have not been so fond of everybody since I was a girl,' she wrote to her husband, who had gone on the Friday after the address, to spend a few peaceful days at Scotsbrig, where a slight sprain detained him.

The ankle was slow in mending, and Carlyle was writing to his wife in Chelsea on April 19, the day which was her last on earth, for on that day her weary pilgrimage ended softly in death.

On that day she had written to her husband and spoken of a tea-party she intended having on the Saturday. It was to include Mrs. Oliphant, Principal Tulloch, Mr. and Mrs. Froude, and others; Miss Jewsbury was also to be one of the party. The letter written on this last day of her life was posted by her own hand. Some few hours later, Mr. Froude received a message that something had happened to Mrs.

Carlyle, and he was desired to go at once to St. George's Hospital. Calling for Miss Jewsbury on his way, he went to the hospital at once, and there,

on a bed in a small room lay Mrs. Carlyle—beautifully dressed—dressed as she always was, in perfect taste. Nothing had been touched. Her bonnet had not been taken off. It was as if she had sate upon the bed after leaving the brougham, and had fallen back upon it asleep. But there was an expression on her face which was not sleep, and which, long as I had known her, resembled nothing which I had ever seen there. The forehead, which had been contracted in life by continual pain, had spread out to its natural breadth, and I saw for the first time how magnificent it was! The brilliant mockery, the sad softness with which the mockery alternated, both were alike gone. The features lay composed in a stern, majestic calm. I have seen many faces beautiful in death, but none so grand as hers. I can write no more of it.

And this was what had happened: again we quote from Mr. Froude:

'Mrs. Carlyle had gone on that last afternoon for her customary airing,' driving round Hyde Park, taking her little dog with her. . . . Near Victoria Gate she had put the dog out to run, a passing carriage went over its foot, and, more frightened than hurt, it lay on the road on its back, crying. She sprang out, caught the dog in her arms, took it with her into the brougham, and was never more seen alive. Coming a second time near to the Achilles Statue, and surprised to receive no directions, he turned round, saw indistinctly that something was wrong, and asked a gentleman near to look into the carriage. The gentleman told him briefly to take the lady to St. George's Hospital, which was not two hundred yards distant. She was sitting with her hands folded on her lap—*dead*.

So it was all over—the long, long pain and exhaustion—no more steps for the tired feet to take, not a farewell, and, we must trust, not a pang; only the stern, sweet peace of the newly-dead, left to tell of the end of all pain for her. On that first solemn night—'the last of danger and distress,'—Mrs. Warren lighted the two candles, about which such earnest directions had been given by the departed. She slept at last !

A telegram was sent to John Carlyle at Edinburgh, Carlyle's own whereabouts being a little uncertain. It was in his sister's house at Dumfries that the fatal news reached him. He was stunned. Sixteen hours after the arrival of the telegram, arrived a letter from *her*, a cheery and merry one ! *His* last to her, posted too late, lay unopened on his table at Chelsea on his return, and was endorsed by him: 'Never read ! Alas, alas !' Its tender words never reached her.

On the Monday his brother, Dr. John Carlyle, accompanied him to London. 'Never,' says Carlyle, 'for 1,000 years should I forget that arrival here of ours, my first unwelcomed by her. She lay in her coffin, lovely in death.'

What thoughts must those have been which came to Carlyle when he looked on the face of his wife, his ' dear life partner ? ' We cannot dwell on this part of the tragedy. There is no need.

Arrived again from London at Haddington, where his wife had wished to be laid by her father, Carlyle was, on the whole, less desperately unhappy. His brother John, with Forster and other friends, accompanied him on the journey with his ' sacred burden.'

I looked out (he says) upon the spring fields, the everlasting skies, in silence. . . . I went out to walk in the moonlit, silent streets. . . . I looked up at the windows of the old room, where I had first seen her, on a summer evening after sunset, six-and-forty years ago. . . . I retired to my room, slept none all night, . . . but lay silent in the great silence.

Thursday, April 26, wandered out into the churchyard. . . . At 1 P. M. came the funeral . . . silent, small, only twelve old friends and two volunteers besides us there. Very beautiful and noble to me, and I laid her in the grave of her father, according to covenant of forty years back—and all was ended. In the nave of the old Abbey Kirk, long a ruin, now being saved from further decay, with the skies looking down on her, there sleeps my little Jeannie, and the light of her face will never shine on me more!

We give here the epitaph composed by Carlyle, and engraved on the tombstone of her father in the chancel of Haddington Church: *

Here likewise now rests

JANE WELSH CARLYLE

Spouse of THOMAS CARLYLE, Chelsea, London.

She was born at Haddington 14th July, 1801, only daughter of the above JOHN WELSH, and of GRACE WELSH, Capelgill, Dumfriesshire, his wife.
In her bright existence she had more sorrows than are common; but also a soft Invincibility, a clearness of discernment, and a noble loyalty of heart which are rare.
For forty years she was the true and ever-loving helpmate of her husband, and, by act and word, unweariedly forwarded him as none else could, in all of worthy that he did or attempted.
She died at London, 21st April, 1866, suddenly snatched away from him, and the light of his life as if gone out.

There is little to add to the telling record. The bright promise of childhood was checked by early and keen sorrow—the death of a father shadowed over that time of youth—already touched by the pain inseparable from some phases of a woman's experience.

It would be idle to discuss here the question whether great intellect is a happy gift for a woman to possess. We feel that is too wide a field to enter upon.

Jane Welsh Carlyle seems 'a creature whom only a little change of earthly fortune; a little kinder smile of Him who sent her hither, and one true heart to encourage

---

* 'The grave,' says Mr. D. G. Ritchie, ' is in the chancel.'

and direct her, might have made all that a woman could be!'

Had she even shared to the full, the literary interests of the man of genius whose overwhelming personality left her so lonely, she would doubtless have entered the lists as a brilliant and successful authoress. But her share seemed, for the most part, limited to the listening to Carlyle's tremendous denunciations of all people, things, and systems, since the creation of the world. On her sofa she lay, night after night, exhausted, with nerves 'all shattered to pieces,' and gave her word of sympathy when she could. To the casual visitor these fierce and powerful monologues of Carlyle's were fascinating—to her, they must have been almost intolerable at times.

Had she been placed in a congenial companionship, with a man many degrees less intellectual than Thomas Carlyle—a man with whom the deeper sympathies of a woman's heart had met full response—we cannot doubt that the world would have known Jane Welsh Carlyle as a writer. But that career was closed to her, and all connected with literature seemed interwoven with the loneliness and disappointment of her own lot.

When we think of the eager, bright-eyed, spirited child, fenced round from the world's cold, by softest nurture and love; of the young girl gay, arch, sparkling, confident—when these images are brought face to face with the wasted, almost despairing, stern woman who lived to lose every token of her shining youth, but the 'bit smile,' we cannot but lament so inadequate a result to the world, as this deeply touching record of sharp and peculiar suffering. With the slackening of the acute tension of her agony, however, came the 'loosening of the golden cord.'

That, after all, she died, as it were, of joy and triumph, not of lingering and repeated misery—is our most soothing thought. The summons came so softly at last. Even the thought of that lonely, unsheltered spot where she was laid, ceases to give pain, when we remember that it was there her heart clung so fondly, over her father's grave—it was there she wished to rest. It has been said, 'Happy is the nation that has no history.' More truly, possibly, may the remark be applied to woman:

Where the light is brightest, the shadow is deepest.

And it is not in the intellectual life that woman can find warmth. Surely the sphere sacredly and peculiarly her own —the sanctuary of her home, filled and enfolded by loving blessedness—must, to a large extent, bound the possibilities of her perfect happiness.

We cannot guess what Jane Welsh Carlyle would have been in the sunshine of motherhood! had she also known its keen anxieties and unremitting cares. It must remain a mystery what would have resulted from that tender and natural tie—what blossoming of softer, sweeter manifestations might have sprung forth at the touch of baby hands, and lips— caressing and winding round the very hearts of mothers— 'Dream-children'—Alas!

And into the region of dreams, or of dreams made realities, this noble-hearted, suffering woman has passed—she to whom so much was given—from whom so much was withheld.

APPENDIX.

I. *THE WELSH ANCESTRY.*

WE are indebted for the following to an old and valued friend of later branches of the family.

The family of Welsh seems to have been settled, at a remote date, in the valley of the Nith, Dumfriesshire, and to have been of considerable standing and repute. We find, in the year 1480, a 'Nicolas Welsch,' Lord Abbot of Holywood; a foundation of the twelfth century, and better known under its Latinised name of 'de Sacrobosco.' Collistoun, the principal landed possession of the family, was, in all probability, a portion of the Abbey lands, which the Welshes obtained firm hold of at the Reformation, as, both before and after that great event, they are found holding the important office of 'hereditary deputy baillies' of the Abbey: a position which placed great opportunities in their hands at the dissolution and sequestration of the monastic lands and revenues.

The family seem to have had distinctly ecclesiastical proclivities all through its history; as, beside the Abbot, we find the following beneficed clergy: Schir Herbert Velsche, Chaplain, Dumfries; John Velsche, Vicar of Dumfries; another 'John,' Vicar of Dunscore; Dean Robert Velsche, of Tynron (1568), with Schir Galbert Velsche, his brother, being probably, from their designations, ecclesiastics under the old Faith, in their early days. Of distinctly post-Reformation times, we have, first, the still famous Rev. Maister John Welsch, Minister of Ayr, surnamed 'The Incomparable,' a man of stirring life, who married Elizabeth, third daughter of John Knox and Dame Margaret Stewart, daughter of Lord Stewart of Ochilltree, of the kindred of Queen Mary herself; secondly, the Rev. Josias Welsh, a minister of note in the North of Ireland, where he took refuge during the troublous times in Scotland; and thirdly, another minister of the name of Welsh, the Rev. John Welsh of Irongray, son of Josias, settled not far from the hereditary lands of Collistoun: a very determined Covenanter, originator of the 'open air Conventicle,' which played so great a part in the civil and religious history of Scotland. Craigenputtock, the patrimony of Jane Welsh Carlyle, seems originally to have formed one of the possessions of the family of Collistoun, and must, sometime after the year 1685, have been detached by family arrangement, by marriage or otherwise, from the more ancient 'holding,' and become the property of one of the numerous cousins of the main house.*

II. DR. JOHN WELSH.

JOHN WELSH was born at Craigenputtock, in Dumfriesshire, in 1772; studied medicine at Edinburgh, and obtained his surgeon's diploma in 1796, when he was appointed surgeon to the regiment of Perthshire Fencibles, which he held until 1798, when he went to Haddington. He shortly thereafter joined Mr. George Somner, a surgeon in that town, in partnership. The practice was carried on very successfully under the title of Somner and Welsh. Mr. Somner died in June 1815, Dr. Welsh having previously assumed as a partner a former apprentice of the firm, Mr. Thomas Howden, surgeon, and the practice was carried on under their names until the death of Dr. John Welsh from typhus fever, contracted whilst attending a patient for that disease in September 1819. Mr. Howden assumed as a partner Mr. Welsh's younger brother, Benjamin Welsh, M. D. These gentlemen continued in connection till 1826, when Mr. Welsh died. Mr. Howden then took a Mr. Fyffe as a partner, which partnership lasted till 1833, when they separated, and Mr. Howden's son joined him, and it became Howden and Son. With that son (Dr. Howden) it now goes on with another partner. Dr. John

* A full and able detailed account of the Welsh ancestry is given by Mr. J. C. Aitken, in a paper read before the Natural History and Antiquarian Society at Dumfries, and published in the Dumfries and Galloway *Courier and Herald* on January 9, 1889.

Welsh was a surgeon of great skill, always ready to relieve suffering humanity, whether occurring amongst the rich or poor, by all of whom, who had the opportunity of knowing him, or who came under his treatment, he was greatly loved and esteemed and greatly regretted after his decease. Dr. Welsh wrote a book on fever, which was well received.

The house in which Dr. Welsh lived, and from which the wife of Thomas Carlyle was married, is still standing. It is not of large size, but, like the homes of many who have become either great themselves, or have become connected with great names, it is small but comfortable. Being a little off the street, it seems like a narrow strip packed behind other high buildings. It is one room in width from east to west, having its access up a close or passage four feet wide. On the first floor there are dining room, consulting-room, and surgery, a kitchen and offices; second floor, drawing-room and two bedrooms, and an attic flat of three low bedrooms. The property belongs to Mr. W. Howden, son of Mr. Howden.

III. THE DEATH OF DR. JOHN WELSH.

'IT was in the beginning of 1872,' says Lieutenant-Colonel Davidson, ' that I found myself at the door of old Betty's " poor cottage at Greenend." Betty opened to my knock, and exclaimed, " Eh, Maister Davidson ! " I was soon seated beside her in her tidy little room, and deep in the memories of auld langsyne. Among other subjects we came upon Dr. Welsh. She said, in reference to his regard for religion: " Some folk didna think sae muckle o' the doctor, but I thought a hantle o' him. Ye see, when he got auld, he didna tak' the lang rides he used to tak', but he got a kerridge; and just aboot that time I was takin' in a Bible an' commentary in pairts—that's it on the table there— and as the Doctor gaed his veesits, mony a read he had o't. I mind as weel as yesterday his sayin', as he cam' thro' the kitchen to his kerridge, ' Betty, could ye obleege me wi' a bit o' yer Bible?' Says I, 'What pairt wad ye like, Doctor?' Says he —for the Doctor was aye pelite—' Weel, Betty, if it's quite convenient for you, I wad like a bit o' the gospel o' John !' Ay, he was fond o' the Bible." Then I was telling how I remembered that solemn Sabbath morning when he died, which led her to go into the circumstances of his illness and death. "Ye see," said she, "the Doctor was a regular man in his habits. He used to come hame at four o'clock, an' tak' a bath before his denner; but yae Thursday he cam' hame, an' took naither his bath nor his denner, but gaed straight to his naked bed. The next day he was in a high fever, an' word was sent to Edinburgh for a grand doctor (Hamilton, I think he was ca'ed), and he cam' wi' his cocket hat, an' gold-headed stick, an' had a long consultation wi' Dr. Howden. Whan it was ower, he cam' thro' the kitchen, for that was the nearest way to the kerridge. Mrs. Welsh was wi' him, wi' a bottle in her han', for she wanted to gie him a glass o' wine, but we couldna find the screw; so she just took a knife an' nicket aff the head o' the bottle. As he was takin' the wine, he saw I was lookin' at him, an' he said, 'Ow he'll get roon; he'll get roon!' But he didna get roon ava, for the next day he was waur, an' on the Sabbath morning he was sae bad they put a laddie on a horse to ride to Edinburgh for the doctor, but before the laddie was weel awa', the breath gaed clean oot o' him! There was deid silence in the hoose for aboot half an oor, and the first that brak it was Miss Jean. She was sitting on the stair, when up she got wi' a scream, an' cried, 'I maun see my father?' an' rushed to the locked door o' his room; but, before she could open it, Dr. Howden gat her in his airms, an' she fainted clean awa'. He carried her thro' the drawing-room, ye ken, to the little bedroom aff it, an' laid her on the bed beside her puir mother that was lying there in a deid swoon; and there they were like twa deid corpses! Eh, but it was waefu'! I thocht I wad look in an' say a word, whan the mistress brak oot into sic a fit o' greetin' I thocht she wad brak her heart. So I went to Dr. Howden, an' telt him to come an' see her, for I thocht she wad dee, but he said, 'Oh, Betty, I'm gled o't, for it's just the best thing that could happen to her;' an' he only wished Miss Jean could get a gude greet too." Such was Betty's account of this tragic event, which caused a gloom over the whole town and countryside."*

* From Lieut.-Colonel Davidson's *Memorials of a Long Life*, Edinburgh: David Douglas.

IV. MRS. CARLYLE AND DE QUINCEY.

An incident connected with De Quincey finds place here. Mr. James Hogg—co-editor, with his father, of a weekly periodical called 'The Instructor,' which was succeeded by 'Titan,' to both of which De Quincey contributed—has written an article in 'Harper's New Monthly Magazine' for January 1890, entitled 'Nights and Days with De Quincey.' In this article mention is made of the Carlyles, and a touching incident is related of Mrs. Carlyle's kindness, which we give in Mr. Hogg's own words.

'Many, many times De Quincey referred, with the most touching, almost tearful earnestness, to Mrs. Carlyle and her kindly care of him during that severe illness which he had some time about the period when the " Confessions " appeared. Mrs. Carlyle had nursed him, if I remember rightly, at their own home, and he ever afterwards retained the most profound feeling of gratitude for her motherly kindness, combined with the highest possible opinion of her character and intellectual power. More than once, while dwelling on her qualities of heart and head, he exclaimed, " She was, indeed, the most angelic woman I ever met upon this God's earth !"

'Afterwards, when I was about to transfer myself to London, De Quincey said, " If ever you meet Carlyle, will you tell him from me——;" and he charged me with a solemn and moving message. I dare only say that it referred to Mrs. Carlyle.'

Mr. Hogg did not see Carlyle until 1876. One day, being in Chelsea, the thought struck him that he ought to deliver De Quincey's message, and that if he did not make haste, he might never have the chance. He called and found Carlyle at home, apparently very nervous and feeble.

'At first I let the conversation drift hither and thither, but gradually bent it to De Quincey, and their old working days. By this time he had become animated, and seemed to gain nervous power. I then told him I had a message to him from an old friend, now no more. I gave De Quincey's words as faithfully as I could. As I spoke, Carlyle started and quivered, and the tears sprang to his eyes. It was some little time before the tremor ceased. Slowly, sadly, tenderly, he murmured little ejaculatory recollections of those old days, and after the first thrill of emotion it seemed to do him good.'

Mr. Hogg is in error in assigning the date of Mrs. Carlyle's kind act to the period when the 'Confessions' appeared. These papers were first published in the 'London Magazine' in 1821, and in a volume the year after. It was while the Carlyles resided at Comely Bank, Edinburgh, after their marriage and before their going to Craigenputtock, that the incident must have occurred, namely, between 1826 and 1828. That, however, is a slight matter, and in no way detracts from the deep interest of Mr. Hogg's narration.

Dr. A. H. Japp, in a brief but truly able sketch of Mrs. Carlyle in 'True and Noble Women' (Isbister), says: 'The bright and versatile woman must have liked the erratic, melodious-voiced little man, for, to her honour, she assiduously nursed him through an illness which he had in Edinburgh at that time, with no one to look after him; for his own wife . . . was still left behind in Westmoreland, with her little brood of chickens.'

V. *CARLYLE'S ACCOUNT OF THE BAKING OF THE FIRST LOAF.*

IN connection with this account of the first loaf we cannot but contrast the description given by Mrs. Carlyle—thirty years after the event—with that given by Carlyle in the 'Reminiscences,' nearly forty years after that memorable baking. According to their individual characters each deals with the subject. Mrs. Carlyle speaks of her sobbing and despair—at three in the morning. Carlyle says, 'I can remember very well her coming in to me, late at night (eleven or so) with her *first loaf*, looking mere triumph and quizzical gaiety: "See!" The loaf was excellent, only the crust a little burnt. And she compared herself to Cellini and his Perseus, of whom we had been reading. From that hour we never wanted excellent bread.'

In this case, we must feel that each wrote what was, to each, the truth; yet the impression given is not the same in the two narratives. Carlyle adds: 'The saving charm of her life at Craigenputtock, which to another young lady of her years might have been so gloomy and vacant, was that of conquering the innumerable practical problems that had arisen for her there. . . . Dairy, poultry-yard, piggery. That of milking with her own little hand, I think, could never have been necessary, even by accident—(plenty of milkmaids within call), and I conclude must have had a spice of frolic or adventure in it, for which she had abundant spirit. . . . From the baking of a loaf, or the darning of a stocking, up to comporting herself in the highest scenes or the most intricate emergencies—all was insight, veracity, graceful success.'

VI.

HERE are the verses written by Mrs. Carlyle to Jeffrey about 1832. 'There were rose-leaves along with them,' says Mr. Froude. The sad tone of the lines is very apparent; their literary merit not less apparent.

To a Swallow building under our Eaves.

Thou, too, hast travelled, little fluttering thing,
Hast seen the world, and now thy weary wing
   Thou too must rest.
But much, my little bird, could'st thou but tell,
I'd give to know why here thou lik'st so well
   To build thy nest.

For thou hast passed fair places in thy flight;
A world lay all beneath thee where to light:
   And strange thy taste,
Of all the varied scenes that met thine eye,
Of all the spots for building 'neath the sky,
   To choose this waste!

Did fortune try thee? Was thy little purse
Perchance run low, and thou, afraid of worse,
   Felt here secure?
Ah, no! thou need'st not gold, thou happy one!
Thou know'st it not. Of all God's creatures, man
   Alone is poor!

What was it, then? Some mystic turn of thought,
Caught under German eaves, and hither brought,
　　Marring thine eye
For the world's loveliness, till thou art grown
A sober thing that doth but mope and moan,
　　Not knowing why?

Nay, if thy mind be sound I need not ask,
Since here I see thee working at thy task
　　With wing and beak.
A well laid scheme doth that small head contain
At which thou work'st, brave bird, with might and main;
　　No more need'st seek.

In truth, I rather take it thou hast got
By instinct wise much sense about thy lot,
　　And hast small care
Whether an Eden or a desert be
Thy home, so thou remain'st alive and free
　　To skim the air.

God speed thee, pretty bird; may thy small nest
With little ones all in good time be blest;
　　I love thee much;
For well thou managest that life of thine,
While I! Oh ask not what I do with mine!
　　Would I were such!
　　　　　　　　　　　　　　The Desert.

VII. *CARLYLE LOCALITIES IN EDINBURGH.**

March 15, 1881.

　SIR,—It may interest Edinburgh readers of the Carlyle 'Reminiscences' to have a jotting of some of the localities referred to there in connection with his sojourns in our city. When he came to commence his college career in November 1809, being yet nearly a month short of fourteen years of age, he lodged in Simon Square. This was a dingy little court, entering off Nicolson

* *Scotsman*, March 15, 1881.

Street, nearly opposite the United Presbyterian Church. By recent improvements it has been made part of a street, connecting old Davie Street with new Howden Street, running between West Richmond Street and Crosscauseway. A much humbler locality this than that of Alison Square close at hand, but now similarly obliterated almost out of recognition, and named Marshall Street, in which Thomas Campbell, ten winters before, in a 'dusky lodging,' wrote the 'Pleasures of Hope.' Carlyle's companion was 'one Tom Smail, who had already been to College last year.' ' Tom and I,' he says (vol. ii. p. 4), ' had entered Edinburgh, after twenty miles of walking, between two and three P.M., got a clean-looking most cheap lodging (Simon Square—the poor locality), had got ourselves brushed, some morsel of dinner perhaps, and Palinurus Tom sallied out into the street with me to show the novice mind a little of Edinburgh before sundown.' Then follows the wonderfully vivid description of the hall of the Parliament House, and the impression which it made on the 'novice mind.' When Carlyle returned to Edinburgh, after school-mastering at Annan and Kirkcaldy between 1814 and 1818, to support himself here by taking pupils, it does not appear where he lived. ' Irving,' he says, ' lived in Bristo Street, more expensive rooms than mine, used to give breakfasts to intellectualities he fell in with—I often a guest with them. They were but stupid intellectualities,' &c. (vol. i. p. 141). Very likely he had gone back to Simon Square, for he speaks (p. 152), of being out in Nicolson Street for his walk 'one blessed Sunday morning, perhaps 7 or 8 A. M., in the 'fierce Radical and anti-Radical times,' when he met ' the Lothian Yeomanry, Mid or East I know not, getting under way for Glasgow,' and no doubt joined in the contemptuous shout which ' rose from the crowd by way of farewell cheer,' saying, as plain as words, ' may the devil go with you, ye peculiarly contemptible and dead to the distresses of your fellow-creatures.' It was at the door of ' Peddie's Meeting House, a large, fine place behind Bristo Street,' that the strangely and suddenly pathetic farewell took place (p. 109) between Carlyle and his former landlady in Annan. Mrs. Glen, whose look 'stuck in my heart like an arrow . . . all that night and for some three days more.' It was surely that kind of pity which is akin to love that thus troubled the poor lad, caused him ' such a bitterness of sorrow as I hardly recollect otherwise,' and engaged him with Irving in a mad sort of enterprise to intercept in a yawl from Kirkcaldy Sands 'the outward bound big ship' in which Mrs. Glen and her husband were sailing forth on their Astrachan missionary enterprise. In 1822, when he had become tutor to Charles Buller and his younger brother, Carlyle says, 'I still lodged in my old rural rooms, 3 Moray Place, Pilrig Street,' showing he had some time left Simon Square, or other like lodging. He should have written Moray *Street*, not Place; it is a small street opening off Pilrig Street, and runs parallel to Leith Walk. Here his brother John lodged with him (pp. 199-200). After his marriage in 1826, he took up his abode at Comely Bank, in that ante-Dean Bridge era, a sufficiently retired suburb. It was there that Jeffrey visited them first, and often; and there as he records, his wife subdued Mr. William Tait, rudely enough, certainly, seeing that Mr. Tait was only doing a good-natured thing:—In Edinburgh, Bookseller Tait (a foolish, goosey, innocent, but very vulgar kind of mortal), 'Oh, Mrs. Carlyle, fine criticism in the *Scotsman*, you will find it at, I think you will find it at ——.' 'But what good will it do me?' answered Mrs. Carlyle, with great good humour, to the miraculous collapse of Tait, &c. (vol. ii. p. 201). After eighteen months' residence, the Carlyles left Edinburgh for Craigenputtock; but returned to Edinburgh for some time in the winter of 1833; and unfortunate experience there determined their final departure and settlement in London. 'The Jeffreys absent in official regions, a most dreary, contemptible kind of element we found Edinburgh to be (partly by accident, or baddish behaviour of two individuals, Dr. Irving one of them, in reference to his poor kinswoman's furnished house); a locality and life-element never to be spoken of in comparison with London and the frank friends there.' Still, for many years there were frequent visits to Edinburgh; to the Jeffreys especially, at Moray Place or Craigcrook—'one of the prettiest places in the world.' At his visit in 1866 to deliver his Rectorial Address he was the guest of Mr. Erskine of Linlathen. But from the 'crowding and shouting' of the students at the Music Hall he took nearer refuge, 'having hurried joyfully over to my brother's lodging (73 George Street, near by)' (vol. ii. p. 296). An outsider, a friend of Dr. John Carlyle's, who happened to be present, describes the scene as one of strange hilarity. The old gentlemen—three brothers they were in all—laughing loudly all round, like schoolboys who had got unexpected holiday. Once again, three weeks after, the same outsider saw Carlyle at the Waverley Station, seated in the railway carriage for London, after the burial of his wife at Haddington; his right cheek lent on his right hand in the manner familiar by photograph; the rugged face full of infinite sadness, yet also of silent, resolute submission. — I am, &c., A.

VIII. A REMEMBRANCE OF SUNNY BANK.*

Our contributor, to whom we are mainly indebted for the following sketch, writes as follows: 'Jane Welsh Carlyle was the most genial, charming, and affectionate woman I ever had the happiness to meet. Retaining in her warm heart the most tender recollections of her childhood's home, and always clinging fondly to past memories and the friends of her youth, she was even in her declining years a most deeply interesting and delightful being.

'It was in the summer of 1857 that I had the pleasure of seeing her for the first time. She was the only child of Dr. Welsh, a medical man in Haddington, and was deeply attached to the place of her birth, which was also that of her celebrated ancestor John Knox, the great Reformer; and delighted to look back upon that joyous, girlish period of her existence. She had come to that town to visit some kindly old ladies at Sunny Bank (as it was then called); and knowing how she prized anything belonging to her old home, which was now ours, I sent her a basket of pears from the tree where, no doubt, she had often gathered them in bygone days, and encircled them with the prettiest flowers I could find. She was much pleased with the little offering, and sent with the empty basket the following gracious note:—

'"My dear Woman,—You don't know how the sight of that fruit and those flowers gathered from the dear old garden affected me. Thank you, thank you *so* much ! I love the 'Auld Hoose,

* From *Chambers' Journal* of February 26, 1881.

so dearly, that I know you will pardon me if I do not come to see it and you; the sight of the familiar rooms would be too much for me. But come to Sunny Bank, dear, and see *me*. And believe me, ever yours affectionately,

"JANE WELSH CARLYLE."'

IX. LETTER TO MRS. CARLYLE FROM HER HUSBAND.*

THERE is in the possession of Mr. Robert Thomson, Thornhill, an unpublished letter of Thomas Carlyle, addressed by him to his wife while she was staying with Dr. Russell in Thornhill, and suffering from illness. It reveals the writer in an amiable domestic light, and is interesting also because of the opinion which he incidentally expresses regarding the relative value of the advice of the practising and consulting physician. We append the letter *in extenso*:—

Chelsea: (Tuesday) July 27, 1864.

'Dearest,—It was well they kept their Pharisaic Sabbath, and preventing yr. telling me, what wd. not have lightened the gloom of mind. Oh dear ! Oh dear !—and but little sleep yet, in spite of all the chances and all the kindnesses! Nevertheless, hold on to yr. *milk*, to yr. dietings, to yr. bathings, under Dr. R.'s direction and the kind lady's nursing. What strange old days (sunk like old ages) you look out upon from yr. windows there, my poor little heavy-laden woman ! Yes; but it is for ever true "The Eternal rules above us," and in us and round us; and this is not Hell or Hades, but the "Place of Hope"—the Place where what is *right* will be *fulfilled!* And you know that too in yr. way, my own little Jeannie—and you will not and must not forget it; forgetting it one might go mad.

'I think with you of Dr. Russell, that his advice is probably worth *more* than that of all the doctors you have yet had. A sound-headed, honest-hearted man, passing his life in silent company with *facts*, earnestly studying Disease at a thousand *bedsides*, with an eye only to knowing and helping it—what a

* From the *Glasgow Herald*, June 30, 1890.

difft. man from one, or from a thousand ones, who are always "on the stage," and have no time to think of anything except of claptrap, and how they shall get a reputation in a totally stupid world! I beg him very much to survey and investigate your case, and to throw what light on it he can. *Darkness* he will not throw on it; I suppose there is but little "light" except what our own common sense might lead us to. "Time and the hour," which wear out the roughest day, are what I have looked to from the first.

'This morng. at 8, Ann Craik stole out softly as a dream. I heard her, having been awake and smoking, but said nothing. She has been perfect, poor little soul; nevertheless I am glad to be in perfect solitude; rather I intend to *work* with double energy; no other resource for me to keep the demons chained in their caves. I have this note from Craik since she went—hardly read it. I had given her the Bank *viaticum* last night, wh. she protested was too, &c., &c.; but all in a modest natural way. The Poulterer, &c., were discovered to be right, and to-day I have paid accordingly. Every Monday I am to count and reckon, and will. The girls look fairly promising; and I do not fear mischance on that side. My floor (bed-room) is stripped bare, bed ld. off; extremely cool and clean [two words undecipherable] does me no damage. Where cd. I be better—were my poor sick Dear back to me, as by God's blessing she will be, perhaps a little better were the heat gone somewhat. Don't mind writing me above a word when you feel weary: one word (as you say) to keep away worse. Heaven grant it be a good one to-morrow. Adieu, my own dear Jeannie.*

'T. C.'

X. EXTRACT FROM A LETTER TO MR. CARLYLE WRITTEN SOME TIME AFTER HIS WIFE'S DEATH.*

(By Lieutenant-Colonel Davidson.)

MY DEAR SIR,—Often lately have I felt a strong impulse to write to you a few lines on the subject that has moved our hearts so deeply, but as often have I shrunk from it. 'The

* *Memorials of a Long Life.*

heart knoweth its own bitterness, and a stranger doth not intermeddle with its joy.' And I doubt not most men at this time, —even those you were in a sense familiar with,—have been peculiarly strangers to you. You have felt how few there were, if any, who could go down into the deep waters with you. I know but One who could do so fully. Yet I cannot be altogether silent. I have been looking over some of your dear lost one's letters, which are more precious than ever, and I draw from one of them an argument for writing. When inviting me to repeat my call, I having missed her, she says, ' Don't you think it would have been pleasing to our mothers, dear friends as they were, that we should be meeting again in this great foreign London?' and so now I think it would be pleasing to her who is gone that we exchanged a word of sympathy, and so I write. If I may not speak of your bitterness, may I not of my own? I have lost in her a true friend. She was one on whom my heart could rely most perfectly. Perhaps our strongest bond was the early association we both cherished so deeply. Singularly enough, after twenty years' absence from the scenes of our youth, we, on our way to Haddington, were sitting face to face in the same railway carriage—looking out from the same window on scenes that awoke the same emotions, and yet time had so changed us, that when our eyes met, they met as the eyes of strangers! It was some years afterwards that we sat together in the drawing-room at Chelsea, and got into each other's hearts, drew out our little treasured memories, showed them to each other, and wept over them. She was perhaps the only one who had freely entered this secret chamber of my heart; and, now that she is gone, I feel as if its doors were for ever closed. Hers was the hand that touched chords which now no living hand can cause to vibrate. Dear friend, I feel as if I were one of those who have a right to weep with you, though, as compared with yours, my grief must take a secondary place.

XI. CARLYLE AT THE GRAVE OF HIS WIFE.*

THE following little story of Carlyle, which we find in a pamphlet by John Swinton descriptive of a recent brief visit to Europe, will disclose to many readers of that rugged and vehement essayist an almost unsuspected trait of gentleness in his character. It is a very touching picture of Carlyle in his lonely old age which it presents. Mr. Swinton found the grave of Mrs. Carlyle in the ruined church at Haddington, and on the stone is cut Carlyle's tribute to her, in which, after referring to her long years of helpful companionship, he says that by her death 'the light of his life is gone out.' Mr. Swinton continues—' And Mr. Carlyle,' said the sexton, ' comes here from London now and then to see this grave. He is a gaunt, shaggy, weird kind of old man, looking very old the last time he was here.' 'He is eighty-six now,' said I. 'Ay,' he repeated, 'eighty-six, and comes here to this grave all the way from London.' And I told him that Carlyle was a great man, the greatest man of the age in books, and that his name was known all over the world; but the sexton thought there were other great men lying near at hand, though I told him their fame did not reach beyond the graveyard, and brought him back to talk of Carlyle. 'Mr. Carlyle himself,' said the gravedigger softly, ' is to be brought here to be buried with his wife. Ay, he comes here lonesome and alone,' continued the gravedigger, 'when he visits the wife's grave. His niece keeps him company to the gate, but he leaves her there, and she stays there for him. The last time he was here I got a sight of him, and he was bowed down under his white hairs, and he took his way up by that ruined wall of the old cathedral, and round there and in here by the gateway, and he tottered up here to this spot.' Softly spake the gravedigger, and paused. Softer still, in the broad dialect of the Lothians, he proceeded—' And he stood here awhile in the grass, and then he kneeled down and stayed on his knees at the grave; then he bent over and I saw him kiss the

* *San Francisco Bulletin.*

ground—ay, he kissed it again and again, and he kept kneeling, and it was a long time before he rose and tottered out of the cathedral, and wandered through the graveyard to the gate, where his niece was waiting for him.*

* We regret that we have not the exact date of Mr. Swinton's visit to Haddington Church, but it was presumably towards the close of Carlyle's life, though, born in 1795 and dying in 1881, he can hardly have been 86 at the time of this, his last visit to his wife's grave.

INDEX

AGR

'AGRIPPINA,' name given in joke to Mrs. Carlyle by Lady Ashburton, 214
Aitken, Mrs., *see* Jean Carlyle
Alfieri, 37
Ashburton, the first Lady (Lady Harriet Baring, *née* Montagu), 171, 182, 184, 189–191 (character); 193, 194, 195, 196, 197, 198, 214, 223, 233, 235, 242, 243, 246, 247 (death)
Ashburton, the second Lady (*née* Miss Stuart Mackenzie), 254, 270, 271, 295
Ashburton, Lord, 248, 271, 272

BADAMS, 122
Baillie, Miss, became maternal grandmother of Jane Welsh, 4
Baillie, Matthew, Gipsy ancestor of Jane Welsh, 88
Baring, Lady Harriet, *see* Ashburton, Lady
Barnes, Dr., 274
Barnes, Miss (Mrs. Simmonds), 269; letter of Mrs. Carlyle to, 279
Bell, Dr. (John or Charles?), Dr. Welsh assistant to, 3
Blakiston, Dr., 284, 286
Bölte, Miss, 178
Bradfute, John, 19, 24, 31, 37, 116
Braid, Mrs. ('Betty'), her account of Dr. Welsh's death, 311
Brewster, Sir David, 97
Bromley, Miss Davenport, 271, 288, 291, 297

CAR

Bullers, Carlyle tutor to the, 35, 43, 44; Charles Buller, 127, 318; Mrs. Buller, 146; Reginald Buller, 170, 171
Byron, 35, 41

CAMPBELL, Thomas, 317
Carlyle, Alexander, 45, 48, 60, 66, 98, 101, 103, 107, 118
Carlyle, James, senr., *see* Carlyle's father
Carlyle, James, 139, 140
Carlyle, Jean (Mrs. Aitken), 69, 97, 99, 123, 126, 139, 208
Carlyle, Dr. John Aitken, 40, 90, 91, 96, 98, 122, 147, 178, 197 (discussing Dante with Mazzini), 224, 227, 229, 287, 289, 291, 305, 318
Carlyle, Margaret, 115
Carlyle, Mary, 103, 244
Carlyle, Thomas, first meets Jane Welsh, 25, 29; directs her reading, 30, 34; described by J. W., 32, 33; proposes marriage, 38; relations to J. W., 41, 42, 47–59 (for the rest see *Analytical Contents*); his *Cromwell*, 164, 166, 181, 183, 187, 223; *Frederick the Great*, 223, 227, 231, 249, 250, 254, 264, 267, 281, 282, 286, 295; *French Revolution*, 145, 148, 150, 153, 156, 163; 'German Literature,' lectures on, 156; *Latter Day Pamphlets*, 215; *Life of Schiller*, 45; *Past and Present*, 177; *Sartor Resartus*, 91, 119, 120

325

CAR

Carlyle's father, 66; death of, 128
Carlyle's mother, 37, 66, 69, 97, 99, 123, 229, 230
Cavaignac, Godefroi, 149, 153
Cellini, Benvenuto, 111, 314
Cheyne Row, Chelsea, the Carlyles settle at, 144
Christison, Prof., 12
Cicero, 37
Clough, Arthur Hugh, 192, 207, 267
Cobbett's *Cottage Economy*, 111
Collins, Wilkie, 302
Comely Bank, Edinburgh, 83, 95, 97
Craigenputtock, home of the Welshes, 2, 310; 47, 49, 51, 61, 100, 101, 103-106 (description of it), 111, 128, 129, 131, 141; revisited by Mrs. Carlyle, 252
Craik, Mrs., *see* Miss Mulock
Cunningham, Allan, 44, 127, 145
Cunningham, George, 34

DANTE, 197
Darwin, Erasmus, 163, 216
Davidson, Lieut.-Col. David, his *Memorials of a Long Life* quoted, 214, 311, 321
Delane, J. T. (of the *Times*), 212
De Quincey, Thomas, 97; nursed by Mrs. Carlyle, 313
Dickens, Charles, 174, 183, 211, 302; his *David Copperfield*, 200
Don Quixote, 114
Donaldson, the Misses, 195, 201, 245, 248, 265, 319

EDINBURGH, Jane Welsh at school in, 19; Carlyle's various residences in, 316-319 (Appendix vii.)
Edinburgh Review, The, 137
Edinburgh University, Carlyle elected Rector of, 301
Emerson, Ralph Waldo, visits Carlyle at Craigenputtock, 137-139, 163
Erskine, Thomas, of Linlathen, 185, 222, 225, 232, 298, 302, 318

HOG

FOLKESTONE, Mrs. Carlyle's visit to, 297
Foreign Review, The, 137
Forster, John, 165, 183, 195, 197, 199, 211, 212, 288, 300, 302, 303, 305
Forster, W. E., 194, 200, 202
Fox, Caroline, 232, 233
Fraser, James (proprietor of the magazine), 127
Froude, J. A., first introduction to Carlyle, 207; Carlyle's reference to, 278; his edition of the *Letters and Memorials*, 2; Mr. Froude quoted or referred to, 35, 36, 42, 82, 85, 101, 105, 107, 116, 130, 138, 142, 151, 167, 195, 242, 247, 258, 272, 281, 289, 291, 298, 301, 304
Fyffe, Dr., of Haddington, 39, 310

GALT, John, 127
Garnier, 178
Gipsy ancestry of Mrs. Carlyle, 88, 147, 174, 202
Goethe, 35, 41, 106, 117; *Wilhelm Meister* quoted, 158
Gordon, Margaret (Lady Bannerman), 26
Gully, Dr., 220
Gully, Miss, letter of, quoted, 220, 221
Guthrie, Rev. Thomas, 246

HADDINGTON, Jane Welsh born at, 2; Dr. Welsh's house, 311; the school, 8, 11; references to, 22, 23, 79, 83; revisited by Mrs. Carlyle, 201, 245, 248; Mrs. Carlyle's grave at, 305, 323
Hall, Miss, Jane Welsh at her school, 19
Hamilton, Sir William, 97
Hoddam Hill, Carlyle living at, 60; Jane Welsh visits the Carlyles at, 65, 66
Hogg, James (the Ettrick Shepherd), 127
Hogg, James, writer of article on De Quincey in *Harper's Magazine*, quoted, 313, 314

HOL

Holmes, O. Wendell, quoted, 81
Houghton, Lord (Monckton Milnes), 171, 190, 212, 247, 293, 301
Howden, Thomas, partner of Dr. Welsh, 3, 4, 310, 312
Howden, Dr. (Junior), 248, 310
Humbie (near Aberdour), the Carlyles at, 255-257
Hunt, Leigh, 145, 146
Hunter, Miss, married John Welsh, paternal grandfather of Jane Welsh, 3, 8
Huxley, Prof., 302

IRELAND, Mr. Alexander, his acquaintance with Emerson, 137, 138
Irving, Edward, fellow-student of Carlyle's, 317, 318; teacher of Jane Welsh, 11, 12, 13; introduces Carlyle to her, 25, 26; relations between, and Jane Welsh, 28, 29, 33, 34, 36, 42, 46, 47, 63, 106; letter to Carlyle quoted, 35; goes to London, 35; in London, 43, 44, 61-63; advises Carlyle to stand for professorship in London, 104; his 'blessing,' 115; Carlyle meets again in London, 122, 125, 126; makes his one call on the Carlyles at Cheyne Row, 146; referred to by Mrs. Carlyle, 164

JAPP, Dr., quoted, 88, 147, 314
Jeffrey, Francis (Lord Jeffrey), 14, 99, 103, 106, 112, 113, 114, 118, 119, 120, 123, 127, 129, 130, 132, 140, 164, 201, 315, 318
Jewsbury, Miss Geraldine, 133, 151, 172, 182, 189, 198, 199, 206, 212, 232, 234, 246, 265, 268, 299, 303, 304

KANT, read by Carlyle, to fortify him against the wedding ceremony, 90
Kirkcaldy, Irving schoolmaster in, 25; Carlyle schoolmaster in, 35

MON

Knox, John, ancestor of Jane Welsh, 2, 111, 202, 309, 319

LARKIN, Henry, 250, 251-253, 265, 274, 275; quoted, 276, 277, 281, 285, 294
Leslie, Sir J., 12
Liverpool, Jane Welsh's 'Uncle John' at, 5; her visit to, 22; the Carlyles return from London by coach to Liverpool, and steamer thence to Annan, 128, 129; journey to London by same route, 144; Mrs. Carlyle hears at Liverpool of her mother's death, 169; visits her relations in, 181
Lockhart, John Gibson, 127
London, Carlyle's first visit to, 43, 45; second visit to, 120; Mrs. Carlyle joins him, 125; Carlyle's opinion of, 128; resolves to settle in, 141; arrival at Cheyne Row, 144
Lothian, Marquis of, 270
Lowe, Robert, 212

MACAULAY, 222
Mackenzie, Mr. A. K., 19
Macready, 183
Macready, Mrs., 222
Mainhill, Carlyle at, 37
Malvern, the Carlyles visit, 220
Martin, Miss, engaged to Edward Irving, 25, 26, 27, 36
Martineau, Harriet, 156, 198
Masson, Prof., quoted, 106
Mathew, Father, Mrs. Carlyle's meeting with, 175-177
Maurice, F. D., 149
Mazzini, 149, 183, 186, 187 (his letter of counsel to Mrs. Carlyle), 197 (discussing Dante with Dr. J. Carlyle), 222, 233 (his farewell words to Mrs. Carlyle)
Mill, J. S., 128, 145, 148, 164
Milman, Dean, 298
Milnes, R. Monckton, *see* Lord Houghton
Montagu, Basil, 153

Montagu, Mrs. Basil, 'the noble lady,' 44, 61-64, 122, 126, 127, 129
Moore's melodies, 37
Mulock, Miss (Mrs. Craik), author of *John Halifax*, 211

'NERO,' Mrs. Carlyle's dog, 211, 212, 214, 250, 255, 259

OLIPHANT, Mrs., 272, 303; her *Life of Edward Irving* quoted, 11

PAULET, Mr., 182
Paulet, Mrs., 173, 174, 181, 186, 199
Penfillan, 3, 4; 'Pen,' pet name of Jane Welsh, 6
Pepoli, Count, 152, 163
Pepoli, Countess (Elizabeth Fergus), 216, 269
Plattnauer, 182
Procter, B. W. (Barry Cornwall), 44, 99

QUAIN, Dr., 273, 297, 300

RAMSGATE, Mrs. Carlyle's visit to, 268
Renan quoted, 155
Rennie, George, 31, 32, 33, 34, 147, 150, 163, 260-262 (Mrs. Carlyle's letter, telling how she watched by his death-bed)
Ritchie, D. G., editor of *Early Letters of Jane Welsh Carlyle*, 18, 19, 40, 306
Rousseau, 35. *La Nouvelle Héloïse*, 31, 32
Ruskin, J., 298
Russell, Dr., of Thornhill, 168
Ryde, Mrs Carlyle visits, 175

St. GEORGE'S HOSPITAL, 304
St. Leonards, 272, 284, 286, 287
Sandwich, Lady, 254, 269
Schiller, 35, 37; Carlyle's *Life of*, 45
Scott, Thomas, *Commentary on the Bible*, 99

Scott, Sir Walter, 90, 202
'Shandy,' Jane Welsh's dog, 213, 214
Sherborne, 222
Scotsbrig, (near Ecclefechan), Carlyle's parents settle at, 70, 72, 76, 77: Mrs. Carlyle nursing Carlyle's mother at, 229
Sinclair, Sir George, 264
Smith, John Stores, 173, 296, 299
Somner, George, partner of Dr. Welsh, 3, 310
Spedding, James, 149, 207, 208
Spedding [elder brother of James], 298
Spring Rice, Mr., 171
Stanley, Dean, 298
Stanleys, the, of Alderley, 259, 264
Sterling, Edward (of the *Times*), 175, 177, 195
Sterling, John, 148, 156, 157, 163, 166, 167, 168, 175, 201
Sterling, Mrs., 151, 152, 163
Stodart, Eliza, early friendship with Jane Welsh, 19

TAIT, William, bookseller in Edinburgh, 318
Taylor, [Sir] Henry, 149, 233
Templand, home of Walter Welsh, 4, 22, 65; Jane Welsh and Carlyle married at, 87; becomes home of Mrs. Welsh, 83, 87; visits to, 103, 114, 115, 153, 165
Tennyson, 183, 219
Thackeray, 209, 210
Thirlwall, Bishop, 174
Tulloch, Principal, 303
Twisleton, Hon. Edward, 288
Tyndall, Prof., 301, 302, 303

VIRGIL, read by Jane Welsh as a girl, 11; effect on her, 13

WALLACE, William, Jane Welsh's mother traced her pedigree to, 4
Walrond, Mrs., at school with Jane Welsh, 19

WEL

Welsh family, *see* Appendix I., p. 309
Welsh, Ann, sister of Dr. Welsh, 202, 245
Welsh, Benjamin, brother of Dr. Welsh, 4, 310
Welsh, Elizabeth, sister of Dr. Welsh, 202
Welsh, Grace, wife of Dr. Welsh and mother of Jane Welsh, 4; her character, 5, 15; references to her, 67, 71, 74, 75, 76, 77, 83, 95, 114, 123, 134, 151, 152, 153, 155; death of, 168; her grave, 169, 270
Welsh, Grace, sister of Dr. Welsh, 202
Welsh, Helen, daughter of John Welsh of Liverpool, 163, 174, 193, 195, 206
Welsh, Jane (Aunt Jeannie), youngest sister of Mrs. Welsh, 95, 226
Welsh, 'Jeannie,' daughter of John Welsh of Liverpool, 170

WOR

Welsh, John, minister of Ayr, married daughter of John Knox, 2, 111, 309
Welsh, John, name of lairds of Craigenputtock, 2
Welsh, John, of Penfillan, father of Dr. Welsh, 3, 8
Welsh, Dr. John, father of Jane Welsh, 3–5, 6; his death, 17, 311, 312; references to, 20, 89, 225, 241; trees at Craigenputtock planted by, 136; Mrs. Carlyle visits his grave, 203
Welsh, Robert, brother of Dr. Welsh, 22, 37
Welsh, Walter, father of Mrs. Welsh, 4, 6, 7, 65, 71, 77, 134
Welsh, Rev. Walter, cousin of Mrs. Carlyle, minister of Auchtertool, 188, 271
Woolner, Thomas (the sculptor), 288
Wordsworth, 137

www.ingramcontent.com/pod-product-compliance
Lightning Source LLC
Chambersburg PA
CBHW030318240426
43673CB00040B/1207